I0105462

DEVELOPING THE SERVICES SECTOR FOR ECONOMIC DIVERSIFICATION IN CAREC COUNTRIES

DECEMBER 2021

CAREC
Central Asia Regional Economic Cooperation Program

ADB

Creative Commons Attribution 3.0 IGO license (CC BY 3.0 IGO)

© 2021 Asian Development Bank
6 ADB Avenue, Mandaluyong City, 1550 Metro Manila, Philippines
Tel +63 2 8632 4444; Fax +63 2 8636 2444
www.adb.org

Some rights reserved. Published in 2021.

ISBN 978-92-9269-241-4 (print); 978-92-9269-242-1 (electronic); 978-92-9269-243-8 (ebook)
Publication Stock No. TCS210505-2
DOI: http://dx.doi.org/10.22617/TCS210505-2

The views expressed in this publication are those of the authors and do not necessarily reflect the views and policies of the Asian Development Bank (ADB) or its Board of Governors or the governments they represent.

ADB does not guarantee the accuracy of the data included in this publication and accepts no responsibility for any consequence of their use. The mention of specific companies or products of manufacturers does not imply that they are endorsed or recommended by ADB in preference to others of a similar nature that are not mentioned.

By making any designation of or reference to a particular territory or geographic area, or by using the term "country" in this document, ADB does not intend to make any judgments as to the legal or other status of any territory or area.

This work is available under the Creative Commons Attribution 3.0 IGO license (CC BY 3.0 IGO) https://creativecommons.org/licenses/by/3.0/igo/. By using the content of this publication, you agree to be bound by the terms of this license. For attribution, translations, adaptations, and permissions, please read the provisions and terms of use at https://www.adb.org/terms-use#openaccess.

This CC license does not apply to non-ADB copyright materials in this publication. If the material is attributed to another source, please contact the copyright owner or publisher of that source for permission to reproduce it. ADB cannot be held liable for any claims that arise as a result of your use of the material.

Please contact pubsmarketing@adb.org if you have questions or comments with respect to content, or if you wish to obtain copyright permission for your intended use that does not fall within these terms, or for permission to use the ADB logo.

Corrigenda to ADB publications may be found at http://www.adb.org/publications/corrigenda.

Notes:
In this publication, "$" refers to United States dollars unless otherwise indicated.
ADB recognizes "Hong Kong" as Hong Kong, China; "Kyrgyzstan" as the Kyrgyz Republic; "China" as the People's Republic of China; and "Korea" and "South Korea" as the Republic of Korea.

Cover design by Mike Cortes.

CONTENTS

Tables, Figures, and Boxes   v
Acknowledgments   ix
Abbreviations   x
Executive Summary   xi

1. ENABLING THE SERVICES SECTOR TO SUPPORT ECONOMIC DEVELOPMENT   1
    1.1 The Role of the Services Sector in Economic Development   2
    1.2 International Experience with Service-Led Economic Diversification   9
    1.3 Implications of the COVID-19 Pandemic   11

2. THE ECONOMIC STRUCTURE OF CAREC COUNTRIES   12
    2.1 Growth and Sector Composition of Gross Domestic Product   12
    2.2 Sector Composition of Employment   16
    2.3 Inflows of Foreign Direct Investment   17
    2.4 Aggregate Exports and Imports of Goods   20
    2.5 Composition and Direction of Exports of Goods   21
    2.6 Aggregate Exports and Imports of Services   23
    2.7 Composition of Exports and Imports of Services   26
    2.8 Services Trade by Mode of Supply   27

3. KEY SERVICES SUBSECTORS AND INDUSTRIES FOR ECONOMIC
    DIVERSIFICATION IN CAREC COUNTRIES   30
    3.1 Telecommunication and Information Services   31
    3.2 Financial Services   35
    3.3 Education, Research, and Experimental Development Services   41
    3.4 Tourism-Related Services   48
    3.5 Freight Transportation and Storage Services   51
    3.6 Quality Testing and Certification Services   54
    3.7 Other Agriculture-Related Services   55

4.   CREATING AN ENABLING ENVIRONMENT FOR THE DEVELOPMENT   57
OF THE SERVICES SECTOR IN CAREC COUNTRIES
4.1 Improving Governance   57
4.2 Enhancing Market Competition   61
4.3 Deepening Regional Cooperation and Integration   68
4.4 Raising the Efficiency and Quality of the Labor Market   75
4.5 Developing Physical and Digital Infrastructure   76

5.   CONCLUSION, RECOMMENDATIONS, AND POSSIBLE PROJECTS   78
5.1 Conclusion   78
5.2 Policy Recommendations   79

APPENDIXES   86
1 CAREC Countries' Exports and Imports of Services by Value   86
2 CAREC Countries' Exports and Imports of Services by Mode of Supply   96
3 Contribution of Service Industries to Output and Exports of Selected Sectors   106
   in CAREC and OECD Countries
4 Horizontal Commitments of CAREC Countries Under GATS   110
5 Summary of CAREC Countries' GATS Commitments by Sector   113
6 Summary of CAREC Countries' GATS Commitments by Subsector   114

REFERENCES   121

TABLES, FIGURES, AND BOXES

TABLES

1.2.1	Services Entering the Bread Value Chain	4
1.2.2	Interface Between Services and Government Policies and Regulations in the Bread Value Chain	6
1.3.1	Services Entering the Apparel Value Chain in Indonesia	7
2.1	CAREC Countries—Average Annual Growth Rates of Gross Domestic Product and Gross Value Added in Selected Sectors at Constant Prices, 2001–2020	13
2.2	CAREC Countries—Shares of Selected Sectors in Gross Domestic Product at Current Prices, 2000 and 2020	14
2.3	CAREC Countries—Share of Selected Service Industries in Gross Value Added Created in the Services Sector, 2000 and 2019	15
2.4	CAREC Countries—Share of Selected Sectors in Employment, 2000 and 2019	16
2.5	CAREC Countries—Share of Service Industries in Total Employment in Services Sector, 2019	18
2.6	CAREC Countries—Selected Indicators of Merchandise Exports and Imports, 2000–2020	20
2.7	CAREC Countries—Composition of Merchandise Exports by Product Groups, 2020	22
3.1	CAREC Countries—Selected Indicators of Development of Communication Services, 2019	32
3.2	CAREC Countries—Speedtest Global Index, May 2021	33
3.3	CAREC Countries—Selected Indicators of Development of Banking Sector, 2019	36
3.4	CAREC Countries—Selected Indicators of Development of Nonbank Financial Sector, 2017	37
3.5	CAREC Countries—Ranking in Selected Global Competitiveness Index 2019 Components Relating to Depth of Financial System	38
3.6	CAREC Countries—Selected Indicators of Use of Formal Financial Services by Adult Population, 2017	38
3.7	CAREC Countries—Selected Indicators of School Enrollment, 2019	42
3.8	CAREC Countries—Rank in Selected Global Competitiveness Index 2019 Components Relating to Workforce Skills	43
3.9	CAREC Countries—Selected Indicators Relating to Research and Development, 2018	44
3.10	CAREC Countries—Number of Resident Patent, Trademark, and Industrial Design Applications, 2019	46
3.11	CAREC Countries—Selected Indicators Relating to International Tourism, 2019	49

3.12	CAREC Countries—Selected Logistics Performance Indicators, 2018	52
3.13	CAREC Countries—Number of Valid Certificates for Selected ISO Standards, 2018	55
4.1	CAREC Countries—Measures of Concentration and Competition in Banking Sector	62
4.2	CAREC Countries—Foreign Direct Investment Restrictiveness Index for Selected Sectors, 2020	64
4.3	Number of CAREC WTO Member-Specific Subsectoral Commitments	65
4.5	CAREC Countries—Membership/Participation in Selected Regional Organizations and Regional Cooperation Initiatives	70
4.6	Service Industry Coverage of Selected Regional Organizations and Regional Cooperation Initiatives	70
4.7	Regional Trade Agreements Entered into by CAREC Countries with Services Commitments	71
4.8	CAREC Countries—Ranking in Global Competitiveness Index 2019 Components Relating to Labor Market	75
4.9	CAREC Countries—Ranking in Selected Global Competitiveness Index 2019 and Travel and Tourism Competitiveness Index 2019 Components Relating to Infrastructure	76
5.1	Possible Projects for CAREC Countries	81
A1.1	Afghanistan—Exports and Imports of Services, 2005–2019	86
A1.2	Azerbaijan—Exports and Imports of Services, 2005–2019	87
A1.3	Georgia—Exports and Imports of Services, 2005–2019	88
A1.4	Kazakhstan—Exports and Imports of Services, 2005–2019	89
A1.5	Kyrgyz Republic—Exports and Imports of Services, 2005–2019	90
A1.6	Mongolia—Exports and Imports of Services, 2005–2019	91
A1.7	Pakistan—Exports and Imports of Services, 2005–2019	92
A1.8	Tajikistan—Exports and Imports of Services, 2005–2019	93
A1.9	Turkmenistan—Exports and Imports of Services, 2005-2019	94
A1.10	Uzbekistan—Exports and Imports of Services, 2005–2019	95
A2.1	Afghanistan—Exports and Imports of Services by Mode of Supply, 2017	96
A2.2	Azerbaijan—Exports and Imports of Services by Mode of Supply, 2017	97
A2.3	Georgia—Exports and Imports of Services by Mode of Supply, 2017	98
A2.4	Kazakhstan—Exports and Imports of Services by Mode of Supply, 2017	99
A2.5	Kyrgyz Republic—Exports and Imports of Services by Mode of Supply, 2017	100
A2.6	Mongolia—Exports and Imports of Services by Mode of Supply, 2017	101
A2.7	Pakistan—Exports and Imports of Services by Mode of Supply, 2017	102
A2.8	Tajikistan—Exports and Imports of Services by Mode of Supply, 2017	103
A2.9	Turkmenistan—Exports and Imports of Services by Mode of Supply, 2017	104
A2.10	Uzbekistan—Exports and Imports of Services by Mode of Supply, 2017	105
A3.1	Contribution of Services Industries to Gross Output and Exports of Agriculture, Forestry, and Fishing in Selected Countries, 2015	107
A3.2	Contribution of Services Industries to Gross Output and Exports of Food Industry in Selected Countries, 2015	107

A3.3   Contribution of Services Industries to Gross Output and Exports of Textile   108
        and Apparel Industry in Selected Countries, 2015
A3.4   Contribution of Services Industries to Gross Output and Exports of   108
        Chemical/Pharmaceutical Industry in Selected Countries, 2015
A3.5   Contribution of Services Industries to Gross Output and Exports of Electronics   109
        Industry in Selected Countries, 2015
A3.6   Contribution of Services Industries to Gross Output and Exports of Transport   109
        Equipment Industry in Selected Countries, 2015

FIGURES

2.1   CAREC Countries—Selected Indicators of Inward Foreign Direct Investment, 2001–2019   17
2.2   Georgia—Sector Distribution of Cumulative FDI Inflows, 2007–2018   19
2.3   Kyrgyz Republic—Sector Distribution of Cumulative FDI Inflows, 2011–2018   19
2.4   CAREC Countries—Product Concentration Index for Exports and Share of Top Five   21
        Markets in Merchandise Exports, 2020
2.5   CAREC Countries—Ranking in Economic Complexity Index, 2019   22
2.6   Exports of Services in CAREC, 2005–2019   25
2.7   Imports of Services in CAREC, 2005–2019   26
2.8   Services Export by Mode of Supply, 2017   27
2.9   Services Import by Mode of Supply, 2017   28
3.1   Key Services Subsectors for Economic Diversification in CAREC Countries   31
3.2   CAREC Countries—B2C E-commerce Index, 2020   34
B3.2.1 Gross Expenditure on Research and Development in Selected Countries, 1991–2019   45
3.3   CAREC Countries—Ranking in Global Innovation Index 2019 and Its Sub-Indexes   46
3.4   CAREC Countries—Ranking in Travel and Tourism Competitiveness Index, 2019   50
B3.4.1 Georgia—International Visitor Arrivals and International Tourism Receipts, 2010–2019 50
4.1   CAREC Countries—Corruption Perception Index Scores and Rank, 2012 and 2019   58
4.2   CAREC Countries—Average Worldwide Governance Indicator Scores, 2010 and 2018   59
4.3   CAREC Countries—Selected Global Competitiveness Index 2019 Components   59
        Relating to Quality of Institutions
4.4   CAREC Countries—Selected Global Competitiveness Index 2019 Components   62
        Relating to Domestic Competition

BOXES

1.1   Growing Importance of the Services Sector   2
1.2   Role of Services in Bread Value Chain from Manufacture in Shenzhen   4
        to Retail in Hong Kong, China
1.3   Role of Services and Government Interventions in the Apparel Value Chain in Indonesia 7
1.4   International Experiences in Economic Diversification   9
2.1   Identifying Services Inputs   24

3.1 Role of Financial Services in Diversification and Development in Selected   40
    CAREC Countries
3.2 Research and Development in the People's Republic of China   45
3.3 Education, Research, and Upgrading Opportunities—The Case of Wheat in Kazakhstan   47
3.4 The Tourism Industry in Georgia   49
3.5 Freight, Transport, and Storage Services in Uzbekistan's Horticultural Value Chains 53
3.6 Improving Livestock Production Systems in Central Mongolia   56
4.1 Regulatory Impact Assessment   60
4.2 Expanding Trade in Services under the CAREC Trade Agenda   69
4.3 GATS Commitments in Regional Trade Agreements   72
4.4 Regional Cooperation: Implications for the Kyrgyz Republic Garment Industry   74

ACKNOWLEDGMENTS

This technical study was prepared by the Public Management, Financial Sector, and Regional Cooperation Division (EAPF) of the East Asia Department (EARD) of the Asian Development Bank (ADB) under the supervision of Emma Fan, director of EAPF. Management's overall guidance and support throughout the production particularly from M. Teresa Kho, director general, EARD; and Safdar Parvez, advisor of EARD is gratefully acknowledged.

The study team was led by Dorothea Lazaro, regional cooperation specialist, EAPF. The study builds on a comprehensive assessment prepared by Patrick Low and Bahodir Ganiev in December 2020. Loreli de Dios, Camille Cyn Isles, Julius Irving Santos, and Aiken Rose Tafgar (EAPF consultants) provided research assistance including updating of data in September 2021.

Valuable comments and suggestions were received from ADB staff: Akiko Hagiwara and Yumiko Tamura of EARD; Saad Paracha, Xinglan Hu, Joao Pedro Farinha, and Aziz Haydarov of Central and West Asia Regional Department; Donghyun Park and Matthias Helble (on leave) from Economic Research and Regional Cooperation Department; Yuebin Zhang of Sustainable Development and Climate Change Department; Sameer Khatiwada of Southeast Asia Department; and Rosalind McKenzie of Pacific Department. Mia Mikic (then director of the United Nations Economic and Social Commission for Asia and the Pacific's Trade, Investment, and Innovation Division) provided external feedback.

The study benefited from feedback of country delegates and development partners at the Central Asia Regional Economic Cooperation (CAREC) Webinar on Facilitating Diversification—and Economic Recovery—through the Services Sector on 2 September 2020. The technical and coordination support by the CAREC program's advisors and regional cooperation coordinators is highly appreciated.

Richard Vokey and Samantha Brown provided content review and copyediting. Mike Cortez created the cover art and Joe Mark Ganaban did the typesetting. EARD's Edith Joan Nacpil, Genny Mabunga, and Sophia Castillo-Plaza, and Department of Communications' Rodel Bautista supported the publication process.

The study is prepared under ADB's Technical Assistance 9712: Implementing the Integrated Trade Agenda in the CAREC Program, cofinanced by the Regional Cooperation and Integration Fund and the People's Republic of China Poverty Reduction and Regional Cooperation Fund.

ABBREVIATIONS

ADB	Asian Development Bank
CAREC	Central Asia Regional Economic Cooperation
COVID-19	coronavirus disease
FDI	foreign direct investment
GATS	General Agreement on Trade in Services
GDP	gross domestic product
GERD	gross expenditure on research and development
ICT	information and communication technology
OECD	Organisation for Economic Co-operation and Development
PRC	People's Republic of China
RIA	regulatory impact assessment
RTA	regional trade agreement
RVC	regional value chain
WTO	World Trade Organization

EXECUTIVE SUMMARY

Economic diversification is a fundamental feature of economic development. However, production and exports in many countries of the Central Asia Regional Economic Cooperation (CAREC) Program are dominated by resource intensive and primary commodities such as crude oil, metals, and agricultural products. Exports also tend to be concentrated geographically. The CAREC member countries need economic diversification to grow faster, raise incomes, and increase productivity. The long-term strategy—the CAREC 2030—aims to strengthen CAREC's role as a catalyst for trade expansion and economic diversification. In this context, the *CAREC Integrated Trade Agenda 2030* aims to create an enabling environment for greater economic diversification by supporting reforms to enhance the policy and regulatory environment, ensuring adequate financing, and linking CAREC countries with regional and global value chains.

The services sector has become a key driver of economic development and diversification. Efficient, cost-effective supply of services is essential for productivity, export growth, job creation, and poverty reduction. Diversification stemming from the services sector also increases economic resilience. The coronavirus disease (COVID-19) pandemic has underscored the need to accelerate economic diversification into the services sector and demonstrated the potential for technological advances and digital transformation.

The services sector has made a significant contribution to the economic growth of CAREC countries. The growth rate of gross value added in the services sector is much faster than in agriculture in all CAREC countries as well as in the manufacturing sector in most of them. Exports of services had positive annual growth over the 2005–2019 period. However, services inputs broadly considered to support diversification are lacking, and there remains a high concentration of natural resource-dependent manufacturing economies.

CAREC countries could further foster growth of their services sector, especially their services subsectors and industries which are critical to economic diversification and sustainable development. These include (i) telecommunication and information services, (ii) financial services, (iii) education and research and development services, (iv) tourism-related services, (v) freight transport and storage services, (vi) quality testing and certification services, and (vi) other agriculture-related services. Most of these service subsectors are producer services—that is, they are inputs into other economic activities. The efficient functioning of these service subsectors is a precondition for the strong performance of the rest of the economy. The quality of the institutions that are the interface of the government and the economy is also a factor in how well and to what extent services promote a country's growth and advancement.

Several enabling or facilitating conditions are essential for robust development of the services sector and economic diversification, including (i) improving governance, (ii) enhancing market competition, (iii) deepening regional cooperation and integration, (iv) raising the efficiency of the labor market, and (v) developing physical and digital infrastructure. Most CAREC countries have undertaken efforts to improve governance but more needs to be done. Competition remains weak in many sectors. By leveling the playing field, the private sector can play a greater role in the development of producer services. Eight of the 11 CAREC countries are members of the World Trade Organization and have broadly committed to a higher level of specific commitments under the General Agreement on Trade in Services. By modes of supply, CAREC commitments on services trade appear to be open and liberal in terms of commercial presence—where the service supplier is in the territory of another member country. However, the presence of natural persons—where the individual service supplier is in the territory of another country—is most restrictive in terms of market access and national treatment provisions.

CAREC countries need to adopt a coherent and comprehensive approach to the balanced development of the interdependent services subsectors. Establishing and maintaining favorable legal and regulatory frameworks for the overall services sector will deliver the greatest net benefit.

Liberalizing trade in services—by lowering barriers to foreign direct investment for example—is an effective way to enhance competition in the services sectors. However, market opening needs to be carried out carefully to effectively manage the adjustment costs. For example, as countries liberalize their services trade, they should strengthen labor market institutions and vocational training. It is also crucial to build and upgrade critical infrastructure to nurture the development of the services sector.

Despite the growth of the services sector's contribution to the global economy, the economic shift to services sector has not been accompanied by commensurate improvement in policies and regulations for its faster development. Fostering greater regional cooperation and integration can help improve domestic regulations, facilitate policy coherence and mutual recognition, and pursue reciprocal liberalization of trade in services. Platforms for knowledge-sharing and policy dialogue—such as under the CAREC program—can help create mutual trust. Experiences from CAREC countries and beyond show that strong cooperation arrangements can pave the way for closer economic relations and greater links with global and regional value chains.

Chapter 1

ENABLING THE SERVICES SECTOR TO SUPPORT ECONOMIC DEVELOPMENT

Economic diversification is a critical step in the development of many countries. A greater variety of product lines and more sophisticated products are essential for incomes and employment to grow. Diversification can lead to higher value-added production and make a nation's economy less vulnerable. Productivity increases, incomes rise, and the growth in demand that results will provide additional stimulus for new production patterns to emerge.

The member countries of the Central Asia Regional Economic Cooperation (CAREC) Program need to diversify their economies to grow faster, raise incomes, and increase their productivity.[1] Primary commodities such as crude oil, metals, and agricultural products often dominate their current production and exports.[2] Export destinations tend to be geographically concentrated. This leaves CAREC economies vulnerable to commodity market downturns and economic conjunctures in a few major trading partners.

Just how exposed their primary commodity-heavy merchandise export baskets leave most CAREC countries to the vagaries of world markets was illustrated in 2014–2015. Global price drops had a significant adverse effect on exports and growth in many CAREC economies (Capannelli and Kanbur 2019; IMF 2018a; World Bank 2017a). Overly concentrating on only a few export markets also leaves CAREC economies particularly sensitive to adverse changes in their top trading partners and even unfavorable turns in bilateral relations. In 2008–2009, for instance, the People's Republic of China (PRC) exports and gross domestic product (GDP) growth slowed markedly, due largely to a recession in the United States (US), the destination market for about one-fifth of its merchandise exports. The PRC is one of the top five export markets for all other CAREC countries (except Azerbaijan and Georgia), and their exports and growth suffered adversely in turn (ADB 2009; ADB 2010).

---

[1] The CAREC Program is a partnership of 11 countries (Afghanistan, Azerbaijan, Georgia, Kazakhstan, the Kyrgyz Republic, Mongolia, Pakistan, the People's Republic of China, Tajikistan, Turkmenistan, and Uzbekistan) and development partners working together to promote development through cooperation, leading to accelerated economic growth and poverty reduction. Following the government change in Afghanistan in mid-August 2021, the Asian Development Bank placed on hold its assistance in Afghanistan effective 15 August 2021.

[2] The lack of diversification in production and exports is often associated with macroeconomic volatility (Koren and Tenreyro 2007). Poverty-reducing, trade-driven growth has been particularly difficult to achieve in countries with economies concentrated in commodity and natural resources sectors (World Bank 2017a).

The long-term strategy—the CAREC 2030—aims to strengthen CAREC's role as a catalyst for trade expansion and economic diversification. There is a need for CAREC countries to substantially expand the range of products they produce and export to fully participate and benefit from the emerging global and regional supply chain. It is in this context that the *CAREC Integrated Trade Agenda 2030* aims to support reforms to enhance the policy and regulatory environment, ensure adequate financing, and link CAREC countries with regional and global value chains (ADB 2019a).

The repercussions from the coronavirus disease (COVID-19) pandemic have further amplified the need for economic diversification in the CAREC countries. World prices for crude oil and other primary commodities that dominate their exports dropped sharply in 2020. Stronger-than-expected recovery in 2021 was driven by the upsurge in economic activity boosted by fiscal stimulus, supply shortfalls, and rising global commodity prices between the second half of 2020 and the first half of 2021. However, the outlook is still uncertain given renewed COVID-19 outbreaks and divergent recoveries (ADB 2021a; ADB 2021c). Overall, countries in developing Asia that fared worst during the pandemic tended to be those reliant on a single product, service, or export commodity. Creating more diverse, high-value economies will lead to greater resilience and sustainability (ADB 2021b).

The Role of the Services Sector in Economic Development

Services are recognized as a mainstay of growth and development, and indispensable to progress in practically every aspect of economic activity. Studies demonstrate the increasing role of services in productivity growth, as inputs to manufacturing, and as drivers for job creation and socioeconomic inclusion (Box 1.1). Empirical evidence further suggests that a services sector can support economic growth and progress even in countries that do not yet have a manufacturing core (Nayyar, Cruz, and Zhu 2018; Nayyar and Cruz 2018). Policies to develop both manufacturing and services sectors together can help achieve a country's competitiveness objectives.

Box 1.1: Growing Importance of the Services Sector

As dynamic sources of productivity growth

In the past, productivity growth in the services sector was presumed to be lower than that of manufacturing (Baumol and Bowen 1965). However, subsequent empirical work suggests a more nuanced and changing reality. Drawing on a sample of 18 Organisation for Economic Co-operation and Development countries and data spanning 1970–2005, Yong Young (2014) finds that goods and services have experienced similar total factor productivity growth rates since 1970. Similarly, Jorgensen and Timmer (2011) found that market services' productivity growth in Japan and the United States predominated over that of goods production from 1980, although this was not the case in the European Union. They identify distribution services as a rapid productivity-growth sector that has become a major engine of aggregate productivity growth in all regions. The International Monetary Fund has argued that a shift in employment from manufacturing to services need not hinder the overall economy's productivity growth (IMF 2018a). The IMF study notes that average productivity growth in services has surpassed that of manufacturing in many developing countries. These include India, the People's Republic of China, and some of the nations of sub-Saharan Africa.

continued on next page

Box **1.1** *continued*

As important inputs to manufactured exports

The line between services and manufacturing is also becoming blurred as the latter increasingly relies on services inputs to produce and market wares (Miroudot 2019). This is sometimes called the "servicification" of manufacturing. Manufacturing firms are making more intensive use of services as intermediate inputs and employ workers to perform service-related functions such as design, logistics, marketing, and sales. Manufacturing firms also increasingly sell services bundled with manufactured goods to create more value. Examples are warranties or aftersales services for a product sold, or a smartphone that enables its purchaser to download applications (Mercer-Blackman and Ablaza 2018).

Recently, some services industries or subsectors—especially information and communication technology-enabled services—benefited enormously from digitalization. Digitalization has reduced search costs for these services and lessened the so-called "proximity burden" associated with consummating services transactions. This has expanded both the domestic and international markets for a variety of services, making them more tradable. Developing an efficient services sector can therefore promote manufacturing sectors and help produce competitive manufacturing exports. In this way, the services sector continues to expand its contribution to output and value-added trade.

As a source of job creation and inclusion

The services sector employs about half of the world's workers. The proportions change depending on the stage of economic development, rising from about a quarter in low-income countries to three-quarters in high-income countries. The sector's capacity for creating employment and boosting inclusion is made apparent by the experiences of many developing countries. India's information and communication technology sector employs roughly 3.5 million people and has created many jobs for women and outlying cities (Hoekman and te Velde 2017). Business process outsourcing companies in the Philippines have 1.2 million full-time employees (Price, Francisco, and Caboverde 2016). A 2019 study in Mexico found that a 10% increase in local hotel revenues can raise employment by 2.5% in each municipality and increase its nominal gross domestic product by 4% (Faber and Gaubert 2019).

Economic growth cannot bring about better living standards on its own, particularly for the poor and the excluded. Improving basic services such as health care and education also has far-reaching effects. Improving and expanding education services can help achieve a multitude of social goals. Education enhances people's ability to make informed decisions, cope with and adjust to economic and other shocks, and be effective stewards of the natural environment (World Bank 2011a). It is a powerful force for improving social mobility and reducing inequality, including gender inequality. A well-educated population is equipped not to fear technological change in this age of digital transformation and instead, to adapt to and benefit from it.

Sources: Baumol, W. J., and W. G Bowen. 1965. On the Performing Arts: The Anatomy of Their Economic Problems. *American Economic Review.* 55 (1/2):495–502; Hoekman, B., and D. W te Velde. 2017. *Trade in Services and Economic Transformation: A New Development Policy Priority.* London: Overseas Development Institute; Faber, B., and C. Gaubert. 2019. Tourism and Economic Development: Evidence from Mexico's Coastline. *American Economic Review.* 109(6):2245–2293; IMF. 2018. *World Economic Outlook April 2018: Cyclical Upswing, Structural Change.* Washington, DC: International Monetary Fund; Jorgensen, W., and M. P. Timmer. 2011. Structural Change in Advanced Nations: A New Set of Stylised Facts. *Scandinavian Journal of Economics.* 113(1):1–29; Mercer-Blackman, V., and C. Ablaza. 2018. The Servicification of Manufacturing in Asia: Redefining the Sources of Labor Productivity. *ADBI Working Paper Series 902.* Tokyo: ADBI; Miroudot, S. 2019. Services and Manufacturing in Global Value Chains: Is the Distinction Obsolete? *ADBI Working Paper.* No. 927. Tokyo: ADBI; Price, N. A., J. P. Francisco, and C. E. Caboverde. 2016. IT-BPO in the Philippines: A Driver of Shared Prosperity? *Working Paper 16-002.* Philippines: Asian Institute of Management; World Bank. 2011a. *Learning for All: Investing in People's Knowledge and Skills to Promote Development.* Washington, DC: World Bank; Yong, A. 2014. Structural Transformation, the Mismeasurement of Productivity Growth, and the Cost Disease of Services. *American Economic Review.* 104(11):3635–3667.

Case studies also show that specific value chains at individual manufacturing firms are highly dependent on services inputs. The heavy reliance on the inputs of a diverse mix of services highlights the need for government policies to support the efficient and competitive supply of services that can help ensure that such firms and a country's overall economy prosper.

One such case study involved a company that manufactures, distributes, and sells a wide range of bakery products in Guangzhou and Shenzhen in Guangdong Province in the PRC; Hong Kong, China; and Macau, China (Box 1.2). The supply chain for bread manufactured in the firm's Shenzhen factory and retailed in Hong Kong, China was selected for study. A second study examined the supply chain for a branded outerwear jacket manufactured in Indonesia for export (Box 1.3). The firm involved is an Indonesia-based multinational garment manufacturer with facilities in Indonesia and Viet Nam that produce a variety of products for worldwide markets. Since many service inputs in these value chains are outsourced, the studies restricted the analysis to only the first tier of such outsourced services. The rest of the inputs that go into the "bundle of value" that is sold as an input into the supply chain were disregarded for purposes of the studies.

Box 1.2: Role of Services in Bread Value Chain from Manufacture in Shenzhen to Retail in Hong Kong, China

The value chain studied was a relatively simple one—that of a prepackaged loaf of bread. The chain begins with the procurement and transport of inputs to the factory in Shenzhen. Imported ingredients from other parts of Asia—sugar, salted butter, and margarine—land at the port, and are then unloaded, cleared through customs, and transported to the factory. Other ingredients are procured in the People's Republic of China and shipped to the factory. These include eggs, butter, salt, oil, wheat flour, yeast, rapeseed, turmeric, condensed milk, and packaging materials. The bread produced in the firm's Shenzhen factory is then trucked across the border daily to the firm's warehouse in Hong Kong, China. From there it is transported to the firm's local retail outlets two to six times a day. The frequency depends on store turnover and the availability of in-store storage space and delivery trucks. The value chain ends at a retail outlet with a purchase by the consumer.

The 30 services identified as sources of value in this chain accounted for 72% of the costs of production. They are grouped according to stages of production: (i) services upon importation of ingredients, (ii) in-factory and factory-related services, (iii) transporting the bread from the factory to the retail outlet, (iv) retail store services, and (v) business processes (back office support) (Table 1.2.1) based on the UN's Central Product Classification Version 2 codes.[a]

Table 1.2.1: Services Entering the Bread Value Chain

Services upon importation of ingredients
1. Customs-related services
2. Quality assurance services
In-factory and factory-related services
3. Auditing services to meet standards such as that of International Organization for Standardization (ISO) and Hazard Analysis Critical Control Point (HACCP)

continued on next page

Box 1.2 *continued*

Services upon importation of ingredients
4. Production administration—production management services
5. Production administration—repair and maintenance of factory equipment
6. Production administration—quality assurance services
7. Cleaning services
8. Personnel search and referral services—recruitment of factory workers
9. Dormitory services for factory workers
10. Social insurance services for factory workers
11. Local transport services for staff in Shenzhen
Transporting the bread from the factory to the retail outlet
12. Customs-related services for bread exports to Hong Kong, China
13. Cross-border freight transport services (Shenzhen—Hong Kong, China warehouse)
14. Storage and warehousing services
15. Inland freight forwarding services (from warehouse to retail outlets)
16. Repair and maintenance services (for trucks)
Retail store services
17. Retail services
18. Retail administration—operation management services
19. Retail administration—site development services for new shops
20. Security services (cash delivery)
Business processes (back office support)
21. Financial accounts auditing services
22. Internal auditing services (including audits of financial accounts and corporate governance)
23. Retail administration—advertising services
24. Back office support—human resources services
25. Back office support—information technology services
26. Back office support—estate management services
27. Financial services
28. Company secretary services
29. Legal services
30. Training services

The list of services in Table 1.2.1 is self-explanatory. Some services were intrinsic to the actual production processes, and others reflected the regulatory framework within which the supply chain operated (such as customs, social insurance, and auditing services regulations). This list, however, does not fully capture the extent of the interface between government policies and regulations on the one hand, and services and the value chain on the other hand (Table 1.2.2).

continued on next page

Box 1.2 *continued*

Table 1.2.2: Interface Between Services and Government Policies and Regulations in the Bread Value Chain

Policies upon importation
Port services—port safety and emergency response services regulations
Customs inspection—collection of revenue
Import licensing for flour, sugar, milk
Regulations on imported food—registration and inspection and quarantine clearance
Policies affecting in-factory and factory-related services
Occupational safety inspections and hygiene requirements for workers
On-site inspection of food production facilities and processes
Environmental regulations—wastewater disposal regulations
Environmental regulations and carbon emission trading scheme
Electricity supply regulation or tariffs
Policies affecting the transportation of bread from the factory to the retail outlet
Food safety standards—supervision and administration over exported food (People's Republic of China)
Food safety standards (for retail in Hong Kong, China)
Policies at the retail level
Food business licenses
Food safety regulations

Most of the government policies and regulations listed could be seen as potential value-added to the bread supply chain. On the one hand, many are concerned with public policy and action on health, safety, and other socioeconomic and environmental imperatives which the market does not provide. On the other hand, the related costs could be netted out of the value they add as public policy if their design or administration place unnecessary burdens on the firm and production. Considering the many ways that policy impacts activity in a modern economy, an **efficient and cost-effective public policy intervention can be an important determinant of competitiveness**. The same can be said of those producer services that any enterprise relies on, whether these are financial, information and communication, transport, logistics, business, or distribution services.

ᵃ The Central Product Classification refers to a standard central product classification developed by the UN Statistical Commission to serve as an instrument for assembling and tabulating all kinds of statistics requiring product detail. See https://unstats.un.org/unsd/classifications/Family/Detail/1074.

Source: Cheung, D. Low P., and Sit, D. 2014. Case Study: Hong Kong-based Bakery Chain, FGI Services in Global Value Chains Project. Hong Kong, China: Fung Global Institute (unpublished).

Box 1.3: Role of Services and Government Interventions in the Apparel Value Chain in Indonesia

This case study examined the supply chain to produce a single item of clothing—an outerwear jacket—that was made for a major United States clothing brand in one of its factories in Jakarta, Indonesia. The manufacturing firm is part of a multinational in Indonesia that can produce 75 million pieces a year, mostly for branding by such global apparel leaders as Adidas, Nike, Amer Group, The North Face, Lacoste, and Calvin Klein. The group was a large exporter to Europe and the United States, but Asia became its primary market in 2013. Production is centered in Indonesia but growing in Viet Nam.

Although details can vary significantly between the products the firm produces, particularly during post-production processes, the value chain studied represents the standard procedure for most of the firm's lines. The value chain was segmented into four stages for ease of analysis: (i) product design (contracting, sampling, and costing); (ii) pre-production (engineering, sourcing, freight, and logistics); (iii) production (quality assurance, cutting, sewing, embossing, and packaging); and (iv) post-production (freight and logistics, customs, and tax). **The study identified 42 services** that contribute to the manufacture of a piece of clothing either entering the garment manufacturing value chain directly or as supporting services and first-tier outsourced services (Table 1.3.1). **They accounted for 30% of total production costs and included government-supplied services**.

Table 1.3.1: Services Entering the Apparel Value Chain in Indonesia

Stages and Services	Direct Regulatory Requirement
Establishment stage	
Government liaison services	X
Company registration and licensing services	X
Business consultant services	
Staff training	
Safety standards and inspection services	X
Personnel search and referral services	
Pre-production stage	
Procurement agent services	
Customs-related services	X
Quality assurance services	
Freight transport services	
Repair and maintenance services for fleets	
Storage services for raw materials	
Design of manufacturing machinery	
Product research and development	
Design and production of manufacturing templates	
Conception and design of products	

continued on next page

Box 1.3 *continued*

Stages and Services	Direct Regulatory Requirement
Production stage	
Production administration services	
Engineering services	
Government inspection services	X
Compliance management services	
Testing and trial services	
Cleaning services	
Security services	
Waste treatment services	
Repair and maintenance services	
Logistics services	
Truck hire services	
Utility services	
Storage and warehouse services	
Post-production – back office	
Auditing services	
Internal auditing services	
Insurance services	
Accounting services	
Banking services	
Legal services	
General management services	
Communication and marketing services	
Estate management services	
Human resources services	
Courier and postal services	
Telecommunications services	
IT services	

Five government-supplied services were identified to have a direct impact on the apparel value chain. The regulatory interface with the subject apparel value chain, however, goes much further than these direct interactions. It also involves government interventions affecting the supply of utilities, auditing and accounting, banking services, legal services, postal services, and telecommunications. The pricing, quality, and reliability of all these services are crucial to diversification objectives in an economy.

Source: Elms, D. and Haines, W. 2015. *Case Study: An Apparel Firm in Indonesia, FGI Services in Global Value Chains Project.* Hong Kong, China: Fung Global Institute (unpublished).

International Experience with Service-Led Economic Diversification

Services can make direct contributions to economic competitiveness and diversification. For many industries, in fact, competitiveness often depends on an ability to obtain high-quality producer services at a low cost (Francois and Hoekman 2010). Country-wide experiences—including in low-, middle-, and high-income countries in the Middle East, Asia, Sub-Saharan Africa, and Central and Eastern Europe—demonstrate how diversification was achieved through the development of their services industries or subsectors and the role of policy on services development (Box 1.4). While countries differ, what they have in common is the recognition that services are a vital gateway to broad-based economic diversification. Their diversification efforts have also been focused on both home and international markets. In this connection, they have not concentrated only on creating profitable market opportunities domestically, but also looked beyond their borders to exploit possibilities in their geographic regions and globally.

Box 1.4: International Experiences in Economic Diversification

Malaysia is a good model for many Central Asia Regional Economic Cooperation (CAREC) countries. It was once a commodity exporter but succeeded in diversifying its economy beyond overdependence on such products as palm oil, tin ore, and rubber. Its transition began in the 1980s. The manufacturing sector's share in gross domestic product (GDP) rose to nearly a quarter during the decade, and textiles, chemicals, and electronics became a prominent part of its exports. The share of agriculture and natural resources fell from around half of GDP in the early 1960s to less than 10% in 2018. Manufacturing and services grew in importance over time. Malaysia's recipe for diversification had several key ingredients (Ali 2016). These included capable political leadership, equitable distribution of the fruits of economic success, and investment in human resources. The country's economic development was marked by several distinct policy regimes. The first involved import substitution, which spurred industrial and manufacturing growth. Most manufacturing was in labor and resource-intensive sectors at this stage (Yusof 2013). Malaysia's home market was small, however, and policymakers recognized this policy's limits. Like many countries in Asia, it turned to **export-led development**. Supported by inflows of foreign direct investment and technological know-how, this strategy helped create a thriving, globally competitive export-oriented electronics and electrical products sector. Services also expanded as the economy diversified. Having leapt to upper middle-income status, Malaysia aims to become a developed economy by fostering further growth of the services sector and knowledge-based sectors.

Diversification helped the **Republic of Korea** vault within a couple of generations from the ruins of war to membership in the Organisation for Economic Co-operation and Development. This involved a seismic shift from an economy with little industry and dominated by agriculture to one powered by globally competitive high-tech manufacturing. Its fast-growing services sector now makes up more than half of GDP and includes construction, information and communication services, transportation, tourism, and wholesale and retail trade. The state played a decisive role in this **diversification by nurturing key services industries** for rapid growth (Woo 2016). This support was allocated with great discipline, however, with governments monitoring export market performance as a key criterion for continuing or ending assistance.

The members of the Gulf Cooperation Council—including the **Emirate of Dubai**—are some of the richest in the world. However, most members have struggled with the challenge of diversifying away from the oil sector industries that largely created this wealth (Cherif and Hasanov 2016). Between 2010 and 2018, per capita GDP stagnated for most Gulf Cooperation Council countries, remaining either significantly below or at about the same levels that they achieved nearly 4 decades ago. Oil reserves are fast running out in some cases, making diversification more urgent. Reliance on **service-led diversification** has been a key feature of the model in Dubai. Nearly 90% of Dubai's economic activity is centered on services. These include construction, real estate, finance, transportation and storage, accommodation and food services, and wholesale and retail trade.

Some similarities exist between Dubai's circumstances and those of many CAREC countries. Dubai straddles the trade route between the great markets of Europe and Asia, making it a natural maritime and air transport hub for passengers and cargo and a convenient headquarters for suppliers servicing the needs of Asia–Europe trade. Central

continued on next page

Box 1.4 *continued*

Asia is a land link between the People's Republic of China and Europe and can play a similarly vital role in providing such services as transport and logistics to support what is expected to be rapidly expanding trade between the two regions. Several ongoing regional initiatives create enormous opportunities for service providers in CAREC countries to scale up and grow in tandem with the expanding transit and cross-border trade.

The services sector has also helped spearhead the efforts of economic diversification and development in several nations in **Sub-Saharan Africa**. Better transport services meant more export opportunities in **Ethiopia**. For example, Ethiopian Airlines' expansion of its regional network and cargo capacity has enabled the country to transport high-value, time-sensitive exports much more quickly and cheaply. This has increased trade in transport services, spurred growth in other sectors as a valuable services input, and led to overall economic growth. Better air transport also enabled Ethiopia's cut flower industry to thrive and exports of cut flowers to explode nearly 60-fold from $12 million in 2005 to $662 million in 2014 (Hoekman and te Velde 2017).

In **Kenya**, regulatory reform has boosted financial services through a more open finance sector, establishment of diversified financial hubs, and modification of the tax regime for the sector. These, along with growth in mobile banking, have deepened and boosted trade in financial services, generated jobs—accounting for 2.8% of Kenya's formal employment in 2017—and made the country a leader and hub for financial services in East Africa. M-PESA, the leading player in the country, serves about 19 million users and has an estimated daily turnover of $150 million including loans and saving products. Kenya's banks and financial institutions also expanded internationally, establishing subsidiaries and overseas banks in other countries (WTO 2019a).

Mauritius maintains a remarkably open trade and investment regime. Nearly 90% of its most favored nation tariff lines are duty free, and there are very few restrictions on foreign investment (WTO 2015). Such policies have afforded the economy the flexibility needed to diversify, including to develop services subsectors. For instance, when it perceived an opportunity to promote medical travel, Mauritius invested in health care facilities. These investments boosted the number of foreign patients receiving health care in the country by 1,500% during 2005–2011. Reduced trade barriers also supported more efficient and internationally competitive information and communication technology services. Exports of these services rose from $300 million in 2005 to $1.3 billion in 2015, and their share of overall service export value doubled from 18.5% to 37.0% (Hoekman and te Velde 2017). Mauritius also fostered the export of financial services and business process outsourcing. In 1988, offshore banking was introduced to transform the economy into an international financial center (Zafar 2011).

In **Croatia**, tourism has had the greatest diversification impact on the country's economy. International tourist arrivals almost tripled from 5.8 million in 2000 to 15.6 million in 2017. Tourism also provides the foreign exchange needed to import capital goods and helped spur economic growth (Hajdinjak 2014; Pavlić, Tolić, and Svilokos 2015). By 2019, tourism accounted for nearly a quarter of Croatia's GDP and employment, and 40% of its total exports (World Travel and Tourism Council 2021). Since most employees in the tourism services industry are young and female, the sector also contributed to inclusive growth, reduced income inequality, and raised aggregate welfare in the country (Gatti 2013).

Based on firm-level data from the **Czech Republic**, Arnold, Javorcik, and Mattoo shows a positive relationship between pivotal services sector policy reforms and the performance of domestic firms in downstream manufacturing. Liberalization of domestic services—mainly through commercial presence—appears to have contributed to the improved performance of the manufacturing sector. In 2017, a large manufacturing sector made up 24.1% of the country's GDP and almost 91% of merchandise exports.

CAREC = Central Asia Regional Economic Cooperation.

Sources: Ali, A. T. 2016. Malaysia's Move Toward a High-Income Economy: Five Decades of Nation Building—A View from Within. In R. Cherif, F. Hasanov, and M. Zhu, eds. *Breaking the Oil Spell: The Gulf Falcons' Path to Diversification*. Washington, DC: International Monetary Fund; Woo, M. 2016. Industrial Diversification in Korea: History in Search of Lessons. In Cherif, R., F. Hasanov and M. Zhu, eds. *Breaking the Oil Spell: The Gulf Falcons' Path to Diversification*. Washington, DC: IMF, pp. 93–101; Arnold, J. M., Javorcik, B. S. and Mattoo, A. 2011. Does Services Liberalization Benefit Manufacturing Firms? Evidence from the Czech Republic. *Journal of International Economics*. 85(1):136–146; Gatti, P. 2013. Tourism, welfare and income distribution: The Case of Croatia. *Tourism*. 61(1):53–71; Cherif, R. and F. Hasanov. 2016. Soaring of the Gulf Falcons: Diversification in the GCC Oil Exporters in Seven Propositions. In R. Cherif, F. Hasanov, and M. Zhu, eds. *Breaking the Oil Spell: The Gulf Falcons' Path to Diversification*. Washington, DC: IMF; Hajdinjak, S. 2014. Impact of Tourism on Economic Growth in Croatia. *Enlightening Tourism. A Pathmaking Journal*. 4(1):30–51; Hoekman, B. and te Velde, D. W. 2017. Trade in Services and Economic Transformation: A New Development Policy Priority. London: Overseas Development Institute; Pavlić, I., M. Š. Tolić, and T. Svilokos. 2015. Tourism, Real Effective Exchange Rate and Economic Growth: Empirical Evidence for Croatia. *International Journal of Tourism Research*. 17:282–291; Woo, M. 2016. Industrial Diversification in Korea: History in Search of Lessons. In Cherif, R., F. Hasanov, and M. Zhu, eds. *Breaking the Oil Spell: The Gulf Falcons' Path to Diversification*. Washington, DC: IMF; World Trade Organization (WTO). 2015. Trade Policy Review: Report by the Secretariat. Mauritius. Geneva: WTO. WT/TPR/S/304/Rev.1; WTO. 2019. Trade Policy Review of the East African Community (EAC). Geneva: WTO; World Travel and Tourism Council. 2021. Croatia: 2021. *Annual Research: Key Highlights*. London: WTTC. Yusof, Z. 2013. Economic Diversification: The Case of Malaysia. New York: Revenue Watch Institute; Zafar, A. 2011. Mauritius: An Economic Success Story. Chapter 5 in Punam Chuhan-Pole and Manka Angwafo, eds. *Yes Africa Can: Success Stories from a Dynamic Continent*. Washington DC: World Bank.

Implications of the COVID-19 Pandemic

The COVID-19 pandemic has fundamentally changed the options and priorities that will influence the economic prospects of the CAREC countries. The pandemic's largely unanticipated onslaught early in 2020 has wreaked massive damage across the globe. Millions of people have been infected by the virus and have died. Efforts to contain the spread have severely dented economies and imposed overwhelming pressure on many nations' health systems. Along with the great social hardships, disparities in income and opportunity widened. In 2020, merchandise trade volume declined by 5.3%. The drop is even larger in nominal US dollar terms: merchandise goods declined by nearly 8% while commercial services exports declined by 20% (WTO 2021). However, economies are beginning to rebound in developing Asia. Regional growth is forecast to reach 7.1% in 2021 and level out at 5.4% in 2022 (ADB 2021c). A similar recovery is expected in Central Asia as rising world commodity prices trigger a resumption in economic activity. The uncertain future course of the pandemic will nonetheless continue to pose a threat.

As CAREC countries attempt to bolster jobs and output at home during the recovery phases, the risk may grow that international value chains will be eschewed and resort will be made to tariffs, other trade restrictions, and subsidies to promote domestic economic activities. Whatever the short-term gains in output and jobs, this will ultimately deprive countries of the significant economic benefits provided by specialization. No country's economy can gain in the long term from turning inward. To do so would put it on the path to slower, not greater, growth and development. Trade policy decisions made in the CAREC region and the rest of the world will be crucial in determining overall regional and national outcomes.

Services production and trade have been profoundly affected by the pandemic. The many services associated with the trading of goods have seen demand severely contract. Transport, distribution, and trade-related financial services will take time to pick up. Tourism and other services that are associated with this industry have also been hard hit both worldwide and in most of the CAREC economies. Demand has obviously surged for health care services and most countries are struggling to manage a supply shortage.

Nonetheless, new opportunities are emerging, and some services subsectors have benefited from the health crisis. These include the financial and insurance services, professional and consulting services, audiovisual and other recreational services, and particularly information and communication technology (ICT). These subsectors are likely to further evolve and grow because of long-term changes in personal and business behaviors, practices, and preferences resulting from the pandemic. This underlines the importance of prioritizing development of the ICT sector across the five CAREC 2030 operational clusters, and the importance of implementing the *CAREC Digital Strategy 2030*.[3] As CAREC governments face considerable challenges adapting to changed circumstances created by the COVID-19 pandemic, regional collaboration and cooperation will provide mutual benefits and lighten each country's burden in managing the shock. Collective actions will also give the region more influence over the policies of others beyond CAREC members.

---

[3] *CAREC Digital Strategy 2030: Accelerating Digital Transformation for Regional Competitiveness*. The strategy is intended as a catalyst for regional cooperation on digital matters and a mechanism to promote policy design, capacity-building and dialogue on the ways social and economic challenges in the region can be addressed with the help of digital technologies.

Chapter 2

THE ECONOMIC STRUCTURE OF CAREC COUNTRIES

Growth of the CAREC economies has generally been strong since the turn of the millennium. However, even though the services sector has expanded, it remains underdeveloped in most of the CAREC members, as does manufacturing. The energy and/or mining sectors have accounted for the bulk of inward foreign direct investment (FDI) in many countries, and exports are concentrated in terms of products and destinations in all of them. Primary commodities dominate the merchandise exports of most. The same narrow concentration is seen in services sector, with transport, travel, and construction preponderant for the most part on both the import and export sides.

Growth and Sector Composition of Gross Domestic Product

The main drivers, services gaining ground. Average annual real GDP growth rates varied across the region during the 2001–2020 period—from 3.8% in the Kyrgyz Republic to 8.7% in the PRC—but were considerably higher than the world average (Table 2.1). The energy and/or mining sectors were the main drivers, especially in Azerbaijan, Kazakhstan, Mongolia, Turkmenistan, and Uzbekistan. Manufacturing performed well in some countries. Agriculture underperformed in comparison with industry and services across the region overall, although it showed healthy expansions in several countries, including Mongolia, Tajikistan, and Uzbekistan. The services sector made a significant economic contribution. Gross value added grew much faster in the services sector (excluding construction) than in agriculture in all CAREC economies, and faster than in the manufacturing sector in most.

Table 2.1: CAREC Countries—Average Annual Growth Rates of Gross Domestic Product and Gross Value Added in Selected Sectors at Constant Prices, 2001–2020

(%)

Country	GDP	Agricultural Value Added[a]	Manufacturing Value Added[b]	Services Value Added[c]
Afghanistan[d]	6.2	3.7	4.7	7.9
Azerbaijan	7.9	4.5	5.9	7.6
China, People's Republic of	8.7	3.9	...	9.5
Georgia	5.0	1.5[e]	4.9[e]	5.4[e]
Kazakhstan	5.9	4.1	5.4	6.5
Kyrgyz Republic	3.8	2.2	2.6	5.7
Mongolia	6.5	5.3	8.7	5.6[f]
Pakistan	4.1	2.4	5.2	4.8
Tajikistan	7.5	7.4	...	9.1
Turkmenistan	8.2	...	...	...
Uzbekistan	6.5	5.3	7.3[f]	7.0
World	2.5	2.7	2.1[g]	2.8[g]

... = data not available, CAREC = Central Asia Regional Economic Cooperation, GDP = gross domestic product.

[a] Includes gross value added created in hunting, forestry, and fishing, and corresponds to Sections A and B (Divisions 1–5) of the International Standard Industrial Classification of All Economic Activities (ISIC), Revision 3 (United Nations, 1990).

[b] Corresponds to Section D (Divisions 15 –37) of the ISIC, Revision 3.

[c] Corresponds to Sections G–Q (Divisions 50–99) of the ISIC, Revision 3.

[d] Data is for 2003–2020.

[e] Data is for 2004–2020.

[f] Data is for 2011–2020.

[g] Data is for 2001–2019.

Source: World Bank. World Development Indicators. https://databank.worldbank.org/source/world-development-indicators (accessed 10 August 2021).

Shifting patterns in national production. This has significantly changed the composition of GDP in CAREC countries, with the decline of agriculture share in GDP in all (Table 2.2).[4] The share of manufacturing fell in five of the eight CAREC countries for which the time series on this indicator is available.[5] While the share of the services sector rose in almost all CAREC countries (except Uzbekistan), the portion of GDP contributed by the services sector remained substantially below the average of Organisation for Economic Co-operation and Development (OECD)

---

[4] This pattern is consistent with economic theory, which predicts that as a country develops—due to a combination of demand- and supply-side factors—the share of agriculture in aggregate output and employment declines, the share of industry first rises and then falls, and the share of services increases. The pattern has been observed in many countries since the 19th century (WTO 2019b).

[5] In many CAREC countries, the share of manufacturing in GDP fell from an already low base, which is a sign of the phenomenon referred to as premature deindustrialization (Rodrik 2016).

Table 2.2: CAREC Countries—Shares of Selected Sectors in Gross Domestic Product at Current Prices, 2000 and 2020
(%)

Country	Agriculture[a] 2000	Agriculture[a] 2020	Manufacturing[b] 2000	Manufacturing[b] 2020	Services[c] 2000	Services[c] 2020
Afghanistan	38.6[d]	27.0	18.8[d]	6.0	36.2[d]	56.1
Azerbaijan	16.1	6.9	5.3	5.8	35.8	42.5
China, People's Republic of	14.7	7.6	32.0[e]	26.2	39.8	54.5
Georgia	20.6	7.4	12.2	9.5	53.2	58.6
Kazakhstan	8.1	5.3	16.5	12.7	48.4	55.8
Kyrgyz Republic	34.2	13.5	18.1	17.0	30.0	49.6
Mongolia	27.4	12.1	6.7	10.7	39.2	40.0
Pakistan	25.6	22.7	10.2	11.6	50.3	52.8
Tajikistan	25.1	23.8	...	13.4[f]	31.5	35.3
Turkmenistan	22.5	10.8[f]	9.8	...	28.9	47.2[f]
Uzbekistan	30.1	26.1	...	20.1	37.2	33.5
Comparator country groups						
OECD countries	1.9	1.4[f]	17.0	12.8[f]	65.8	70.1[f]

... = data not available, CAREC = Central Asia Regional Economic Cooperation, OECD = Organisation for Economic Co-operation and Development.

a   Includes hunting, forestry, and fishing and corresponds to Sections A and B (Divisions 1–5) of the International Standard Industrial Classification of All Economic Activities (ISIC), Revision 3 (United Nations, 1990).

b   Corresponds to Section D (Divisions 15–37) of the ISIC, Revision 3. Includes manufacture of basic metals, which makes up substantial proportions of gross value added created by manufacturing in Georgia, Kazakhstan, the Kyrgyz Republic, Mongolia, Tajikistan, and Uzbekistan. Also note that manufacturing excludes Section C (mining and quarrying), Section E (electricity, gas, steam; water), and Section F (construction); thus, the sum of sectoral shares in gross domestic product is less than 100%.

c   Corresponds to Sections G to Q (Divisions 50–99) of the ISIC, Revision 3.

d   Data is for 2002.

e   Data is for 2004.

f   Data is for 2019.

Source: World Bank. World Development Indicators. https://databank.worldbank.org/source/world-development-indicators (accessed 10 August 2021).

countries.[6] The energy and/or mining industries and the economic activities associated with them—e.g., geological exploration activities, energy and/or mineral product transport, and base metal production—accounted for a large percentage of GDP in Azerbaijan, Kazakhstan, the Kyrgyz Republic, Mongolia, Tajikistan, Turkmenistan, and Uzbekistan.[7]

6   There are several reasons for using the OECD countries as a comparator country group. Data on OECD countries are readily available for many indicators. Most OECD countries have well-diversified economies, with a good business environment and a vibrant services sector. The average OECD performances on many indicators are what CAREC countries should work to match, at least in the medium term.

7   Azerbaijan's large oil and gas reserves are a major contributor to its economy. Exports from the country contracted by 36.6% in 2020. Turkmenistan, a gas-rich country, experienced dramatic decline in external demand and prices for hydrocarbons, which provide more than 80% of exports and 30% of GDP. Kazakhstan, another major oil producer, saw its exports dive by 19.4% during 2020. Economic shocks like the COVID-19 pandemic underline the need for CAREC economies to expand economic diversification in order to be less dependent on one export sector and more resilient. (ADB 2021b).

Services subsector performance. Growth in services has varied substantially between subsectors. Gross value added created in retail and wholesale trade, hotels, restaurants, transport, storage, and communication grew faster than in other services subsectors in most CAREC countries. CAREC countries' "other services" subsector has lower gross value added created compared with global and OECD averages (Table 2.3). The share of these "other services"—comprising the financial and insurance, computer and information-related, professional and consulting, audiovisual and other recreational services—is likely to improve. Amid the pandemic, global trade of "other commercial services"—such as financial services, business services, and charges for the use of intellectual property— have avoided large declines and even increased by 6% in the first quarter of 2021 due to widespread adoption of technologies (e.g., remote work) (WTO 2021).

Table 2.3: CAREC Countries—Share of Selected Service Industries in Gross Value Added Created in the Services Sector, 2000 and 2019
(%)

Country	Wholesale and Retail Trade, Restaurants and Hotels[a]		Transport, Storage, and Communication[b]		Other Services[c]	
	2000	2019	2000	2019	2000	2019
Afghanistan	21.8	19.0	41.6	14.4	36.6	66.6
Azerbaijan	18.7	33.2	33.6	21.0	47.8	45.9
China, People's Republic of	26.1	21.5	15.6	8.1	58.4	70.4
Georgia	27.3	27.5	25.5	13.6	47.3	58.9
Kazakhstan	26.9	32.6	23.7	18.0	49.4	49.4
Kyrgyz Republic	42.9	39.7	13.1	2.7	44.0	47.6
Mongolia	34.2	26.2	21.3	6.2	44.5	57.6
Pakistan	36.8	33.7	22.0	19.3	41.2	47.0
Tajikistan	34.5	36.9	15.1	20.5	50.4	42.6
Turkmenistan	10.0	11.8	18.8	18.0	71.2	70.3
Uzbekistan	30.0	18.1	21.1	20.1	49.0	61.8
Comparator country group						
World	22.2	20.8	13.4	12.8	64.4	66.4
OECD countries	21.5	19.2	13.3	13.2	65.2	67.5

CAREC = Central Asia Regional Economic Cooperation, OECD = Organisation for Economic Co-operation and Development.

[a] Corresponds to Sections G–H (Divisions 50–52 and 55) of the ISIC, Revision 3.

[b] Corresponds to Section I (Divisions 60–64) of the ISIC, Revision 3.

[c] Corresponds to Sections J–P (Divisions 65–99) of the ISIC, Revision 3.

Source: United Nations Conference on Trade and Development. UNCTADStat. https://unctadstat.unctad.org/wds/TableViewer/tableView.aspx (accessed 10 August 2021).

Sector Composition of Employment

The sector composition of overall employment changed even more than that of GDP in the CAREC countries during 2001–2019 (Table 2.4). According to the International Labor Organization estimates, the role of agriculture in employment diminished across the CAREC economies, while manufacturing's contribution increased in most countries. The share of the services sector increased in every country and by more than 10 percentage points for seven CAREC members. However, the share of services in total employment for CAREC countries was relatively smaller than the OECD average.

Table 2.4: CAREC Countries—Share of Selected Sectors in Employment, 2000 and 2019
(%)

Country	Agriculture[a]		Manufacturing[b]		Services[c]	
	2000	2019	2000	2019	2000	2019
Afghanistan	65.8	42.5	3.9	8.1	24.7	39.0
Azerbaijan	41.0	36.0	4.6	5.3	48.1	49.2
China, People's Republic of	50.0	25.3	19.2	19.5	27.5	47.2
Georgia	52.2	38.2	6.0	5.8	38.0	47.6
Kazakhstan	36.4	14.9	7.8	6.8	47.3	64.2
Kyrgyz Republic	53.1	19.3	6.4	12.6	36.5	55.3
Mongolia	48.6	25.3	6.8	7.9	37.2	53.1
Pakistan	43.0	36.9	14.2	16.2	36.1	38.1
Tajikistan	59.4	44.7	4.8	5.6	24.1	39.5
Turkmenistan	34.3	20.7	30.7	31.8	31.0	39.5
Uzbekistan	39.1	25.7	13.0	12.3	39.4	51.3
Comparator country groups						
Upper-middle-income countries	40.9	21.6	17.7	16.8	36.5	53.1
OECD countries	6.8	4.8	...	...	65.8	72.6

... = data not available, CAREC = Central Asia Regional Economic Cooperation, OECD = Organisation for Economic Co-operation and Development.

[a] Includes hunting, forestry, and fishing and corresponds to Sections A and B (Divisions 1–5) of the International Standard Industrial Classification of All Economic Activities (ISIC), Revision 3 (United Nations, 1990).

[b] Corresponds to Section D (Divisions 15–37) of the ISIC, Revision 3. It does not include Section C (mining and quarrying), Section E (electricity, gas, steam; water) or Section F (construction).

[c] Corresponds to Sections G–Q (Divisions 50–99) of the ISIC, Revision 3 (United Nations, 1990).

Sources: International Labor Organization. ILOStat. https://www.ilo.org/shinyapps/bulkexplorer9/?lang=en&segment=indicator&id=EMP_2EMP_SEX_ECO_NB_A; and World Bank. World Development Indicators. https://databank.worldbank.org/source/world-development-indicators (accessed 10 August 2021).

Employment by services subsector. The employment patterns by service subsector in CAREC countries differs significantly from those found in high-income countries. Excluding the Kyrgyz Republic and the PRC, accommodation and food services play a smaller part in overall services sector employment than in upper- and high-income countries (Table 2.5). This is also observed in financial, insurance, and business services throughout the CAREC region. There are indications of underdevelopment in tourism and many modern services industries.[8] Meanwhile, the share of education services in employment for most CAREC countries—generally higher compared with other country groups—could indicate good access to education in the region.

Inflows of Foreign Direct Investment

FDI inflows to CAREC countries were generally strong during 2001–2019. In all CAREC countries except Afghanistan, Pakistan, and Uzbekistan, the average ratio of FDI inflows to GDP was higher than in the world overall (Figure 2.1). Inward FDI stock in 2019 for Azerbaijan, Georgia, Kazakhstan, the Kyrgyz Republic, Mongolia, and Turkmenistan was also higher than the global average.

Figure 2.1: CAREC Countries—Selected Indicators of Inward Foreign Direct Investment, 2001–2019
(% of GDP)

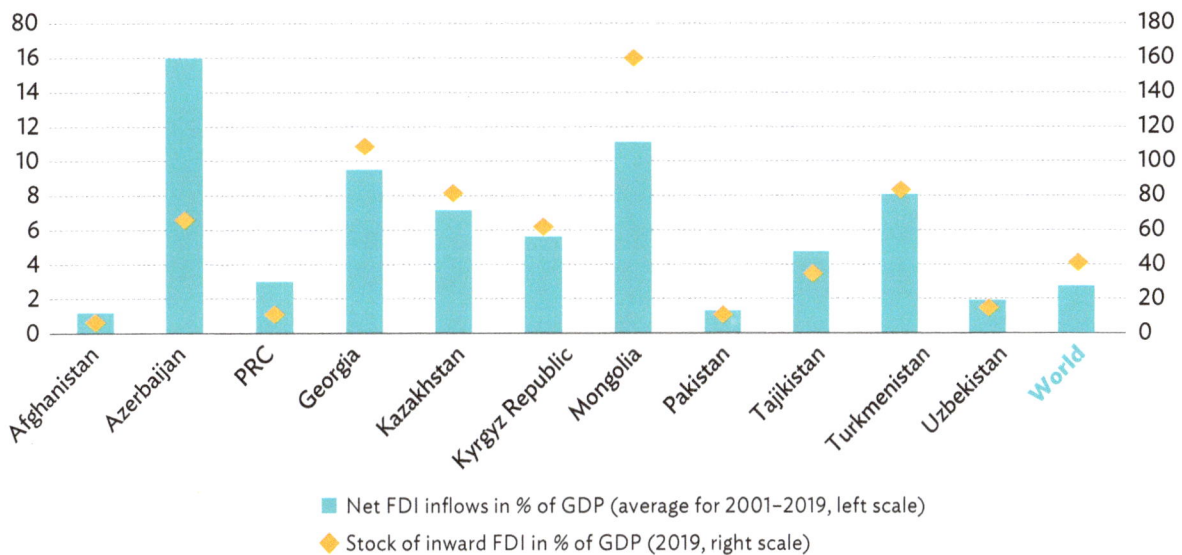

■ Net FDI inflows in % of GDP (average for 2001–2019, left scale)
◆ Stock of inward FDI in % of GDP (2019, right scale)

CAREC = Central Asia Regional Economic Cooperation, FDI = Foreign Direct Investment, GDP = Gross Domestic Product, PRC = People's Republic of China.

Sources: United Nations Conference on Trade and Development. UNCTADStat. https://unctadstat.unctad.org/wds/TableViewer/tableView.aspx; and World Bank. World Development Indicators. https://databank.worldbank.org/source/world-development-indicators (accessed 23 August 2021).

---

8   The share of tourism-related and modern services in CAREC countries' total exports of services is relatively small. Modern services include information and communication, telecommunication, financial intermediation, banking, insurance, computer services, and business and legal services. In comparison, the traditional services are those involving retail and wholesale trade, transport and storage, and personal and social services (ADB 2013).

Table 2.5: CAREC Countries—Share of Service Industries in Total Employment in Services Sector, 2019
(%)

Country	Wholesale and Retail Trade; Repair of Motor Vehicles and Motorcycles	Transport, Storage, and Communication	Accommodation and Food Service Activities	Financial and Insurance Activities	Real estate; Business and Administrative Activities	Public Administration and Defence; Compulsory Social Security	Education	Human Health and Social Work Activities	Other Services
Afghanistan	28.0	15.8	1.1	0.2	2.5	15.7	3.5	26.8	6.4
Azerbaijan	29.3	11.1	3.3	1.1	9.8	11.6	15.7	7.8	10.3
China, People's Republic of	32.2	9.5	9.9	3.1	6.9	11.5	10.4	5.3	11.2
Georgia	24.5	12.6	6.1	3.8	5.7	11.7	19.2	7.5	8.9
Kazakhstan	23.0	14.6	3.8	3.8	10.9	8.9	18.8	8.4	7.8
Kyrgyz Republic	28.4	17.2	11.2	2.8	4.6	7.3	16.5	7.4	4.7
Mongolia	26.4	12.2	6.0	4.0	6.5	14.1	15.8	7.3	7.9
Pakistan	40.1	16.8	5.3	1.5	4.2	6.9	11.3	4.3	9.7
Tajikistan	27.2	14.4	3.6	2.9	2.9	11.7	20.9	10.4	5.9
Turkmenistan	29.9	12.4	1.7	2.3	6.7	13.0	17.1	9.1	7.7
Uzbekistan	19.2	9.6	4.2	1.0	3.2	11.4	13.5	7.2	30.7
Comparator country groups									
World	29.3	12.0	8.1	3.1	9.1	8.5	10.6	8.1	11.1
Upper-middle-income countries	31.2	10.3	9.4	2.9	8.2	10.0	10.5	6.0	11.7
High-income countries	18.7	11.9	7.9	4.6	14.3	7.6	10.7	16.1	8.4

CAREC = Central Asia Regional Economic Cooperation.
Source: International Labor Organization. ILOstat. https://www.ilo.org/shinyapps/bulkexplorer35/?lang=en&segment=indicator&id=EMP_2EMP_SEX_ECO_NB_A (accessed 10 August 2021).

Foreign direct investment patterns. FDI inflows were concentrated in the energy and/or mining sectors in most CAREC countries. The energy sector accounted for the bulk of incoming FDI in Azerbaijan, Kazakhstan, and Turkmenistan, for instance (ADBI 2014; Ganiev 2019; Madhur 2016). So did the mining sector in Mongolia. Elsewhere, the inflows were more diversified as in Georgia, the Kyrgyz Republic, Pakistan, and the PRC. In Georgia, for example, the transport and communication, finance, and hotels and restaurants sector accounted for two-fifths of cumulative FDI inflows during 2007–2018 (Figure 2.2). More than one-third of the cumulative FDI flowing into the Kyrgyz Republic during 2011–2018 went to the financial services and geological exploration activities (Figure 2.3).

Figure 2.2: Georgia—Sector Distribution of Cumulative FDI Inflows, 2007–2018
(%)

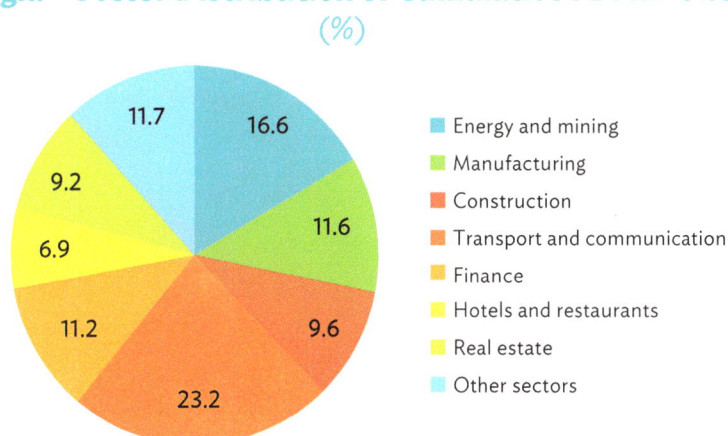

- 11.7
- 16.6
- 11.6
- 9.2
- 6.9
- 9.6
- 11.2
- 23.2

Legend:
- Energy and mining
- Manufacturing
- Construction
- Transport and communication
- Finance
- Hotels and restaurants
- Real estate
- Other sectors

Source: National Statistics Office of Georgia. https://www.geostat.ge/en (accessed September 2020).

Figure 2.3: Kyrgyz Republic—Sector Distribution of Cumulative FDI Inflows, 2011–2018
(%)

- 3.0
- 5.6
- 24.2
- 38.8
- 13.5
- 4.9
- 4.0
- 5.9

Legend:
- Mining and quarrying
- Manufacturing (including gold production)
- Electricity, gas, steam, and air conditioning supply
- Construction
- Wholesale and retail trade; repair of motor vehicles, and motorcycles
- Finance and insurance activities
- Professional, scientific, and technical activities
- Other sectors

Source: National Statistics Committee of the Kyrgyz Republic. http://stat.kg/en/ (accessed September 2020).

Aggregate Exports and Imports of Goods

Merchandise exports and imports grew at higher than world average rates during 2001–2020 in almost all CAREC countries. The exceptions were Pakistan's and Tajikistan's exports and Turkmenistan's imports (Table 2.6). In the CAREC-10 countries (in this study, refer to all CAREC members except the PRC), the rise in merchandise exports came largely (or even mostly) in the form of increases in exports of primary commodities such as oil, gas, coal, ores, metals, vegetables, and fruits. Growth of manufactured exports significantly contributed to the rise of merchandise exports in Georgia, Pakistan and the PRC.

Limited role of merchandise exports and imports in economies. Between 2000 and 2020, the ratio of merchandise exports and imports to GDP rose only in Azerbaijan, Georgia, Pakistan, and Uzbekistan and fell substantially elsewhere (Table 2.6). The decline in Tajikistan was largely due to the reclassification of aluminum from the merchandise to the manufacturing services category and the exclusion of imports of aluminum from merchandise imports. The discontinuation of exports of natural gas to the Russian Federation and the decline in merchandise imports that resulted reduced

Table 2.6: CAREC Countries—Selected Indicators of Merchandise Exports and Imports, 2000–2020
(%)

Country	Cumulative Change in Value of Exports and Imports During 2001–2020 (%)		Ratio of Exports and Imports to GDP (%)	
	Exports	Imports	2000	2020
Afghanistan	471.5	450.6	62.9[a]	36.6
Azerbaijan	687.4	815.6	55.3	57.4
China, People's Republic of	939.8	813.3	39.2	31.6
Georgia	934.7	1,029.9	33.8	71.4
Kazakhstan	427.1	638.5	75.7	49.3
Kyrgyz Republic	284.5	560.2	78.1	73.0
Mongolia	1,313.4	760.8	101.2	97.9
Pakistan	143.4	322.0	24.2	25.7
Tajikistan	134.1	360.7	169.7	60.4
Turkmenistan	184.1	80.6	147.8	27.8[b]
Uzbekistan	371.5	642.3	40.1	57.7
Comparator country groups				
World	172.3	167.7	39.0	42.7
OECD countries	119.6	117.5	35.1	42.1

CAREC = Central Asia Regional Economic Cooperation, GDP = gross domestic product, OECD = Organisation for Economic Co-operation and Development.

[a]   Data is for 2002.

[b]   Data is for 2019.

Source: World Bank. World Development Indicators. https://databank.worldbank.org/source/world-development-indicators (accessed 10 August 2021).

the ratio in Turkmenistan. The ratio varied widely across the CAREC countries in 2020. It stood at 25.7% in Pakistan and reached 97.9% in Mongolia. Overall, however, the ratio was low in most of the CAREC member states compared with many countries of a similar size that have open economies.

Composition and Direction of Exports of Goods

The merchandise exports of most CAREC countries are concentrated in terms of commodity composition and geographic distribution. The product concentration index for merchandise exports is greater than 20 in all the CAREC-10 countries. Their top five markets account for more than 30% of the merchandise exports from all 11 CAREC members (Figure 2.4).

Figure 2.4: CAREC Countries—Product Concentration Index for Exports and Share of Top Five Markets in Merchandise Exports, 2020

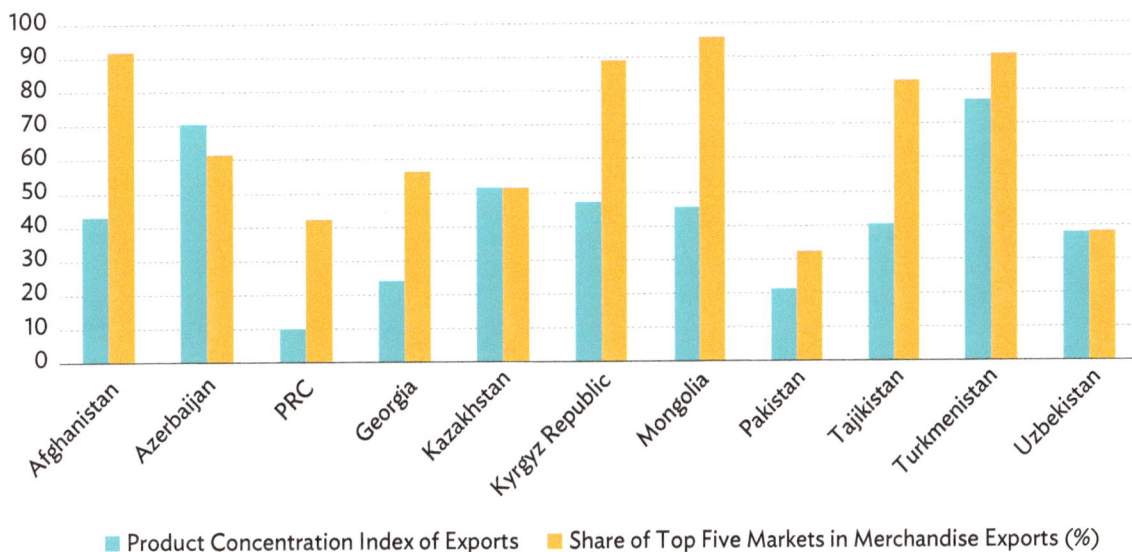

CAREC = Central Asia Regional Economic Cooperation, PRC = People's Republic of China.

Notes: The product concentration index ranges from 0 to 100, with a greater number corresponding to a higher level of product concentration.

Sources: International Monetary Fund. Direction of Trade Statistics. https://data.imf.org/regular.aspx?key=61013712; and United Nations Conference on Trade and Development. UNCTADStat. https://unctadstat.unctad.org/wds/ReportFolders/reportFolders.aspx (accessed 10 August 2021).

Dominance of primary commodities. Primary commodities make up more than half of merchandise exports in all but two CAREC countries.[9] Because a few primary commodities dominate exports of most CAREC countries, most of them rank low in the Economic Complexity Index

---

[9]   The principal primary commodities and commodity groups in the merchandise exports of CAREC countries are: horticulture products (Afghanistan, Azerbaijan, Georgia, the Kyrgyz Republic, Pakistan, Tajikistan, and Uzbekistan); cotton fiber (Pakistan, Tajikistan, Turkmenistan, and Uzbekistan); cereals (Kazakhstan and Pakistan); livestock products (Kazakhstan and Mongolia); crude oil (Azerbaijan and Kazakhstan); natural gas (Turkmenistan and Uzbekistan); coal (Afghanistan and Mongolia); ores and metals (Afghanistan, Georgia, the Kyrgyz Republic, Mongolia, Tajikistan, and Uzbekistan); and uranium (Kazakhstan and Uzbekistan). See also CAREC Trade Information Portal for data on each CAREC country's top exports and imports and their markets. https://trade.carecprogram.org/.

(Figure 2.5). Manufactured goods outstrip primary commodities in the PRC's export basket, and labor- and resource-intensive manufacturers account for most of merchandise exports in Pakistan. Technology-intensive goods comprise a smaller portion of merchandise exports in all the CAREC-10 countries than they do on average in OECD nations (Table 2.7).

Figure 2.5: CAREC Countries—Ranking in Economic Complexity Index, 2019

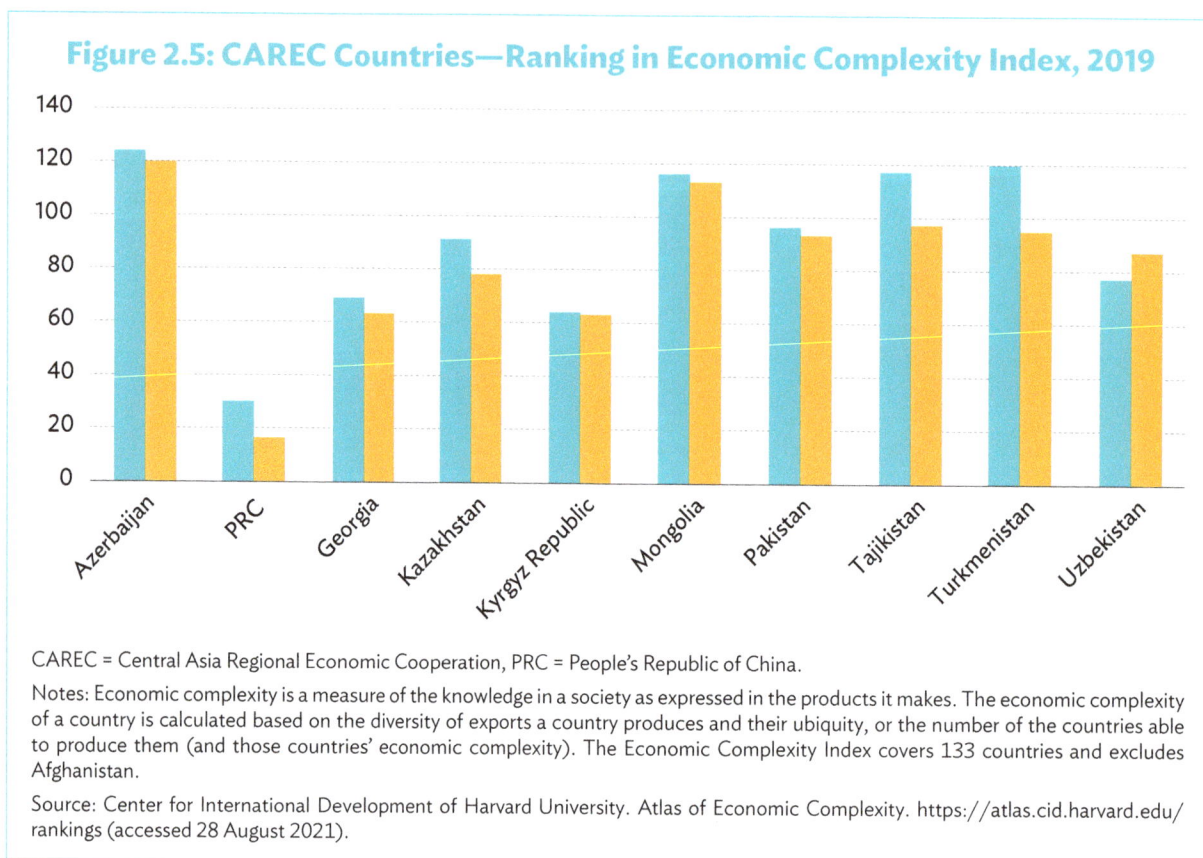

CAREC = Central Asia Regional Economic Cooperation, PRC = People's Republic of China.

Notes: Economic complexity is a measure of the knowledge in a society as expressed in the products it makes. The economic complexity of a country is calculated based on the diversity of exports a country produces and their ubiquity, or the number of the countries able to produce them (and those countries' economic complexity). The Economic Complexity Index covers 133 countries and excludes Afghanistan.

Source: Center for International Development of Harvard University. Atlas of Economic Complexity. https://atlas.cid.harvard.edu/rankings (accessed 28 August 2021).

Table 2.7: CAREC Countries—Composition of Merchandise Exports by Product Groups, 2020
(%)

Country	Primary Commodities[a]	Manufactured Goods			
		Labor- and Resource-Intensive	Low-Skill- and Technology-Intensive	Medium-Skill- and Technology-Intensive	High-Skill- and Technology-Intensive
Afghanistan	94.4	1.6	0.3	1.0	0.8
Azerbaijan	96.2	0.6	0.5	0.5	2.1
China, People's Republic of	5.6	19.6	9.3	27.5	37.0
Georgia	55.8	4.4	10.2	17.6	12.0
Kazakhstan	83.9	0.6	8.2	1.1	6.1
Kyrgyz Republic	82.4	8.9	1.5	5.0	2.2

continued on next page

Table 2.7 *continued*

Country	Primary Commodities[a]	Manufactured Goods			
		Labor- and Resource-Intensive	Low-Skill- and Technology-Intensive	Medium-Skill- and Technology-Intensive	High-Skill- and Technology-Intensive
Mongolia	98.3	1.1	0.2	0.2	0.2
Pakistan	25.0	63.5	1.5	2.9	6.9
Tajikistan	84.1	7.4	1.4	1.3	1.9
Turkmenistan	93.6	3.1	0.2	0.3	2.4
Uzbekistan	73.1	14.8	1.4	3.0	7.5
Comparator country group					
OECD countries	23.4	6.9	6.4	29.0	29.9

CAREC = Central Asia Regional Economic Cooperation, OECD = Organisation for Economic Co-operation and Development.

[a] Includes precious stones and nonmonetary gold.

Note: The sum of the shares of the product groups included in the table may not add up to 100% because some goods are not included in any of these groups.

Source: United Nations Conference on Trade and Development. UNCTADStat. https://unctadstat.unctad.org/wds/ReportFolders/reportFolders.aspx?sCS_ChosenLang=en (accessed 10 August 2021).

Aggregate Exports and Imports of Services

The significant contribution made by the services sector to CAREC countries' GDP growth during 2000–2019 was to be expected as incomes grew, and economies diversified. The services sector has become a more important factor in overall employment in the vast majority of CAREC countries as well.

Modern services growth relatively slow. Performance has varied considerably by services subsector. Growth of the more modern services subsectors, such as financial and business services, has been slower than that in the subsectors less associated with diversified economies. This is also reflected to some extent by observable patterns in services trade flow data, with changes expected due to COVID-19. Gross exports and imports by individual CAREC countries in the major services categories are primarily associated with production—in other words, intermediate services that typically contribute value to other services subsectors and sectors of the economy. However, the contribution of services to production may be statistically underreported. This presents a problem for countries undertaking evidence-based policy making (Box 2.1).

Concentrated exports, volatile prices. Considerable fluctuation is discernible in export and import performance between the selected years of 2005, 2008, 2012, 2015, and 2019 (Appendix 1). The data are in current price terms. This means that they reflect price and output developments at home as well as changes in world prices. Prices tend to be particularly volatile in the mainstay product lines of most CAREC economies—namely, commodities and raw materials. Exogenous price volatility is one reason diversification is a major policy objective of the CAREC countries.

Box 2.1: Identifying Services Inputs

The services sector's characteristics are often intangible and highly customized, which makes hard data sparse. The result is a lack of specific data and precise understanding of the contribution made by services to value.

Value added by services may be underestimated. Services inputs are often hidden in statistical calculations and categories. Any product that goes to market for consumption as either an intermediate input or a final offering will generally be a bundle of goods and services. Yet statistics generally aggregate the values of these two different sources under the single rubric of goods. The value that services inputs contribute dissolves statistically into an overall stated value considered to be that of goods.

An example of underestimation. Think, for example, of the machinery repair and maintenance services and the accounting and advertising services that can go into a business running a clothing factory. Unless these services are supplied by arms-length providers and recorded separately as final products, they will be incorporated statistically in the value attributed to the clothing goods end products themselves. This is one reason that data on goods and services are sensitive to changes in economic structures and particularly to the degree of specialization that occurs, resulting in arms-length transactions that are recorded separately in statistics.

Potential for reverse misclassification. The same type of misclassification, where services are counted as goods, can also occur. Think, for example, of a bakery owned by a hotel that makes bread and cakes for sale on its premises. In this case the output of cake and bread may be classified as part of what the hotel produces and recorded as value attributable to hotel services.

Classifications in trade data. Accurately determining and reporting data on the sources of value in recorded trade flows can be a particular challenge. This is due to the use of different statistical conventions traditionally used for recording goods and services.

One way of measuring gross domestic product (GDP) is as follows: $GDP = C + I + G + X - M$, where C is consumption, I is investment, G is government expenditure, X is exports, and M is imports. Consumption, investment, and government expenditure are all measured in terms of the value that each of these elements of national economic activity was worth in the year concerned. They are, in other words, value-added numbers. By contrast, the values entering the national accounts for exports and imports are gross values.

Because the overall export figure includes and is inflated by the value that was imported, it does not on its own accurately reflect what exports have contributed to the domestic economy. Hence, the need to subtract imports in the national account's calculation. That is an aggregated figure, however; and until recently, very little disaggregated, product-level information on the sources and value of inputs entering trade was available.

New datasets (OECD 2013; Timmer 2012) based on value-added measures identify the services content of production, trade, and consumption by precisely identifying the sources of value. Measured in the traditional way, services are estimated to account for about 25% of trade. This is a gross figure. When sources of value are netted out, however, this number roughly doubles and, due to the disaggregation challenges, is still likely to be underestimated. Case study work that seeks to disaggregate further than is possible with macro datasets demonstrates how significant the services components of production and trade can be. A sample of firm-level case studies undertaken in Asia over 2 years (Low and Pasadilla 2016), showed that 22 firms in a wide array of industries had supply chains through which 37–74 discrete service activities were adding value. The value of these services frequently exceeded the share accounted for by goods on the production side.

Sources: Low, P., and G. Pasadilla. 2016. *Services in Global Value Chains: Manufacturing-Related Services*. Singapore: World Scientific; OECD. 2013. The OECD–WTO Trade in Value Added (TiVA) database. https://www.oecd.org/sti/ind/TIVA_stats%20flyer_ENG.pdf; Timmer, Marcel. 2012. The World Input–Output Database (WIOD): Contents, Sources and Methods. 10.13140/RG.2.1.2863.8802.

Growth in services exports uneven. Services exports by the CAREC countries overall posted growth albeit at varying rates during 2005–2019. Average annual rates cascade from highs of about 15% for Afghanistan, 13% for Georgia, 12% for Azerbaijan, 11% for Uzbekistan and the Kyrgyz Republic, and 9% for Kazakhstan to 8% for Mongolia, 6% for Turkmenistan, 4% for Tajikistan, and 3% for Pakistan.

Services import growth also mixed. The highest annual average import growth rates over the period were in Uzbekistan at about 18% and Mongolia at about 14%. Next came Turkmenistan and Georgia at around 10%, the Kyrgyz Republic at 9%, Afghanistan and Azerbaijan at 6%, and Tajikistan at 5%. The lowest expansion rates were those of Kazakhstan at 3% and Pakistan at 2%. Some but not all the faster growing countries were operating from a lower quantitative base, although this was less true of Turkmenistan.

Caveat on compounded average rates. It should be noted that the calculation of compound average growth rates relies on the first and last recorded values for the year range under consideration. It tells a reliable story only when the trend is uninterrupted throughout the period. Because of widely fluctuating commodity prices and other factors hindering growth at certain times during 2005–2019, the average rates for the period conceal the full picture of services export and import development and can be misleading. Figure 2.6 and Figure 2.7 show how export and import earnings fluctuated within the period.

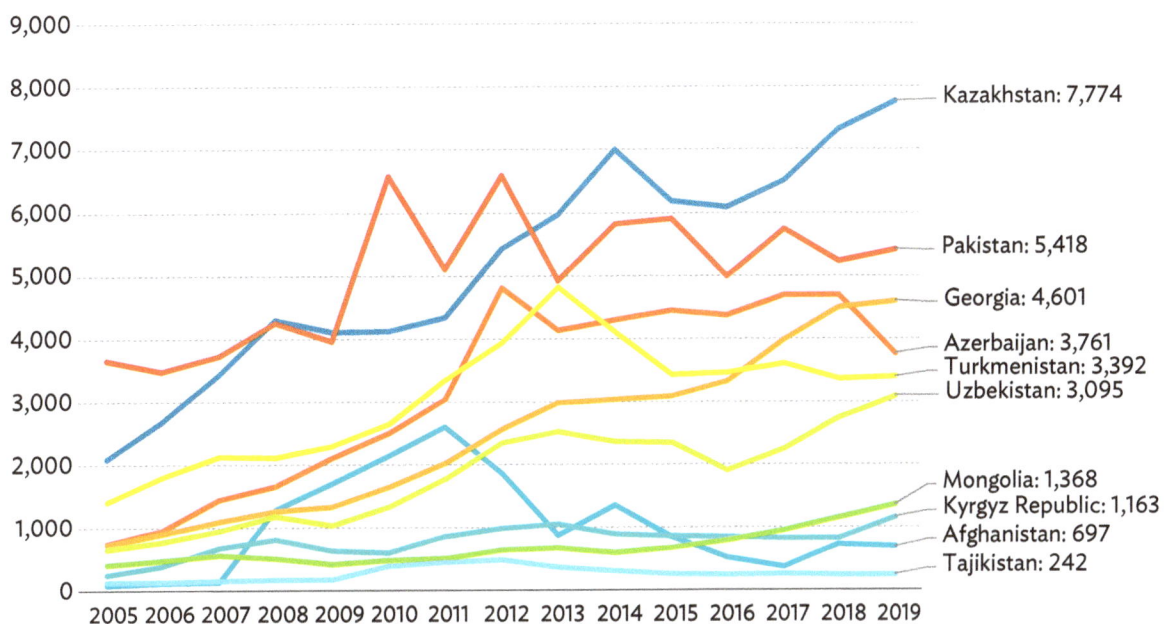

Figure 2.6: Exports of Services in CAREC, 2005–2019
($ million)

CAREC = Central Asia Regional Economic Cooperation.

Source: World Trade Organization. Balanced International Trade in Services Extended Balance of Payments Services 2010. https://www.wto.org/english/res_e/statis_e/trade_datasets_e.htm (accessed March 2021).

Figure 2.7: Imports of Services in CAREC, 2005–2019
($ million)

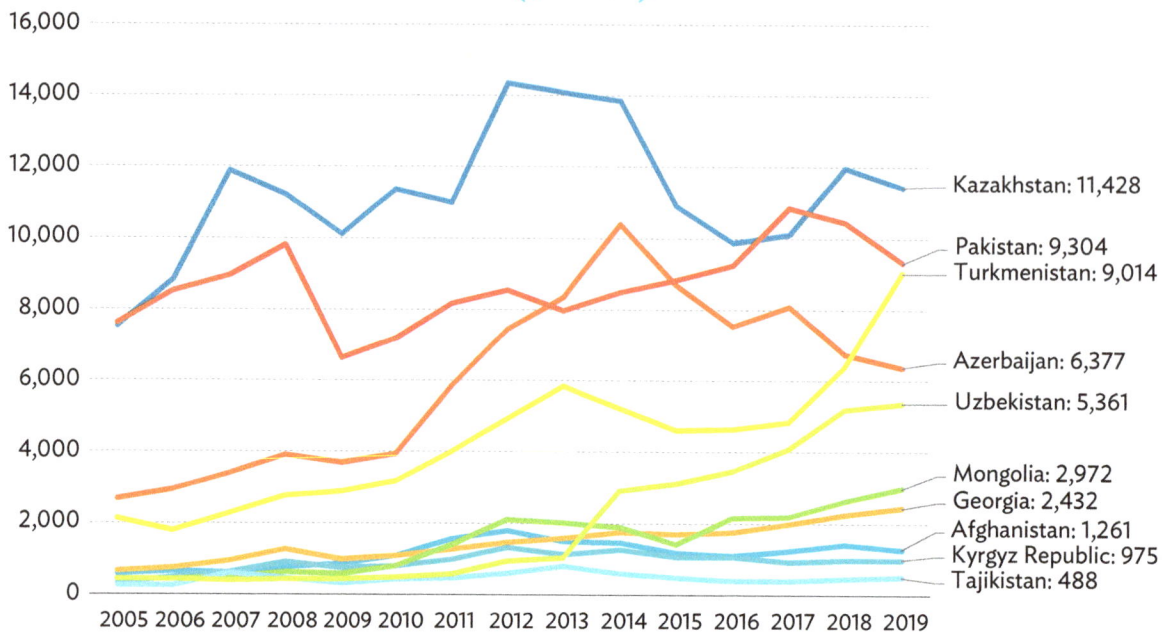

CAREC = Central Asia Regional Economic Cooperation.

Source: World Trade Organization. Balanced International Trade in Services Extended Balance of Payments Services 2010. https://www.wto.org/english/res_e/statis_e/trade_datasets_e.htm (accessed March 2021).

Composition of Exports and Imports of Services

Export patterns concentrated and current account deficits common. Certain patterns appear commonly in the composition of services exports and imports across the CAREC countries. One leading export services subsector is transport. This is the case for CAREC-10. Other relatively significant services are travel (Azerbaijan, Georgia, Kazakhstan, the Kyrgyz Republic, Mongolia, Turkmenistan, and Uzbekistan); construction (Afghanistan); ICT (Pakistan and Uzbekistan); and other business services (Afghanistan, Azerbaijan, Kazakhstan, the Kyrgyz Republic, Mongolia, Pakistan, and Turkmenistan). In recent years, nine CAREC countries (for which data were available and presented in Appendix 1) have run services current account deficits—sometimes very large ones. The two exceptions are Georgia and Uzbekistan.

A lack of modern services imports. Four subsectors dominate CAREC countries' services imports: transport (CAREC-10); travel (Azerbaijan, Georgia, Kazakhstan, the Kyrgyz Republic, Mongolia, Pakistan, Turkmenistan, and Uzbekistan); construction (Azerbaijan, Kazakhstan, Mongolia, and Tajikistan); and other business services (Azerbaijan, Kazakhstan, the Kyrgyz Republic, Mongolia, Pakistan, and Turkmenistan). Except for some business services, these are not the services, such as ICT and financial services, generally considered modern and features of diversified economies. This can reflect either the high concentration of natural resource-dependent manufacturing economies or a domestic supply of these modern services. The former explanation predominates in the CAREC region.

Services Trade by Mode of Supply

An experimental dataset recently developed by the World Trade Organization (WTO) identifies services trade transactions by mode of supply. This trade in services data by mode of supply database (TISMOS) is still a work in progress. In line with the General Agreement on Trade in Services (GATS), transactions are identified under TISMOS as belonging to one of four modes. Mode 1 supply covers cross-border service transactions that are analogous to goods trade transactions. When a service is transacted or consumed in the jurisdiction of the supplier, the transaction comes under Mode 2. This kind of transaction can involve the physical movement of consumers, such as in tourism services, certain kinds of educational offerings, virtual movement such as online distance education, or the consumption by foreigners of financial services in another jurisdiction. The country reporting Mode 2 service transactions is recording exports, not imports. Modes 3 and 4 deal with the movement of factors of production across frontiers and expand beyond WTO rules governing physical goods. Mode 3 covers cross-border investment by juridical persons, that is, capital investment in services enterprises. The temporary cross-border movement of natural persons—in other words, of individual service suppliers employed in a services enterprise—falls under Mode 4.

Economies partly shaped by exports. Appendix 2 divides the data on imports and exports of CAREC-10 countries in 2017 into the four modes of supply. Figures 2.8 and 2.9 provide the overall picture. On the export side, the available data illustrates the role of trade in influencing the economic structures of CAREC countries. The services export numbers are quite modest, particularly at the subsector level. The one exception is the Mode 2 export of tourism and business travel services, which makes a nontrivial contribution to the economies of Azerbaijan, Georgia, Kazakhstan, the Kyrgyz Republic, and Mongolia. Some CAREC countries also record relatively modest exports of transport services, which may be linked to tourism.

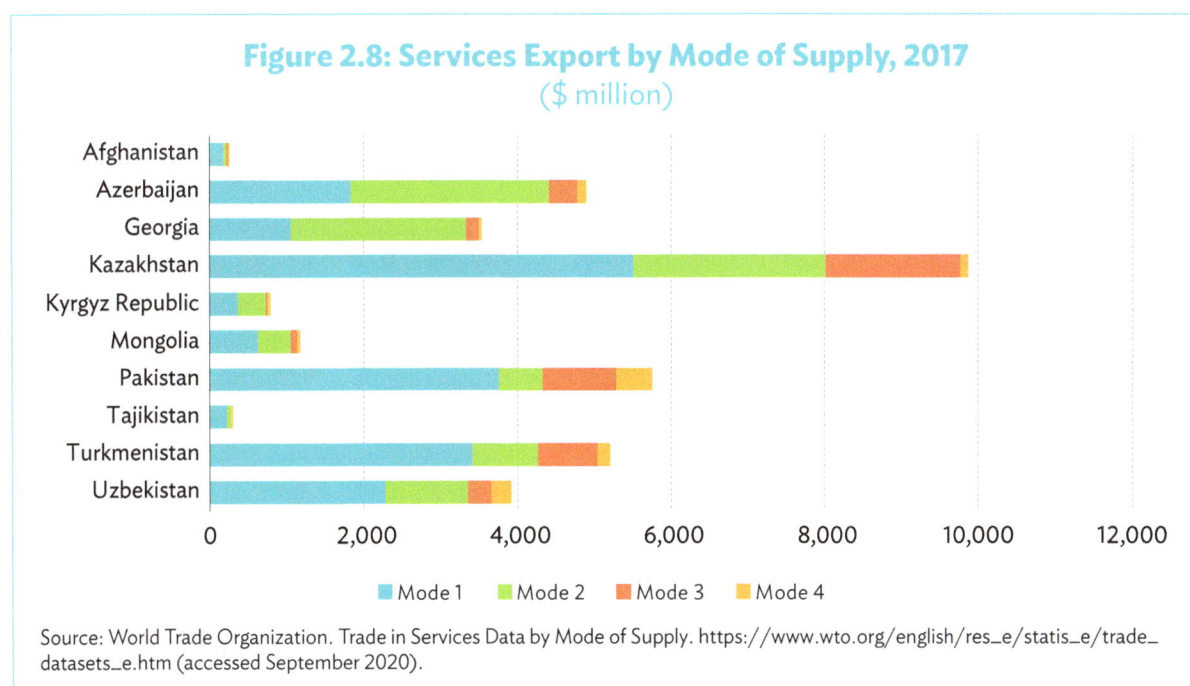

Figure 2.8: Services Export by Mode of Supply, 2017
($ million)

Source: World Trade Organization. Trade in Services Data by Mode of Supply. https://www.wto.org/english/res_e/statis_e/trade_datasets_e.htm (accessed September 2020).

Figure 2.9: Services Import by Mode of Supply, 2017
($ million)

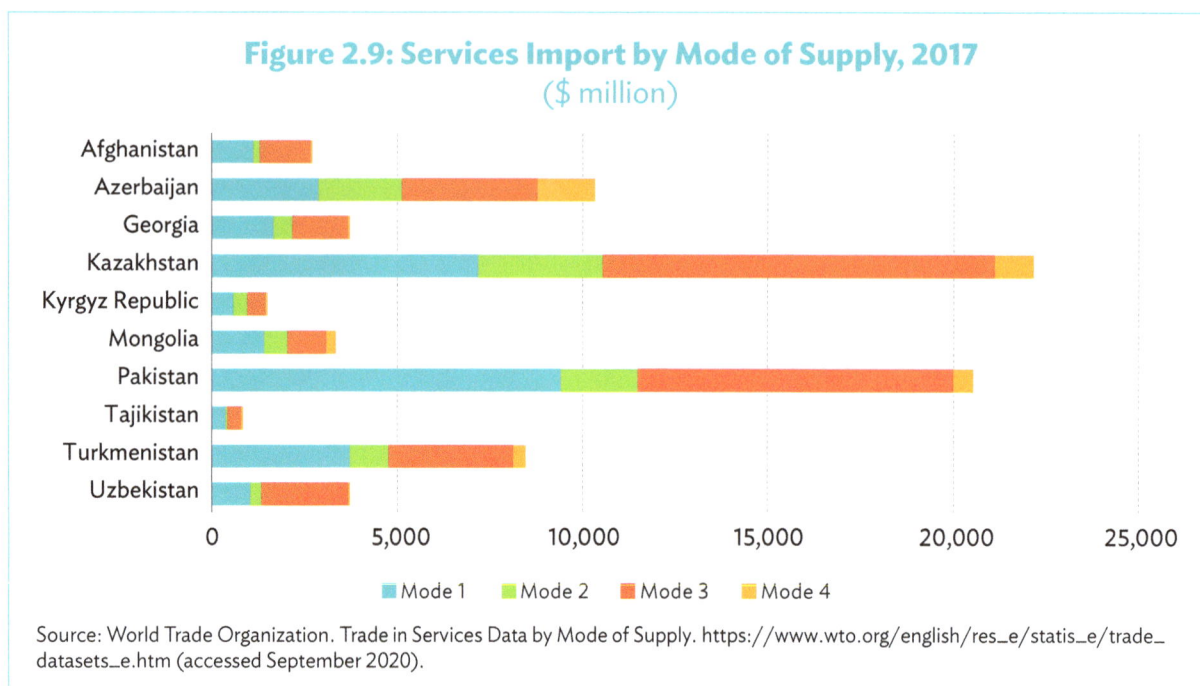

Source: World Trade Organization. Trade in Services Data by Mode of Supply. https://www.wto.org/english/res_e/statis_e/trade_datasets_e.htm (accessed September 2020).

Mode 1 exports of transport, financial, ICT, business, distribution, and health and education services accounted for comparatively small segments of overall export value in 2017. Modes 3 and 4 contributions were slight except in Kazakhstan and Uzbekistan. The bulk of the services exports, aside from Mode 1 tourism services, likely went to other CAREC countries rather than beyond. Appendix 3 illustrates the importance of the services sector, particularly business-related services for exports and economic diversification.

Economies reflected by imports that indicate diversification potential. Modes 1 and 3 dominate services imports by a large margin. Mode 1 values slightly exceeded those of Mode 3 in most countries. The value of Mode 3 imports in the financial, ICT, and construction services subsectors can be viewed as indications of a diversification process. These subsectors are the backbone of potential diversification into manufacturing. Financial and ICT services accounted for significant shares of Mode 3 imports in almost all the CAREC countries. Construction services were important imports for Azerbaijan, Kazakhstan, and the Kyrgyz Republic. While they may not be among the modern services, transport services that also figured prominently in Kazakhstan and Pakistan, and the substantial distribution services imports of most CAREC economies, are increasingly supplied by enterprises established in-country and add to GDP and jobs.

Mode 2 imports depend on foreign demand. Mode 2 service imports are best thought of as exports. They will benefit the importing party less if they involve short-term consumption—by a country's tourists in a foreign country, for example—than if they are long-term human capital imports such as the consumption of a trading partner's education and health services. Most CAREC countries import tourism services. Several also consume imported education services. However, these constitute small parts of the overall picture.

Mode 4 is mainly construction and business services. Mode 4 imports—the temporary presence in a country of individual service suppliers from abroad—also constitute a small share. Predictably, these service suppliers are most evident in construction and business. Azerbaijan, Kazakhstan, Mongolia, and Tajikistan imported construction workers in 2017. The most significant business services importers were Azerbaijan, Kazakhstan, Mongolia, Pakistan, Turkmenistan, and Uzbekistan. Most other CAREC countries imported the above-mentioned services as well, but in smaller quantities. Some also imported Mode 4 ICT, maintenance and repair, research and development, and personal services.

Chapter 3

KEY SERVICES SUBSECTORS AND INDUSTRIES FOR ECONOMIC DIVERSIFICATION IN CAREC COUNTRIES

The services sector encompasses a broad range of economic activities. Service activities differ in how much they can contribute to economic diversification, job creation, productivity growth, and economic development. Modern service activities such as information and telecommunication services create fewer jobs but contribute more to technical progress and productivity growth than traditional service industries such as transport and retail trade. They also require more skilled labor than the traditional service industries (Asian Development Bank Institute 2019; International Monetary Fund 2018b).

CAREC countries should promote robust development of the services sector. However, they also need to pay particular attention to service industries critical for economic diversification and development. As they do so, they need to strike a balance between the labor-intensive service industries that create more jobs and the knowledge-intensive service industries that contribute more to technical progress and productivity growth.

Seven key categories. Figure 3.1 shows the services subsectors found to be important to economic diversification in CAREC countries: (i) telecommunication and information services, including software development and data processing; (ii) financial services, including insurance and other nonbank services; (iii) education and research and development services, including agricultural extension services, vocational training, scientific research and development, and market research; (iv) tourism-related services, including passenger transportation services; (v) freight transportation and storage services, including logistics services and cold storage services for horticulture products; (vi) quality testing and certification services, including those for food; and (vii) other agriculture-related services.

The seven subsectors in Figure 3.1 were identified based on the study's consideration of international experience with economic diversification through the development of the services sector; development priorities of CAREC countries; the potential of various service industries to contribute to job creation, productivity growth, and economic diversification in line with the development priorities of CAREC countries; and global and regional developments and trends that will affect demand for various services over the medium and long term (see also Chapter 1).

**Figure 3.1: Key Services Subsectors for Economic Diversification
in CAREC Countries**

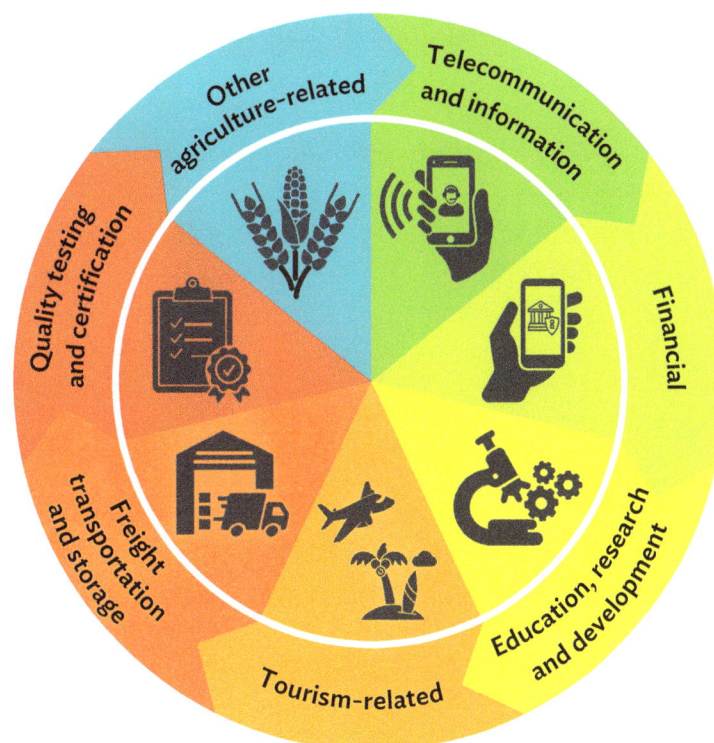

CAREC = Central Asia Regional Economic Cooperation.
Source: ADB.

Certain services subsectors—those referred to sometimes as producer or business services—are critical to the proper functioning of the entire economy. The services they provide are used as inputs by almost every other sector. Thus, these services subsectors or industries must function efficiently for the rest of the economy to perform well.[10] Transport, telecommunications, finance, and water and electricity distribution are prime examples.

Telecommunication and Information Services

Telecommunication and information services play a leading role in the adoption and diffusion of many new technologies, including digital technologies. By doing so, they foster technical progress and productivity growth. In many countries (including Germany, India, and the United States), total factor productivity increased more in information and communication services than in manufacturing during 2006–2015 (ADBI 2019; WTO 2019b). In countries such as Estonia and India, rapid

---

[10]   Another dimension of the critical role of the business services is their part in determining the productivity of the fundamental factors of production, such as labor and capital, that generate knowledge, goods, and other services (Francois and Hoekman 2010).

development of such services contributed in a major way to diversifying the structure of production and exports. These services have spearheaded digital transformation of economies and societies around the world. Owing to the widespread adoption of digital technologies, international trade has become extensive not only in telecommunication and information services, but in many other services as well (WTO 2019b).

Telecommunication and information services have been one of the fastest-growing industries in most CAREC countries. The expansion of wireless telecommunication services has been particularly swift. The mobile cellular subscription rate in many CAREC countries is now higher than the average for OECD countries (Table 3.1). The fixed broadband subscription rate and/or the percentage of the population using the internet are also relatively high in some CAREC countries (e.g., Azerbaijan, Georgia, Kazakhstan, and the PRC).

Table 3.1: CAREC Countries—Selected Indicators of Development of Communication Services, 2019

Country	Fixed Telephone Subscriptions (per 100 people)	Mobile Cellular Subscriptions (per 100 people)	Fixed Broadband Subscriptions (per 100 people)	Individuals Using the Internet (% of population)
Afghanistan	0.4	59.4	<0.1	11.5[a]
Azerbaijan	16.7	107.0	19.3	81.1
China, People's Republic of	13.3	121.8	31.3	54.3[a]
Georgia	13.0	134.7	23.6	68.8
Kazakhstan	16.6	138.6	13.5	81.9
Kyrgyz Republic	4.7	134.4	4.2	38.2[a]
Mongolia	10.9	137.0	9.8	51.1
Pakistan	1.1	76.4	0.8	17.1
Tajikistan	5.4[a]	111.5[a]	<0.1[a]	22.0[a]
Turkmenistan	11.8[a]	162.9[a]	<0.1[a]	21.3[a]
Uzbekistan	10.8	101.2	13.9	55.2[b]
Comparator country groups				
World	12.6	109.4	15.7	49.0[a]
Lower middle-income countries	3.3	98.3	3.2	32.6[a]
Upper middle-income countries	14.1	120.9	24.5	58.8[a]
OECD countries	33.8	123.5	31.9	82.8[b]

CAREC = Central Asia Regional Economic Cooperation, OECD = Organisation for Economic Co-operation and Development.

[a]   Data is for 2017.

[b]   Data is for 2018.

Source: World Bank. World Development Indicators. https://databank.worldbank.org/source/world-development-indicators (accessed 14 July 2021).

However, telecommunication, and especially, information services are underdeveloped in most CAREC countries. Many CAREC countries lag on important indicators of telecommunication services usage (Table 3.1). Only four CAREC countries exceed the global average rate for fixed telephone subscriptions (Azerbaijan, Georgia, Kazakhstan, and the PRC), and only three exceed the world average rate for fixed broadband subscriptions (Azerbaijan, Georgia, and the PRC). Around 45.7% of individuals in CAREC countries use the internet (or 44.8% excluding the PRC), a higher percentage than in lower-middle-income countries, although lower than in the OECD. So is the CAREC region average of 10.6% (or 8.5% for CAREC-10) for the number of fixed broadband subscriptions per 100 people. Afghanistan and Pakistan both fall below the developing country average on all four telecommunications indicators. The cost of accessing the internet is also high in many CAREC countries when compared with their per capita incomes (ADB 2015). The quality of telecommunication services is low and internet connection speed is slow in most of these countries as well. The majority did poorly in speed tests conducted globally in May 2021 (Table 3.2). Of the six CAREC countries covered by the Economist Intelligence Unit's 100-nation Inclusive Internet Index 2020, Kazakhstan, Pakistan, the PRC, and Uzbekistan internet ranked 51st or lower on internet access affordability. Azerbaijan and Mongolia were the exceptions.

Table 3.2: CAREC Countries—Speedtest Global Index, May 2021

Country	Fixed Broadband Internet Connection		Mobile Internet Connection	
	Download Speed (Mbps)	Rank[a]	Download Speed (Mbps)	Rank[b]
Afghanistan	11.20	165	6.86	137
Azerbaijan	23.25	125	36.34	68
China, People's Republic of	178.55	17	153.09	5
Georgia	26.80	111	38.29	64
Kazakhstan	58.35	67	29.70	85
Kyrgyz Republic	46.47	84	24.19	96
Mongolia	46.41	85	20.34	114
Pakistan	11.72	164	19.90	117
Tajikistan	35.60	100	14.79	129
Turkmenistan	4.19	180	...	...
Uzbekistan	40.54	91	18.56	120
Top performers:				
Singapore	250.35	1	82.23	20
Republic of Korea	245.01	2	76.38	25

... = data not available, CAREC = Central Asia Regional Economic Cooperation, Mbps = megabits per second.

[a] Out of 180 countries.

[b] Out of 137 countries.

Source: Ookla. Speedtest Global Index. https://www.speedtest.net/global-index (accessed 14 July 2021).

The underdevelopment of telecommunication and information services has been one reason for the comparatively slow adoption by CAREC countries of digital technologies. This has in turn constrained growth in many other sectors, including agriculture, manufacturing, e-commerce, tourism, and finance. None of the CAREC countries except the PRC has a large electronics manufacturing industry or flourishing e-commerce. As of 2020, half of CAREC countries ranked low on the United Nations Conference on Trade and Development index that measures the preparedness of national economies to support online shopping (Figure 3.2).[11]

Faster growth in telecommunication and information services is essential to diversifying and developing CAREC economies. Such growth will facilitate the adoption of existing digital technologies, which will help CAREC countries raise labor productivity and improve the quality of products and services in agriculture, manufacturing, transport, finance, and other sectors. Prompt adoption of emerging digital technologies such as artificial intelligence, the internet of things, and the use of blockchains will also be enabled. Exports of digitally delivered services (e.g., software development, data processing, market research services, and mining services for the blockchain technology) will grow.[12] The COVID-19 pandemic has led to increased demand for telecommunication and information

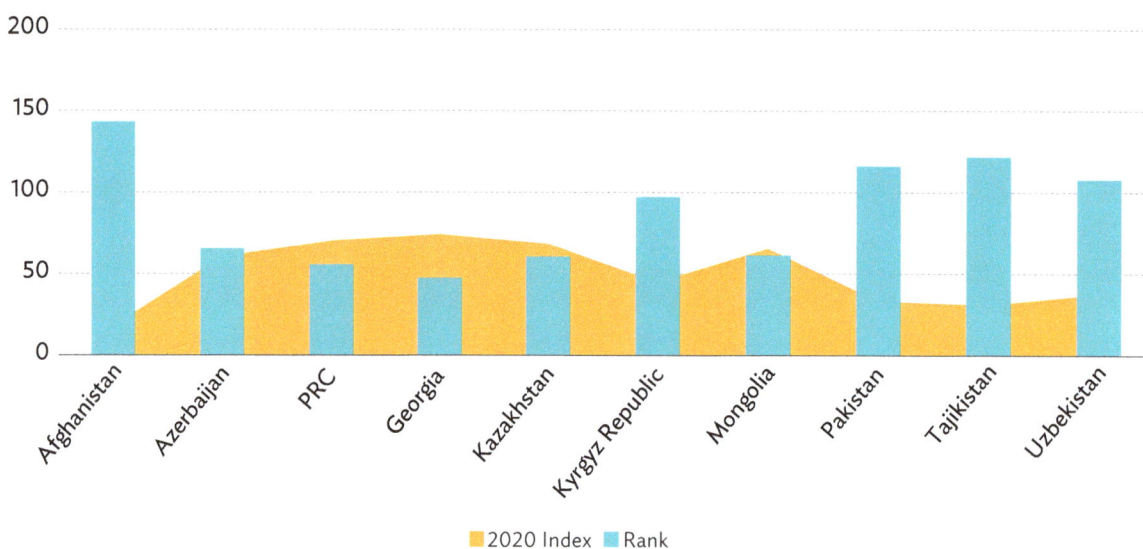

Figure 3.2: CAREC Countries—B2C E-commerce Index, 2020

B2C = business to consumer, CAREC = Central Asia Regional Economic Cooperation, e-commerce = electronic commerce, PRC = People's Republic of China.
Notes: The United Nations Conference on Trade and Development B2C E-Commerce Index measures an economy's preparedness to support online shopping. The B2C E-Commerce Index 2019 covers 152 countries. It does not cover Turkmenistan.
Source: United Nations Conference on Trade and Development. 2020. *The UNCTAD B2C E-Commerce Index 2020: Spotlight on Latin America and the Caribbean. UNCTAD Technical Notes on ICT for Development No. 17.* https://unctad.org/system/files/official-document/tn_unctad_ict4d17_en.pdf.

[11] See also ADB (2018a) for a discussion of the importance of the availability, affordability, and quality of communication and information services for the development of e-commerce.

[12] The global demand for blockchain mining services is likely to grow rapidly over the medium and long terms as the use of blockchain technology expands. This mining is power-intensive, which may give the CAREC countries rich in renewable energy a comparative advantage in competing to offer these services. To exploit this advantage, they need to improve the speed and reliability of their internet connections.

services in many countries and present the CAREC countries with new opportunities to boost their exports. To seize these opportunities, they should foster the development of telecommunication and information services. Many of the region's countries also need to improve the quality of their telecommunication services if they are to attract more international tourists and FDI.[13]

As the telecommunications system is the physical backbone through which digital information must flow, the state of its development is decisive in either enhancing or inhibiting the pace of technological and economic progress. While opportunities from the digital revolution abound, and countries can leapfrog old technologies when they adopt digital communication, these opportunities can only be exploited if businesses and people have access to high-quality telecommunication services. Every CAREC country has its individual digital strategy for achieving universal access to digital technologies. In addition, the CAREC program has a new CAREC Digital Strategy 2030 that aims to provide a vision, road map, and a catalyst for enhancing and transforming digital connectivity in the region.[14]

Financial Services

Financial services have room to leverage much greater growth. According to a WTO study of global data, the distribution and financial services subsectors accounted for the largest shares of total services production, about one-fifth each (WTO 2019b). The financial services subsector is critical on a macroeconomic level and in supporting diversification. Simulations conducted by Francois and Eschenbach (2002) sought to determine what the effects would be if a low-income country had a more open and accessible financial services as seen in high-income countries. The results showed annual GDP per capita growth increasing by 0.4%–0.6%. Mattoo, Rathindran, and Subramanian. (2006) estimated that, with full financial services liberalization, developing countries could grow 2.3% faster.

The evidence also indicates that greater financial inclusion leads to higher economic growth (Sahay, et al. 2015). The more a country's firms (both small and large) that can avail themselves of or already benefit from bank credit and investments, and the fewer that consider finance a major constraint, the better its economic growth prospects will be. There is also a positive relationship between economic growth and the percentage of a nation's adults who have accounts with or a credit card or loan from a formal financial institution.

[13] A large body of empirical evidence indicates that the development of telecommunication and information services reduces information and transaction costs in international trade, boosts exports (especially exports of manufacturers and services), and fosters economic growth (ADB 2018a; Tan 2017; World Bank 2016; WTO 2019b). Clarke (2008), for instance, finds a strong positive correlation between export activity and internet access at the enterprise level in the manufacturing and services sectors in low- and middle-income countries of Eastern Europe and Central Asia. WTO (2019b) finds that the extent of digital connectivity, as measured by mobile phone and broadband coverage, is a significant determinant of trade costs for both services and goods, although much more so for services than for goods. Manyika and Roxburgh (2011) estimate that the internet accounted for more than one-fifth of GDP growth in advanced economies during 2006–2010. Purdy and Daugherty (2016) find that in the 13 OCED countries examined in their study, the deployment of artificial intelligence could raise the annual growth rate of gross value added by 1.8–2.0 percentage points by 2035.

[14] CAREC Digital Strategy 2030: Accelerating Digital Transformation for Regional Competitiveness. The strategy is intended as a catalyst for regional cooperation on digital matters and a mechanism to promote policy design, capacity-building, and dialogue on the ways social and economic challenges in the region can be addressed with the help of digital technologies.

Many CAREC countries have made great strides in developing financial services in recent years. Some of them have done so by adopting innovative approaches. The most notable example is Kazakhstan, which set up the Astana International Financial Centre in 2018 with the aim of creating a regional financial hub.[15] The center is a special economic zone offering tax incentives, easier procedures for foreigners to acquire work permits, and the use of English as the zone's official language. It is regulated by a court and international arbitration center based on English law. The Astana International Exchange, which is based in the Astana International Financial Centre, has entered partnerships with NASDAQ and the Shanghai Stock Exchange. Kazakhstan has also established a partnership with Euroclear (IMF 2018c).

Nonetheless, financial services and nonbank financial services, such as insurance, remain underdeveloped in the CAREC region. Compared with the GDPs of the CAREC-10 countries, domestic credit to the private sector by banks, broad money, stock market capitalization, and total insurance premiums are all small even though some have extensive networks of bank branches and automated teller machines (Tables 3.3 and 3.4). Nonbank financial institution assets

Table 3.3: CAREC Countries—Selected Indicators of Development of Banking Sector, 2019

Country	Commercial Bank Branches (per 100,000 adults)	Automated Teller Machines (per 100,000 adults)	Domestic Credit to Private Sector by Banks (% of GDP)	Broad Money (% of GDP)
Afghanistan	1.9	1.6	3.2	35.0
Azerbaijan	10.7[a]	34.5	23.0	35.2
China, People's Republic of	8.9	95.6	165.4	197.9
Georgia	33.6	85.0	67.7	50.0
Kazakhstan	2.5	85.9	24.3	30.7
Kyrgyz Republic	8.0	39.3	24.6	37.2
Mongolia	63.9	148.8	49.6	55.9
Pakistan	10.4	10.8	18.1	59.0
Tajikistan	24.1[b]	10.6[c]	11.6	28.0
Uzbekistan	34.2	38.5	30.1	17.9
Comparator country groups				
World	11.5	42.8	131.9	125.8
Upper-middle-income countries	15.3	59.6	126.1	148.9
OECD countries	19.4	68.7	144.2	117.3

CAREC= Central Asia Regional Economic Cooperation, OECD = Organisation for Economic Co-operation and Development.
Note: Data not available for Turkmenistan.
[a] Data is for 2015.
[b] Data is for 2017.
[c] Data is for 2013.
Source: World Development Indicators. https://databank.worldbank.org/source/world-development-indicators (accessed 26 August 2021).

---

[15]   Astana International Financial Centre https://aifc.kz/tseli/.

and domestic credit to the private sector are also small in all CAREC countries. Many studies find that access to finance is a major constraint on doing business in some CAREC countries, especially for small and medium-sized enterprises and farmers.[16] Most CAREC countries covered by the World Economic Forum's Global Competitiveness Index 2019 rank low in at least some index components pertaining to the depth of the financial system (Table 3.5).

Table 3.4: CAREC Countries—Selected Indicators of Development of Nonbank Financial Sector, 2017
(% of GDP)

Country	Nonbank Financial Institutions' Assets	Nonbank Financial Institutions' Domestic Credit to Private Sector	Stock Market Capitalization	Insurance Premium
Afghanistan	...	0.1	...	...
Azerbaijan	1.2	1.0	4.5	1.2
China, People's Republic of	...	0.0	70.2	3.9
Georgia	4.1	3.7	1.1	0.6
Kazakhstan	10.7	3.4	25.4	0.6
Kyrgyz Republic	2.0	0.1	3.4	0.2
Mongolia	...	2.3	7.0	0.5
Pakistan	...	0.1	28.7	0.8
Tajikistan	0.7[a]	1.2	0.0	0.4[b]
Comparator country group				
OECD countries	52.0	67.4	74.5	4.5

... = data not available, CAREC = Central Asia Regional Economic Cooperation, GDP = gross domestic product, OECD = Organisation for Economic Co-operation and Development.

Note: Data not available for Turkmenistan and Uzbekistan.

[a] Data is for 2015.

[b] Data is for 2012.

Sources: World Bank. Global Financial Development Database. https://www.worldbank.org/en/publication/gfdr/data/global-financial-development-database (accessed September 2020); and World Bank. World Development Indicators. https://databank.worldbank.org/source/world-development-indicators (accessed September 2020).

---

[16] See, for instance, Morgan, Zhang, and Kydyrbayev (2018) and OECD (2018).

Table 3.5: CAREC Countries—Ranking in Selected Global Competitiveness Index 2019 Components Relating to Depth of Financial System

Index/Country	Financing of SMEs	Venture Capital Availability	Stock Market Capitalization	Insurance Premium
Azerbaijan	24	24	110	118
China, People's Republic of	34	13	30	40
Georgia	83	109	119	112
Kazakhstan	87	89	68	113
Kyrgyz Republic	105	102	114	...
Mongolia	124	124	99	122
Pakistan	66	36	65	104
Tajikistan	59	55	125	...

... = data not available, CAREC = Central Asia Regional Economic Cooperation, SMEs = small and medium-sized enterprises.
Note: The Global Competitiveness Index 2019 covers 141 countries. Data does not cover Afghanistan, Turkmenistan, and Uzbekistan.
Source: Schwab. 2019. *The Global Competitiveness Report 2019*. Geneva.

Household survey data indicate that a substantially smaller proportion of the adult populations of the CAREC countries use formal financial services than the overall average in the OECD, especially in terms of borrowing from financial institutions and using online and mobile banking services. This proportion is also much smaller than even the upper-middle-income country average in all CAREC members except Mongolia, and the PRC, and for some services, Kazakhstan (Table 3.6). The most common reasons given by survey respondents for not having a formal financial institution account include lack of trust in financial institutions (especially in the case of Afghanistan, Azerbaijan, Georgia, and Tajikistan); high prices for financial services (Afghanistan, Azerbaijan, Georgia, the Kyrgyz Republic, Pakistan, and Tajikistan); and the lack of necessary documentation (Afghanistan, Azerbaijan, Georgia, the Kyrgyz Republic, and Turkmenistan) (Demirgüç-Kunt, et al. 2018).

Table 3.6: CAREC Countries—Selected Indicators of Use of Formal Financial Services by Adult Population, 2017
(% of the respondents aged 15+)

Country	Account at Formal Financial Institution	Debit Card Ownership	Saved at Financial Institution in Past Year	Borrowed from Financial Institution or Used Credit Card in Past Year	Used Mobile Phone or Internet to Access Financial Institution Account in Past Year
Afghanistan	14.5	2.7	3.7	3.8	0.6
Azerbaijan	28.6	24.6	4.5	15.1	2.0
China, People's Republic of	80.2	66.8	34.8	22.7	39.8
Georgia	61.2	39.9	4.6	27.4	8.9
Kazakhstan	58.7	39.7	13.9	28.2	18.2

continued on next page

Table 3.6 *continued*

Country	Account at Formal Financial Institution	Debit Card Ownership	Saved at Financial Institution in Past Year	Borrowed from Financial Institution or Used Credit Card in Past Year	Used Mobile Phone or Internet to Access Financial Institution Account in Past Year
Kyrgyz Republic	38.3	19.3	3.0	10.2	3.9
Mongolia	93.0	75.7	19.3	30.4	37.6
Pakistan	18.0	8.3	6.1	2.6	2.0
Tajikistan	47.0	15.9	11.3	15.5	8.3
Turkmenistan	40.6	37.9	4.8	6.8	2.2
Uzbekistan	37.1	24.1	2.3	2.4	6.7
Comparator country groups					
World	67.1	47.7	26.7	22.5	22.8
Upper-middle-income countries	72.8	58.8	26.9	22.4	30.0
OECD countries	91.3	81.7	48.5	46.1	51.3

CAREC= Central Asia Regional Economic Cooperation, OECD = Organisation for Economic Co-operation and Development.

Source: Demirgüç-Kunt, A., L. Klapper, D. Singer, S. Ansar, and J. Hess. 2018. The Global Findex Database 2017: Measuring Financial Inclusion and the Fintech Revolution. Washington, DC: World Bank. https://openknowledge.worldbank.org/handle/10986/29510

Of particular concern regarding the comparatively low level of financial development in CAREC countries overall is the lack of depth in the financial sector and its inability to provide sufficient financial services to the bulk of national populations. Expanding a digital public credit registry and/or a private credit bureau (or establishing one in the case of Turkmenistan) could enhance businesses and households with access to finance. Improvement in these areas is key to enabling the financial sector to contribute more to inclusive economic growth. Economic diversification is dependent in part on the development and growth of nontraditional sectors. The entrepreneurs in emerging sectors require access to financial resources for investment and working capital but are competing for limited financial resources against other firms, many of them incumbents in traditional sectors well known to the banks. Unless the resources of the financial sector in the CAREC region grow and the sector becomes more inclusive, the constraints imposed by small size and limited access to its resources could hinder growth of new players in CAREC countries.

Developing financial services, including nonbank financial services, can help diversify CAREC economies in several ways (Box 3.1). It will improve the mobilization and allocation of savings and enable businesses and households to manage financial risks more effectively; it will help CAREC countries develop other services subsectors, as well as agriculture and manufacturing; and it will help generate increases in the export of services, agricultural products (such as fresh fruits and vegetables), and manufactured goods (such as processed food products). Development of securities markets and such nonbank financial institutions as credit unions, leasing companies, venture capital funds, and insurance agencies is essential to improving businesses' access to long-term finance, especially for innovative projects (World Bank, 2015).

Box 3.1: Role of Financial Services in Diversification and Development in Selected CAREC Countries

Poor access to financial services can be a major constraint on diversification and development in most economic sectors. Inadequate financial inclusion in CAREC countries and elsewhere remains a challenge. Among the impediments on the supply side are asymmetric information, the frequent inability of many potential borrowers to offer acceptable documentation and collateral, and the cost of supplying credit in relatively thin and geographically distant markets. The demand side is affected by the fact that regulatory processes and procedures are often difficult to navigate in remote settings, and potential clients are unaware of or not confident in the financial products and services made available.

The following are some examples of financial services inclusion challenges that are affecting economic diversification and development in CAREC countries.

Financial services in cashmere wool production in Mongolia

In Mongolia, the challenges and opportunities in diversification strategies for building livestock-based value chains were identified by the World Bank (2019a). One commodity studied, cashmere wool, is the product of one of the country's most successful industries. This is partly due to its value-density ratio—i.e., its bulk and weight in relation to its value. Like many other industries, however, a variety of obstacles stand in the way of its further progress.

The quality, pricing, and availability of services on which the industry relies are prominent among these factors. The principal financial services issues are the short supplies of insurance, credit, and adequate acceptable collateral. A particular challenge relates to the time gap between the buying by processors of raw cashmere during April–June and the orders they receive for export production of cashmere goods during August–October. Trade credit and funding for inventories are thus necessary to bridge this gap and manage the prolonged cash-to-cash cycle. In addition to financial services, other services also pose challenges for the value chain of the cashmere-wool industry, including those related to transport and associated infrastructure, logistics, communication, business intermediation, and government regulation. The case study underscored the importance of financial services inputs. Furthermore, it illustrated that the robustness of an enterprise or sector is heavily influenced by its most severe vulnerabilities, and these are very often to be found in services subsectors.

Access to finance for Uzbekistan's small businesses

Between 2013 and 2016, a project—with $50 million financing from ADB—supported a growing number of small businesses in Uzbekistan's economy. In 2012, small businesses accounted for more than half of the country's gross domestic product and three-quarters of employment. However, there was large unmet demand for credit by small businesses and rural women entrepreneurs. Collateral requirements were high and commercial banks' institutional management capacity was inadequate for the financial needs of such businesses. The project aimed to address the market failures that were limiting the access of small Uzbek businesses to credit and financial services. It paid particular attention to enterprises run by women and/or located in rural areas. More than four-fifths of these enterprises are located outside Tashkent.

In 2017, more than 5,900 loans were issued by the participating commercial banks, of which around 76% were onlent to small businesses located outside of Tashkent. Around 32% of all small business borrowers are women. By shrinking the credit gap, the project increased business opportunities for small enterprises, particularly those run by women and located in rural areas. The project generated results on the supply side as well by strengthening the institutional capacity of participating commercial banks to manage risk and diversify their offerings. Simplified and reduced processing times through an online system enhanced bank lending for small businesses. Collateral requirements were relaxed on microfinance loans and a collateral registry was established.

The project also highlighted the need for continuing sector, policy, and institutional reforms. This includes continuous engagement in policy dialogues on regulatory impediments to small business development and prudential supervisory and regulatory mechanisms for banks and other financial institutions.

continued on next page

Box 3.1 *continued*

Inclusive finance to strengthen vegetable value chains in Pakistan

The value chains to produce onions, potatoes, tomatoes, and chilies are important sources of income for about 60% of Pakistan's population. However, these value chains are disrupted by a range of constraints and issues—such as inconsistent quality and quantity of vegetables supplied to the market—confronting the country's low-income rural farmers, particularly in Sindh and Punjab. The challenges posed by poor seed quality, high production costs, and frequent pest infestations and outbreaks of disease are compounded by their poor access to capital and credit. These farmers lack the collateral most formal lenders require and are often charged high interest rates and commissions by the intermediaries who frequently provide them with credit. These financial challenges must be addressed in conjunction with the farmers' other needs, most of which must also be met at least in part by services. These include services to build knowledge and capacity to address production constraints and to improve marketing, post-harvest handling, and access to reliable input supplies.

Sources: ADB. 2018b. Completion Report: Uzbekistan: Small Business and Enterprise Development Project. Manila; Mazhar, Bajwa, McEvilly, Palaniappan, and Kazmi. 2019. Improving Vegetable Value Chains in Pakistan for Sustainable Livelihood of Farming Communities. *Journal of Environmental and Agricultural Sciences*. 18:1–9; and World Bank. 2019a. Mongolia Central Economic Corridor Assessment: A Value Chain Analysis of the Cashmere-Wool, Meat and Leather Industries. Report No. AUS0000216. Washington, DC.

Education, Research, and Experimental Development Services

Educational services are a core determinant of the contribution to GDP of one of the fundamental factors of production: labor. Improving the provision of educational services helps society achieve a multitude of goals by increasing labor productivity, promoting inclusiveness, and enabling workers to better adjust and adapt to economic and technological change.

Rising demand for skilled labor has been a major economic trend over recent decades. This is likely the result of technological change and increased economic integration through globalization. Since 2001, the share of employment in occupations heavy in nonroutine cognitive skills has increased from 19% to 23% in emerging economies and from 33% to 41% in advanced economies (World Bank 2018b). Along with the growing demand by enterprises using a lot more technology for workers to be tech-savvy, the rise of such new digital technologies as artificial intelligence is also casting a shadow over the future availability of certain routine, low-skill jobs (Baldwin 2019). These factors place a premium on enhancing the educational and skill level of a country's work force so that workers can provide the goods and services that today's domestic and international clients demand—and so that they can better cope with a future when more jobs will be put at risk by automation.

Access to primary and secondary education services, most of which are provided by the public sector, is generally good in the CAREC region. Primary and secondary school enrollment rates are generally high in CAREC countries subject to few exceptions. CAREC countries, however, appear to be lagging in providing tertiary-level education,[17] with an average enrollment rate lower than the OECD average. It varies substantially from less than 10% in Afghanistan and Pakistan to more than 60% in Georgia, Kazakhstan, and Mongolia. The private sector's share in both primary and secondary school enrollment is smaller than the OECD average in all the CAREC countries except Pakistan (Table 3.7).

The quality of education services available in most CAREC countries is less than adequate. Competencies provided by the education system and those needed in the workplace are furthermore mismatched.[18] Students from two of the three CAREC countries that participated in the OECD's Program for International Student Assessment survey in 2018 scored below the average for

Table 3.7: CAREC Countries—Selected Indicators of School Enrollment, 2019

Country	Gross Primary School Enrollment (%)	Gross Secondary School Enrollment (%)	Gross Tertiary School Enrollment (%)	Private Primary School Enrollment (% of total)	Private Secondary School Enrollment (% of total)
Afghanistan	104.0	55.4	9.7	6.0	4.5
Azerbaijan	97.9	94.8	31.5	0.8	12.3
China, People's Republic of	101.9	88.2[a]	53.8	8.5	13.7
Georgia	99.3	106.3	63.9	10.7	10.8
Kazakhstan	104.4	113.2	61.7	1.1	4.7
Kyrgyz Republic	106.0	96.4	42.3	2.6	3.0
Mongolia	104.0	91.5[a]	65.6	5.8	7.2[a]
Pakistan	95.4	43.8	9.0[d]	35.7	32.7
Tajikistan	100.9[b]	88.5[c]	31.3[b]	1.1[b]	1.2[c]
Turkmenistan	117.9	89.7	14.2	...	...
Uzbekistan	102.2	97.4	12.6	0.4	0.1
Comparator country groups					
Upper-middle-income countries	104.1	92.2	53.2	12.2	16.4
OECD countries	102.5	104.7	74.4	11.8	18.6

... = data not available, CAREC= Central Asia Regional Economic Cooperation, OECD = Organisation for Economic Co-operation and Development.

Note: Data for Afghanistan and Mongolia are for 2018, unless indicated.

[a] Data is for 2010.

[b] Data is for 2017.

[c] Data is for 2013.

[d] Data is for 2018.

Source: World Development Indicators database. https://databank.worldbank.org/source/world-development-indicators (accessed on 12 August 2021).

---

[17] This education level is frequently used as a threshold for distinguishing between skilled and unskilled workers.

[18] See ADB (2019b) for a discussion of the reasons for the inadequate quality of higher education in CAREC countries. See OECD (2011) for a discussion of the challenges in the technical and vocational education and training systems of Afghanistan, Kazakhstan, the Kyrgyz Republic, Mongolia, Tajikistan, Turkmenistan, and Uzbekistan.

OECD country students (OECD 2019).[19] Georgia, Kazakhstan, the Kyrgyz Republic, and Mongolia ranked low in at least some Global Competitiveness Index 2019 components pertaining to workforce skills (Table 3.8).

Table 3.8: CAREC Countries—Rank in Selected Global Competitiveness Index 2019 Components Relating to Workforce Skills

Country	Skillset of Graduates	Quality of Vocational Training	Digital Skills Among Active Population	Ease of Finding Skilled Employees
Azerbaijan	45	43	19	29
China, People's Republic of	35	41	45	41
Georgia	125	135	107	120
Kazakhstan	95	90	43	81
Kyrgyz Republic	130	125	91	119
Mongolia	119	100	96	140
Pakistan	49	85	73	58
Tajikistan	60	52	57	70

CAREC= Central Asia Regional Economic Cooperation.
Note: The Global Competitiveness Index 2019 covers 141 countries. It does not cover Afghanistan, Turkmenistan, and Uzbekistan.
Source: Schwab. 2019. *The Global Competitiveness Report 2019*. Geneva.

Research and experimental development activities are weak in most CAREC countries. Gross expenditure on research and development makes up less than 1% of GDP in all CAREC-10 countries, compared with more than 2% in the PRC and most OECD nations (Table 3.9). Compared to population size, there are considerably fewer researchers and fewer articles published in scientific and technical journals in the 11 CAREC countries than the average for the OECD region.[20] Of the eight CAREC countries that the Global Competitiveness Report 2019 covers, only the PRC is among the top 10 performers (out of 141 countries) on research and development. Georgia and Pakistan are in the top 75. Azerbaijan, Kazakhstan, the Kyrgyz Republic, and Tajikistan rank below 100 (Schwab 2019). Many of the industries in the CAREC-10 countries are micro and small enterprises that usually do not invest in research and development, and the medium-sized and large enterprises generally invest less in research and development than their peers in advanced economies. Collaboration between universities and industry is weak, and universities play a limited role in research and development.[21] Even in the PRC, where there are many good universities, institutions of higher education account for less than one-tenth of gross expenditure on research and development (Box 3.2).

---

[19] This survey assesses the performance of 15-year-old students in reading, mathematics, and sciences. Scores range from 0 to 1,000, and a higher score reflects better performance. In 2018, students in 79 countries, including Azerbaijan (Baku city), the PRC (Beijing, Shanghai, Jiangsu, and Zhejiang provinces), and Kazakhstan took part in the survey. In all three subjects, the mean score was higher in the PRC but lower in Azerbaijan and Kazakhstan than in the OECD countries.

[20] The relatively small number of the articles published in scientific and technical journals is another indication of inadequate quality of education (especially tertiary) services in most CAREC countries.

[21] See Pillai, Sindila, and Nagornova (2018) for an assessment of university–industry collaboration in Kazakhstan and the Kyrgyz Republic.

Table 3.9: CAREC Countries—Selected Indicators Relating to Research and Development, 2018

Country	Research and Development Expenditure (% of GDP)	Researchers in Research and Development (per million people)	Scientific and Technical Journal Articles (per million people)
Afghanistan	...	...	3.0
Azerbaijan	0.2[a]	...	76.6
China, People's Republic of	2.1[a]	1,113.1[a]	379.3
Georgia	0.1[a]	585.4[a]	147.7
Kazakhstan	0.2[b]	734.1[b]	129.5
Kyrgyz Republic	0.1[a]	...	21.7
Mongolia	0.2[a]	...	44.4
Pakistan	0.3[b]	166.9	60.8
Tajikistan	0.1[b]	...	6.8
Turkmenistan	...	...	0.6
Uzbekistan	0.2[a]	533.7[c]	10.7
Comparator country groups			
Upper-middle-income countries	1.6[a]	1,258.3[d]	333.0
OECD members	2.4[b]	...	1,047.7

... = data not available, GDP = gross domestic product, CAREC= Central Asia Regional Economic Cooperation, OECD = Organisation for Economic Co-operation and Development.

[a]   Data is for 2014.
[b]   Data is for 2013.
[c]   Data is for 2011.
[d]   Data is for 2017.

Source: World Bank. World Development Indicators. https://databank.worldbank.org/source/world-development-indicators (accessed 26 August 2021).

Due largely to an inadequate quality of education and weak research and development activities, most CAREC countries have not been successful in innovation. Compared with the averages for the OECD or even upper-middle-income countries, the number of resident patent applications relative to population size is very small in all CAREC-10 countries. With the exception of Mongolia, and the PRC, the number of resident industrial design applications per million persons is also smaller in CAREC countries than the average for the OECD or upper-middle-income countries (Table 3.10). Many CAREC members rank low on the Global Innovation Index 2019 (Figure 3.3). Because of the relatively high quality of education and robust research and development activity in the country, the PRC clearly stands out among the CAREC countries as a strong performer in patent and industrial design applications and on the Global Innovation Index 2019.

Box 3.2: Research and Development in the People's Republic of China

Research and experimental development activities have expanded rapidly in the People's Republic of China (PRC). The ratio of gross expenditure on research and development (GERD) to gross domestic product rose from 0.9% in 2000 to 2.1% in 2019. The PRC spent more on research and development than Germany, Japan, and the Republic of Korea combined, trailing only the United States in terms of GERD in US dollars at purchasing power parity (Figure B3.2.1).

Businesses finance and use most GERD in the PRC. Universities play a relatively minor role. In 2018, businesses funded 76.6% and utilized 77.4% of GERD, while institutions of higher education utilized only 7.2%. This puts the business share of GERD financing in the PRC above the rates in many Organisation for Economic Cooperation and Development (OECD) member countries, including the United States. At the same time, the share of higher education institutions in GERD use is much smaller in the PRC than in OECD nations. In part because businesses finance and utilize most of GERD, experimental development accounts for the bulk (more than 80%) of GERD in the PRC, and the share of basic and applied research is smaller than in most OECD countries.

Figure B3.2.1: Gross Expenditure on Research and Development in Selected Countries, 1991–2019
(billion $ at purchasing power parity)

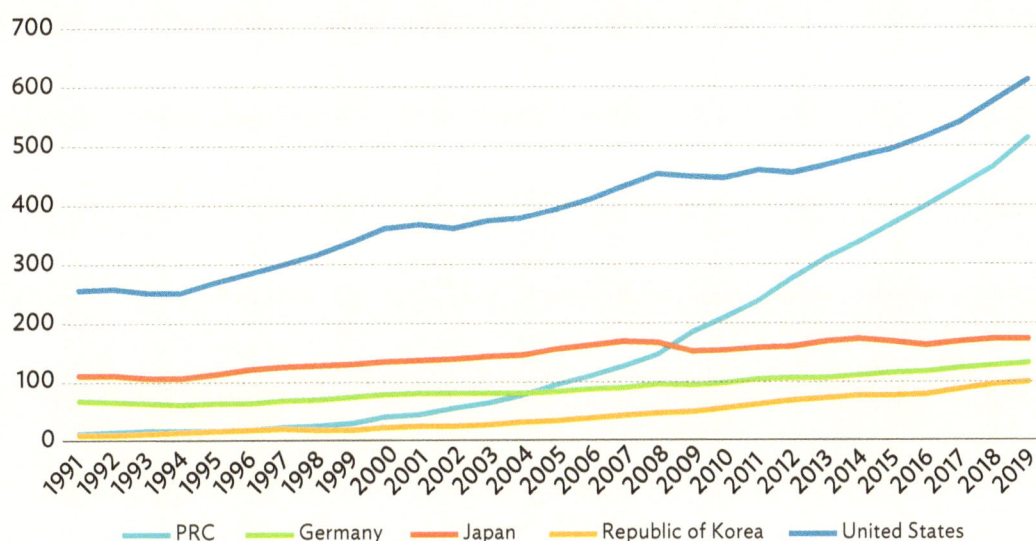

PRC = People's Republic of China.

Sources: World Bank. World Development Indicators. https://databank.worldbank.org/source/world-development-indicators# (accessed 26 August 2021); Organisation for Economic Co-operation and Development. OECD Data. https://data.oecd.org/rd/gross-domestic-spending-on-r-d.htm (accessed 26 August 2021).

Table 3.10: CAREC Countries—Number of Resident Patent, Trademark, and Industrial Design Applications, 2019
(per million people)

Country	Patent Applications	Industrial Design Applications	Trademark Applications
Azerbaijan	14.7	13.9	389.8
China, People's Republic of	889.7	494.9	5,424.9
Georgia	22.9	50.0	797.3
Kazakhstan	43.2[a]	4.5[a]	622.1
Kyrgyz Republic	14.2	1.8[b]	76.5
Mongolia	26.1	265.1	3,355.2
Pakistan	1.4	2.1	151.2
Tajikistan	0.1	0.1[c]	63.8
Uzbekistan	11.1	7.4	239.3
Comparator country groups			
Upper-middle-income countries	514.7	300.2	3,485.1
OECD members	602.8	221.7	2,040.7

CAREC= Central Asia Regional Economic Cooperation, OECD = Organisation for Economic Co-operation and Development.
Note: Data not available for Afghanistan and Turkmenistan.
[a] Data is for 2018.
[b] Data is for 2017.
[c] Data is for 2013.
Source: World Bank. World Development Indicators. https://databank.worldbank.org/source/world-development-indicators# (accessed 26 August 2021).

Many CAREC nations rank low on the Global Innovation Index 2019 (Figure 3.3). Because of the relatively high quality of education and robust research and development activity in the country, the PRC clearly stands out among the CAREC nations as a strong performer in patent and industrial design applications and on the Global Innovation Index 2019.

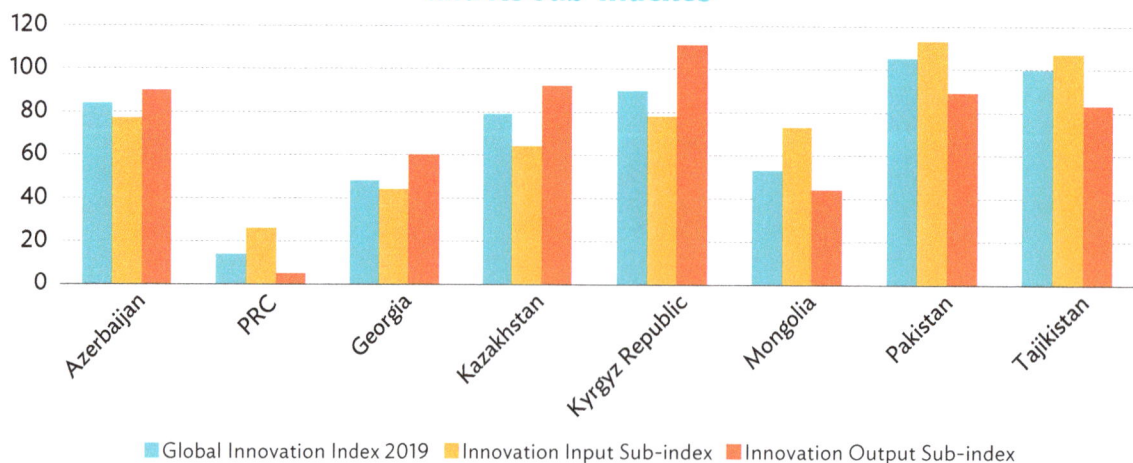

Figure 3.3: CAREC Countries—Ranking in Global Innovation Index 2019 and Its Sub-Indexes

CAREC= Central Asia Regional Economic Cooperation, PRC = People's Republic of China.

Notes: The Global Innovation Index 2019 covers 129 countries. Data excludes Afghanistan, Turkmenistan, and Uzbekistan.

Source: Cornell University, INSEAD and World Intellectual Property Organization. 2019. Global Innovation Index 2019: Creating Healthy Lives—The Future of Medical Innovation. Ithaca, Fontainebleau and Geneva.

CAREC countries need to develop and expand access to education at the secondary (in the case of Afghanistan and Pakistan) and tertiary levels. The quality of education must be improved at all levels.[22] CAREC countries should make education services more responsive to changes in the demand for specific skills in their economies. This will improve the availability of appropriately trained and qualified workers to meet the needs of development and growth in all sectors, including services.

Countries should develop education services (such as vocational training and adult education services) that help people adapt to rapid technical progress and the attendant shifts in skills demand. Several CAREC countries should develop agricultural extension services to introduce modern technologies and raise productivity in agriculture, as well as develop agricultural value chains and increase the volume and diversify the direction of exports of agricultural products (such as fruits and vegetables). Following the PRC's example, the CAREC-10 countries should strengthen research and experimental development to facilitate adoption of new technologies, develop manufacturing and modern service industries, move up the manufacturing value chain, and increase the production and exports of manufactured goods (such as processed food products and chemical and pharmaceutical products). To these ends, the CAREC-10 countries should also strengthen university–industry collaboration. Emphasis should be put on establishing research, development, and production clusters and/or networks of universities, research institutions, and manufacturing firms. Box 3.3 examines some of these matters in the specific case of Kazakhstan's wheat sector.

Box 3.3: Education, Research, and Upgrading Opportunities— The Case of Wheat in Kazakhstan

Wheat, Kazakhstan's leading agricultural crop, occupies 80% of the land under cultivation and absorbs 20% of the labor force. Although the country is a significant global exporter, the value-added per unit of its wheat output is low. This leaves considerable room for diversifying and upgrading the wheat sector value chain to further grow and develop both the domestic and export markets.

Ahmed et al. (2017) suggests in their study that actions by both the government and the private sector to make production more efficient, diversify output, and expand penetration of international markets. One of the study's key recommendations is to reduce the role now played by the state-owned Food Contract Corporation, which controls prices and makes decisions on access priorities to transport and storage facilities, thereby reducing private sector opportunities. Price control stultifies market signaling and inhibits innovation. Incentives to improve seed quality and production and process methods are reduced, leading to lower quality output and diminished volumes. Demand for wheat and export opportunities are growing in the Central Asian region and large markets are nearby, but Kazakhstan will need to upgrade its value chains to benefit. Illustration on next page summarizes the analysis of the situation.

continued on next page

---

[22] Expanding access to education and improving the quality of this education are crucial steps in building the human capital that is needed to grow modern service industries and diversify economies. The Asian Development Bank Institute (2019) highlights the importance of improvements in education to the development of the high-value service industries, such as financial and information services. Goyal (2015) and Sahoo and Dash (2017) underscore the importance of human capital for growth of modern service industries in India. At the same time, the experience of some countries (e.g., Algeria and Saudi Arabia) shows that achieving a high level of human capital, although important, is not a sufficient condition for economic diversification (Cherif, Hasanov, and Zhu 2016).

Box 3.3 *continued*

Strengths	Weaknesses
• Abundance of land • Labor availability • Competitive fertilizer production	• Low private sector development • Inefficient farm management, poor quality control • Lack of workforce skills • Poor institutions—insufficient investments in hard and soft infrastructure, complicated export procedures
Opportunities	**Threats**
• Growing consumption of wheat and food products in the region • Close proximity to large markets, i.e., Iran, the People's Republic of China, and Russian Federation • High profitability of oilseeds and other crops	• High risks in Central Asian markets • Russian Federation becoming a major wheat exporter and possibly replacing Kazakhstan in its markets

The study recommends (i) improvements in quality control and the adoption of best practices; (ii) a better use of tax incentives, and lowering the cost of funds; (iii) alignment of safety and quality standards and certification with international norms; (iv) greater support for the use of high-quality inputs; (v) diversification of production into high value-added products such as oilseeds; (vi) intensified expert training and the inclusion of relevant degree programs in universities; (vii) focus on productivity improvements in the workforce to align skill sets with demand for higher value-added output; and (viii) improved services infrastructure for transport, logistics, and storage facilities. Such reforms would clearly require intensive services inputs in forms such as research, innovation, and training.

Sources: Ahmed G., Baisakalov A., Hamrick D., Iskaliyeva A., Molochanovkiy V., Nahapetyan S., and Seidek S. 2017. *The Wheat Value Chain in Kazakhstan*. National Analytical Center, Nazarbayev University, Astana, and Duke University Global Value Chains Center, Duke University, Durham, North Carolina; and Ghada, et al. 2017. The Wheat Value Chain in Kazakhstan. National Analytical Center (NAC), Nazarbayev University, Astana, and Duke University Global Value Chains Center (GVCC), Duke University, Durham, North Carolina.

Tourism-Related Services

The CAREC countries have considerable untapped potential for accelerating their development of international tourism. International visitor arrivals and international tourism receipts increased substantially in many of them during the 2011–2019 period (Table 3.11). The industry grew particularly fast in Georgia (Box 3.4). Nonetheless, international visitor arrivals remain low in most of the countries on a per-population basis when compared with other nations with similar tourism potential and the overall OECD average. International tourism receipts–GDP ratios are lower in some CAREC countries than the worldwide and OECD averages.

In terms of origin, tourism markets are narrow. Only a few countries accounted for large percentages of international visitor arrivals and international tourism receipts in most CAREC countries. The fragmented data available and anecdotal evidence suggest that domestic tourism is also generally underdeveloped. Most of the CAREC countries covered ranked low on the World Economic Forum's Travel and Tourism Competitiveness Index 2019 (Figure 3.4). Tourism development in the CAREC

Table 3.11: CAREC Countries—Selected Indicators Relating to International Tourism, 2019

Country	International Visitor Arrivals			International Tourism Receipts		
	million persons	% change relative to 2010	per 1,000 local people	$ million	% change relative to 2010	% of GDP
Afghanistan	...	...	...	85	−42.2	0.4
Azerbaijan	3.2	61.5	316.2	2,004	153.0	4.2
China, People's Republic of	162.5	21.5	116.3	...	...	...
Georgia	7.7	280.2	2,076.8	3,551	381.8	20.3
Kazakhstan	8.5	107.8	459.9	2,922	136.4	1.6
Kyrgyz Republic	8.5	595.1	1,317.8	708	234.0	8.0
Mongolia	0.6	14.4	197.5	605	110.1	4.3
Pakistan	1.0[a]	6.5[a]	5.2[a]	948	−5.0	0.3
Tajikistan	1.1[b]	546.9	113.7	179	26.6	2.2
Uzbekistan	6.7	592.2	201.0	1,679	154.4[c]	2.1
Comparator country groups						
World	2,280.1	36.7	297.1	1,815,195	59.5	2.1
Upper-middle- income countries	564.3	35.8	225.6	...	...	...
OECD countries	1,342.2	33.3	983.4	1,008,831	50.6	1.9

... = data not available, CAREC= Central Asia Regional Economic Cooperation, OECD = Organisation for Economic Co-operation and Development.
Note: Data not available for Turkmenistan.
[a]   Data is for 2012.
[b]   Data is for 2018.
[c]   Relative to 2014, not 2010.
Sources: World Bank. World Development Indicators. https://databank.worldbank.org/source/world-development-indicators# (accessed 26 August 2021) and authors' computations.

Box 3.4: The Tourism Industry in Georgia

International tourism has grown swiftly in Georgia since 2010. International visitor arrivals and international tourism receipts more than quadrupled during 2010--2019 (Figure B3.4.1), and the ratio of international tourism receipts to total exports rose from 18.3% to 37.2%. Armenia, Azerbaijan, the Russian Federation, and Turkey. accounted for more than half of international visitors in 2018. The travel and tourism industry generated nearly one-tenth of gross domestic product (GDP) in 2017 and accounted for more than a quarter of all employment.

Such rapid growth in the size and importance of a single slice of the economy has its risks. An estimated 65% drop in tourism receipts in 2020 due to the COVID-19 pandemic was largely responsible for a widening in the current account deficit from 5.1% of GDP in 2019 to 11.3% in 2020.

An important upgrading project for the industry begun in 2015 may help contribute to the economy's recovery. The *Georgia Tourism 2025* initiative has focused on marketing, branding, and promotional strategies to target 26 high-spending tourist markets and create greater value-added in tourism services supply chains. The initiative includes an overall policy framework, capital requirements, and skills development. Digital tourism-related services are receiving special attention, along with the high value-added food and wine segment where emphasis is to be put on unique local offerings. The nature and adventure tourist subsectors are also a focus. Plans also included greater financial support for small and medium-sized tourism-related enterprises and artisanal activities.

continued on next page

Box 3.3 *continued*

Figure B3.4.1: Georgia—International Visitor Arrivals and International Tourism Receipts, 2010–2019

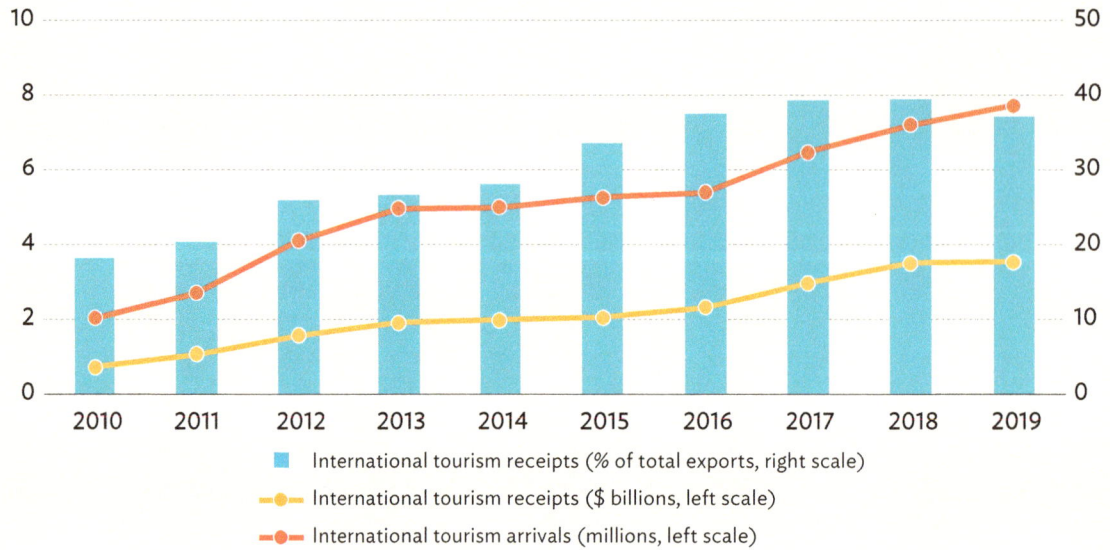

International tourism receipts (% of total exports, right scale)

International tourism receipts ($ billions, left scale)

International tourism arrivals (millions, left scale)

Sources: Ministry of Economy and Sustainable Development of Georgia and Georgian National Tourism Administration. 2015. *Georgian Tourism in Figures: Structure and Industry Data*. Tbilisi. https://gnta.ge/wp-content/uploads/2014/08/ENG-new.pdf; International Monetary Fund. 2020. *Georgia: Staff Report for the Sixth Review under the Extended Arrangement*. Country Report No. 20/149. Washington, DC; World Bank. 2020. Beyond Arrivals: Emerging Opportunities for Georgian Firms in Tourism Value Chains. Report No.: AUS0000777. Washington DC; World Bank. World Development Indicators. https://databank.worldbank.org/source/world-development-indicators (accessed 15 July 2021).

Figure 3.4: CAREC Countries—Ranking in Travel and Tourism Competitiveness Index, 2019

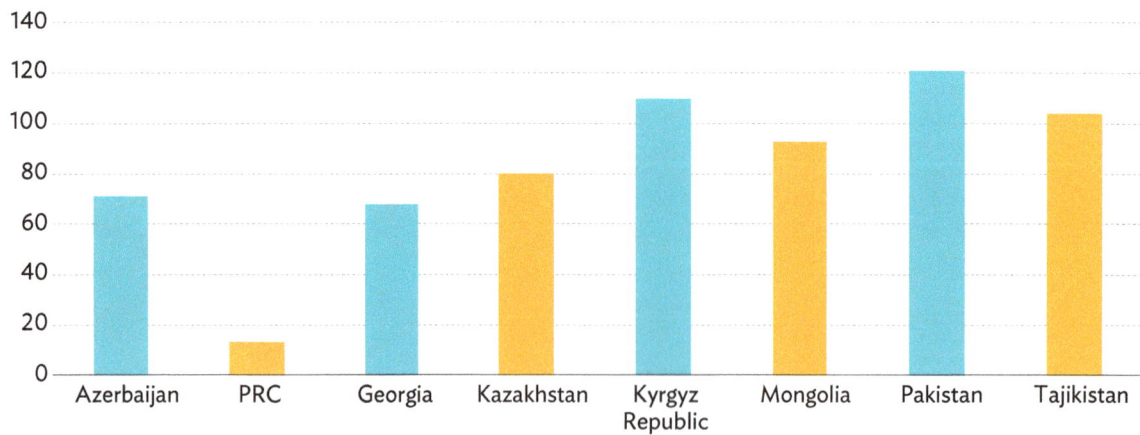

CAREC= Central Asia Regional Economic Cooperation, PRC = People's Republic of China

Note: The Travel & Tourism Competitiveness Index 2019 covers 140 countries. It does not cover Afghanistan, Turkmenistan, and Uzbekistan.

Source: Calderwood and Soshkin. 2019. *The Travel & Tourism Competitiveness Report 2019: Travel and Tourism at a Tipping Point*. Geneva: World Economic Forum.

countries is currently constrained by deficiencies in passenger transport services, inadequacies relating to travel services, complex visa regimes, cumbersome border-crossing procedures, shortages of skilled workers, and the region's weak branding and destination image (ADB 2019a). The CAREC Tourism Strategy 2030 was endorsed in 2020 to address these constraints through the Regional Tourism Investment Framework, 2021–2025. The framework outlines investment and technical assistance projects to support each strategic pillar—connectivity and infrastructure; quality and standards; skills development; marketing and branding; and market intelligence (ADB 2020). Developing support for tourism—through enhanced telecommunication and information services, financial services, quality testing and certification services, and education services—is key to implementing the framework.

The COVID-19 pandemic has drastically reduced demand for tourism-related services. Rebound of the sector depends on availability and roll-out of effective vaccines in the region and beyond. Over the medium and long terms, building and expanding tourism and its related services can make a significant contribution to economic diversification and development in the CAREC countries.[23] This includes historical, ecological, and recreational tourism and such related services as passenger transport, travel agency support, and accommodation. Such growth will create many jobs (particularly for medium-skilled workers), increase the share of services in aggregate output and employment, and boost services exports. To the extent that it widens their sources of international tourist arrivals, tourism development will help CAREC countries diversify the direction of their services exports. By enabling potential foreign investors to gain better knowledge of their countries, tourism will also help CAREC nations attract more FDI. However, risks and contagious diseases such as COVID-19 affect international travel. To prevent or contain the spread of such diseases, CAREC countries will need to implement enhanced safety standards and protocols in the tourism industry.

Freight Transportation and Storage Services

Freight transport and storage and the logistics services that support them are important for the CAREC region, especially the landlocked countries. With the exceptions of Georgia, Pakistan, and the PRC, all CAREC countries are landlocked. Many parts of the region are sparsely populated (e.g., Kazakhstan, Mongolia, Turkmenistan, and the western part of Uzbekistan), and major economic centers are often separated by long distances. Additionally, all members serve—to varying degrees—as transit routes for one another and between other countries beyond the CAREC region. This provides them with the potential to become regional transport hubs and important conduits for international trade flows, including trade between Europe and the PRC, and between Central Asia and South Asia.

---

[23] As noted in WTO (2019b), tourism has many ripple effects due to its many linkages with the rest of the economy. These include backward linkages to those domestic sectors that supply inputs to products and services purchased by tourists.

Freight transport and storage services remain underdeveloped in most CAREC countries. This is especially true of logistics services. All CAREC-10 countries rank low on the World Bank's logistics performance indicators related to transport services (Table 3.12).[24] The PRC, although the highest ranking CAREC country, scores lower than many OECD countries. Most CAREC countries covered by the World Economic Forum's Global Competitiveness Index 2019 also rank low on the efficiency of air transport (Schwab 2019).

Table 3.12: CAREC Countries—Selected Logistics Performance Indicators, 2018

Country	International Shipments[a]		Logistics Competence[b]		Tracking and Tracing[c]		Timeliness[d]	
	Score	Rank	Score	Rank	Score	Rank	Score	Rank
Afghanistan	2.1	152	1.9	158	1.7	159	2.4	153
China, People's Republic of	3.5	18	3.6	27	3.7	27	3.8	27
Georgia	2.4	124	2.3	132	2.3	139	3.0	105
Kazakhstan	2.7	84	2.6	90	2.8	83	3.5	50
Kyrgyz Republic	2.2	138	2.4	114	2.6	99	2.9	106
Mongolia	2.5	117	2.2	140	2.1	152	3.1	93
Pakistan	2.6	97	2.6	89	2.3	136	2.7	136
Tajikistan	2.3	133	2.3	116	2.3	131	3.0	104
Turkmenistan	2.3	136	2.3	120	2.6	107	2.7	130
Uzbekistan	2.4	120	2.6	88	2.7	90	3.1	91
Comparator country groups								
Upper-middle-income countries	2.8	…	2.7	…	2.8	…	3.2	…
High-income OECD countries	3.5	…	3.7	…	3.7	…	4.0	…

… = data not available, CAREC = Central Asia Regional Economic Cooperation, OECD = Organisation for Economic Co-operation and Development.

Note: The Logistics Performance Index 2018 covers 160 countries. It does not cover Azerbaijan. Scores range from 0 to 5 with a higher score corresponding to better performance.

[a]   Refers to the ease of arranging competitively priced shipments.

[d]   Refers to the competence and quality of logistics services (trucking, forwarding, and customs brokerage).

[c]   Refers to the ability to track and trace consignments.

[d]   Refers to the frequency with which shipments reach consignees within scheduled or expected delivery times.

Source: World Bank. 2018a. *Connecting to Compete: Trade Logistics in the Global Economy*. Washington, DC: World Bank.

In part because of their underdeveloped freight transport and storage services, transport costs for international shipments to, from, and through the CAREC-10 countries are high. Transport times for such shipments are also long and unpredictable. This partly explains why manufacturing is underdeveloped in these countries and their merchandise exports are concentrated in terms of commodity composition and geographic distribution (ADB 2006). Technology-intensive manufacturing, which often requires

---

[24]   The geographical constraints of the eight landlocked CAREC countries partly explain their low rankings on the Logistics Performance indicators.

just-in-time delivery, is particularly underdeveloped. These inadequacies also partly explain the inability of CAREC countries so far to fully realize their considerable potential for transit trade, and why many of them (e.g., the Kyrgyz Republic, Tajikistan, and Uzbekistan) have struggled to increase exports of horticulture products.

The further development of transport and storage services is essential to economic diversification in CAREC countries.[25] In particular, it will help CAREC-10 countries increase their participation in global and regional value chains, develop manufacturing, and expand exports of manufactures. It will also help countries such as the Kyrgyz Republic, Tajikistan, and Uzbekistan (Box 3.5) increase the volume and diversify the direction of exports of horticulture products

Box 3.5: Freight, Transport, and Storage Services in Uzbekistan's Horticultural Value Chains

Horticulture is a promising subsector in Uzbekistan's economy. Its contribution to export growth in 2017 was almost twice that of cotton, and it continues to provide higher financial returns to farmers. The subsector, however, is still underdeveloped due to a lack of access to modern production and post-harvest technology and financing. Uzbekistan horticulture had previously suffered from underdeveloped marketing and transport infrastructure, weak and fragmented value chains, and a lack of storage facilities and processing capacity. Up to one-fifth of harvest volumes were lost as a result.

Efforts are underway to modernize and expand Uzbekistan's horticulture subsector. The government's response has helped make the sector more market-driven and increased value-added by supporting the diversification of product lines and increased processing of fruits and vegetables. These efforts are being backed by enhanced financial and technological inputs and the technical assistance components of projects supported by the country's international development partners such as the Asian Development Bank (ADB), the World Bank, and the International Fund for Agricultural Development. Several projects have sought to improve post-harvest logistics through product consolidation, better transport services, and cold storage. Adherence to internationally recognized standards and certification has also been promoted to make Uzbekistan's products more attractive and acceptable abroad, especially in high value-added markets in Europe and elsewhere.

An ongoing ADB project approved in 2018 focuses on creating centers that consolidate agricultural infrastructure and service inputs along horticultural supply chains. These centers, to be established in the cities of Samarkand and Andijan, will support trade, storage, and processing; food safety inspection and certification; customs clearance; transport and shipping; and market advisory, trade finance, and commercial banking services. The availability in one location of this wide variety of key services will strengthen the efficiency and value-addition of the supply chain. The long list only highlights just how dependent product supply chains of all types are on services, as well as how the price and quality of these many essential inputs are fundamental factors in determining efficiency and competitiveness.

Source: ADB. 2018c. Republic of Uzbekistan: Horticulture Value Chain Infrastructure Project. Project Number: 51041-002. https://www.adb.org/projects/51041-002/main.

---

[25] Using a Melitz-type model with heterogeneous firms, Dennis and Shepherd (2007) find that a 1% reduction in the cost of international transport is associated with an export diversification gain of 0.4% in a sample of 118 developing countries. This is because transport costs act like fixed costs to inhibit entry of less efficient firms. A reduction in transport costs reduces fixed costs and enables these marginal firms to start exporting.

by boosting exports of these products to East Asia, South Asia, Europe, and the Middle East. Further, developing transport and storage services will enable CAREC countries to increase transit trade flows and exports of related services. It might lead to some CAREC countries becoming major regional transport hubs.[26]

Quality Testing and Certification Services

Like many other modern business services, quality testing and certification services are underdeveloped in CAREC countries.[27] Product quality testing services and food safety testing services are in short supply, especially outside capital cities. Public entities provide most, if not all, of these services. Testing quality is generally inadequate, and test results are often not accepted by other jurisdictions.

Most CAREC countries have only a few internationally accredited laboratories for testing product quality, or none at all. Foreign entities usually don't recognize test results from CAREC country laboratories.[28] Quality certification services are more widely available, in part due to the many private firms involved in this subsector. However, only a few of these firms can issue international certificates relating to product quality, and all or most are subsidiaries of foreign companies. Their services are expensive, which largely explains why the number of valid certificates for International Organization for Standardization (ISO) standards is relatively low in CAREC countries (Table 3.13).

CAREC countries need to improve the availability, reliability, and affordability of quality testing and certification services. By doing so, they will enhance the competitiveness of local producers in both domestic and foreign markets and help them gain access to new markets. This will in turn help CAREC countries develop other service industries and manufacturing and increase and diversify the direction of their exports. The development of food quality testing and certification services will help CAREC countries such as Afghanistan, Kazakhstan, the Kyrgyz Republic, Mongolia, and Tajikistan establish new international markets for their food products and increase the volume of these exports.[29]

---

[26] The COVID-19 pandemic will likely cause many countries to diversify and shorten supply chains, especially for pharmaceuticals, medical equipment, and food products. At the same time, the heightened tensions between the United States (US) and the PRC is likely to cause the PRC to try to diversify its trade away from the US. These processes are likely to reduce demand for intercontinental freight transport services. However, they may boost demand for local and regional freight transport and storage services, particularly within Eurasia. This will create an opportunity for some CAREC countries to capture a large share of the global market for freight transport and storage services.

[27] Quality testing and certification services are important elements of the quality infrastructure ecosystem, which comprises the organizations (public and private), laws, regulations, policies, and practices that ensure the quality (including the safety and environmental soundness) of goods, services, and processes. Good quality infrastructure is essential for the protection of human health and the environment and the efficient operation of markets. It enhances the competitiveness of local producers and facilitates their access to foreign markets and integration into global value chains (Kellermann 2019).

[28] See ADB (2019c) for an assessment of CAREC countries' sanitary and phytosanitary laboratory capacity.

[29] See World Bank (2011b) for a discussion of the importance of good quality infrastructure (including quality testing and certification services) to economic diversification and development in the countries of Eastern Europe, the South Caucasus, and Central Asia. See GIZ and Euromonitor (2017) for a review of weaknesses of quality infrastructure for horticulture products in Kazakhstan, the Kyrgyz Republic, Tajikistan, and Uzbekistan.

**Table 3.13: CAREC Countries—Number of Valid Certificates
for Selected ISO Standards, 2018**
(per $10 billion of GDP at purchasing power parity valuation)

Country	ISO 9001:2015[a]	ISO 22000:2018[b]	ISO/IEC 27001:2013[c]
Afghanistan	0.6	0.3	0.0
Azerbaijan	11.8	1.1	0.1
China, People's Republic of	116.6	4.6	2.8
Georgia	41.3	19.0	0.5
Kazakhstan	11.3	0.7	0.3
Kyrgyz Republic	4.5	4.9	0.0
Mongolia	10.8	2.1	0.5
Pakistan	19.2	1.9	0.3
Tajikistan	1.0	0.3	0.3
Turkmenistan	4.0	2.0	0.0
Uzbekistan	16.7	1.0	0.0
Comparator			
OECD countries	114.0	4.4	5.2

CAREC = Central Asia Regional Economic Cooperation, GDP = gross domestic product, ISO = International Organization for Standardization, OECD = Organisation for Economic Co-operation and Development.

[a] ISO 9001:2015 Quality management systems.

[b] ISO 22000:2018 Food safety management systems.

[c] ISO/IEC 27001:2013 Information security management systems.

Source: International Organization for Standardization ISO Survey 2019. https://isotc.iso.org/livelink/livelink?func=ll&objId=18808772&objAction=browse&viewType=1; World Bank. World Development Indicators , https://databank.worldbank.org/source/world-development-indicators#; and authors' computations.

Other Agriculture-Related Services

Agriculture, including forestry and fishing, continues to be a major economic sector in CAREC countries. Agriculture accounted for 14.2% of GDP across CAREC members in 2019, compared with the 4% global average. It comprised at least one-fifth of GDP in Afghanistan, Pakistan, and Uzbekistan. The agriculture sector also contributed 33.5% of employment in CAREC countries, higher than the 27% globally. CAREC members have a broad and solid base on which to expand and build new agricultural production, exports, and export markets. The variety and volume of the crops and animals raised, processed, and exported are clear indications of untapped potential for scaling up CAREC's agricultural exports. Facilitating agricultural trade will contribute to CAREC countries' export diversification and sustainable growth. Strong and effective sanitary and phytosanitary measures are also crucial in this regard (Lazaro et al. 2021).

Upgrades along the agricultural value chain, particularly on the services side, are needed for this potential to be fully realized. Agriculture value chain refers to a range of goods and services needed for an agricultural product to move from the farm to the consumers (Rillo and Nugroho 2016). These include support and operation services—mechanization, seed processing, agronomy, plant protection, animal health, business advisory, and marketing services—provided for crop production and animal husbandry. ADB is supporting Mongolia overcome the challenges it faces throughout the meat value chain, which limits access to export markets (Box 3.6).

Box 3.6: Improving Livestock Production Systems in Central Mongolia

Mongolia's agriculture sector remains a key pillar of the economy, with the majority of the poor depending on agriculture and extensive livestock production to sustain their livelihoods. The share of livestock in agriculture output is 84.2%, providing employment to one-third of Mongolia's economically active population. Meat and milk are the primary products of the livestock subsector, contributing to 61.0% of livestock output and 7.0% of gross domestic product.

In June 2021, the Asian Development Bank approved a loan and technical assistance package totaling $31 million to support the improvement of livestock production systems in 20 *soum* (districts) of four *aimag* (provinces) in Central Mongolia. The project will build the climate resilience of herders against the increased frequency of severe weather, promote a reduction in livestock numbers, and increase the quality of livestock products. To improve the quality and health standard of livestock herds and products, the project will coordinate and integrate livestock value chain participants. This will include activities such as establishing standards for health and carcass quality, supporting veterinary units, livestock marketing by establishing linkages between herder households and processors to meet processing and market standards, cashmere marketing including sorting facilities, animal breeding for sheeps and goats, and livestock feeding for hay production and fodder storage.

Source: ADB. 2021d. Mongolia: Climate-Resilient and Sustainable Livestock Development Project. https://www.adb.org/projects/53038-001/main.

Strengthening agricultural value chains in the CAREC region requires overcoming challenges at farm production (e.g., poor production systems and low productivity), processing (e.g., lack of reliable inputs and access to finance) and marketing and distribution (e.g., logistics platforms and trade hubs) stages. The agricultural services supporting the development of value chains could be improved through private–public partnerships and economic corridors. Private–public partnerships involve schemes where the private sector and government work together to provide training programs for farmers and small and medium-sized enterprises and support access to agricultural inputs to improve farmers' productivity. Economic corridors help develop agriculture and agribusiness by linking agribusiness firms and producers through major infrastructure investment areas (Rillo and Nugroho 2016).

Chapter 4

CREATING AN ENABLING ENVIRONMENT FOR THE DEVELOPMENT OF THE SERVICES SECTOR IN CAREC COUNTRIES

Despite the growth of the services sector's contribution to the global economy, governments have not focused their attention on better policies and regulations for even faster development of service subsectors. For instance, global focus on removing services trade barriers—including global technical assistance in relation to services policies—is not commensurate with services' weight in total trade (WTO 2020). The neglect of policy to allow and encourage the development of services (or the maintenance of bad policies) will inhibit growth and progress across a broad swath of economies. Recent work by the WTO (WTO 2019) focuses on key aspects of policy design that influences markets for services. On average, services typically face higher trade barriers than goods. Rather than border tariffs, as in the case of goods, these barriers tend to be regulatory. Opening markets in the services sphere is almost entirely about the intent, design, and administration of regulations. Regulatory systems should, therefore, be a core area for attention. Transparent and efficient regulatory and administrative procedures are crucial to competitive service supply.

Empirical literature highlights the importance of several enabling or facilitating conditions essential for the robust development of the services sector and economic diversification.[30] These conditions, critical for CAREC countries, are classified into five areas: (i) improving governance, (ii) enhancing market competition, (iii) deepening regional cooperation and integration, (iv) raising the efficiency of the labor market, and (v) developing physical and digital infrastructure.

Improving Governance

The quality of institutions at the interface of government policy and the economy greatly influences a country's ability to foster growth and opportunities for advancement. Healthy, sustained development of services sector cannot be achieved without good governance, including a favorable legal and regulatory framework for private sector development (Ghani 2010; Sahoo and Dash 2017; World Bank 2017b; WTO 2019b). Poor governance hinders economic growth generally and services

---

[30] Among them are good governance (or good quality institutions), regional and global economic cooperation and integration, market competition, access to high-quality infrastructure, availability of human capital, efficiency of the labor market, well-managed urbanization, effective public sector interventions addressing market failures, and balanced development of interdependent service industries (Cherif, Hasanov and Zhu 2016; Ghani 2010; Khatiwada and Flaminiano 2019; Linn 2015; OECD 2018; Sahoo and Dash 2017; UNCTAD 2017; World Bank 2017b; WTO 2019b).

sector growth particularly. The damage is done in many ways. Corruption and weak protection of property rights discourage entrepreneurship and private investment by making returns on investment uncertain. Weak protection of intellectual property rights is especially detrimental to the development of innovation-driven services subsectors (such as telecommunication and information services) because it makes returns on investment in research and development more uncertain and discourages innovation. By increasing business expenditure and reducing returns on investment, red tape and corruption also discourage entrepreneurship, private investment, and innovation.[31] Excessive regulatory burdens adversely affect both supply and quality of goods and services.[32] Economies with poor governance tend to specialize in sectors that are less reliant on innovation and complex contracts (Levchenko 2007; Nunn 2007; Silve and Plekhanov 2018). Poor governance fuels brain drain and reduces the stock of available human capital (EBRD 2019). Regulatory and contract-enforcement institutions play a key role in the development of service industries because many of these industries enter complex transactions with the rest of the economy and are more prone to market failures. Overall, therefore, the quality of institutions and the share of the services sector in GDP are positively correlated (Amin and Mattoo 2006).

Most CAREC countries have made efforts to improve governance. They have streamlined business regulations, strengthened the rule of law, and reduced corruption, which helped improve the scores and rankings of most of them in the Corruption Perception Index during 2013–2019 (Figure 4.1). The arithmetic mean of the World Bank's Worldwide Governance Indicator scores for government effectiveness, regulatory quality, rule of law, and control of corruption for all of the CAREC

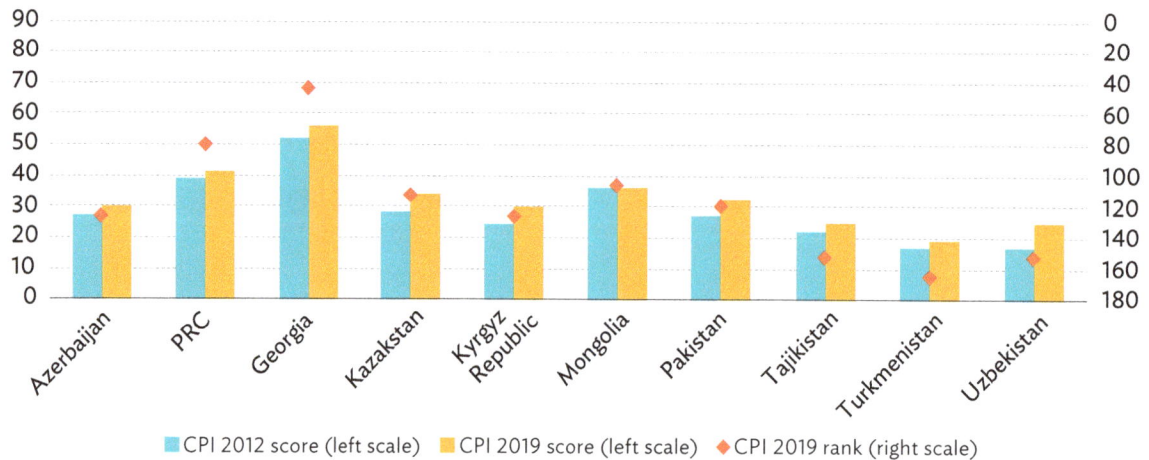

Figure 4.1: CAREC Countries—Corruption Perception Index Scores and Rank, 2012 and 2019

CAREC = Central Asia Regional Economic Cooperation, CPI = Corruption Perception Index, PRC= People's Republic of China.
Note: The Corruption Perception Index score ranges from 0 to 100, with a higher score corresponding to less corruption. The Corruption Perception Index 2019 covers 180 countries. It does not cover Afghanistan.
Source: Transparency International. Corruption Perceptions Index. https://www.transparency.org/en/cpi/2020/index/nzl.

[31]   Fisman and Svensson (2007) find that the detrimental effect of corruption on a firm's growth is three times as great as the adverse impact of extra taxes (where corruption and increased taxation result in outgoing payments of a similar size). This is due to the greater uncertainty and transaction costs associated with corruption.

[32]   Hollweg and Wong (2009) show that there is a negative correlation between the level of restrictiveness of the regulations affecting logistics services and the quality of these services.

countries (except Tajikistan) was also higher in 2018 than in 2010 (Figure 4.2). Despite general improvements, more work is required. For example, most CAREC countries covered by the World Economic Forum's Global Competitiveness Index 2019 rank low on property rights and intellectual property protection (Figure 4.3).

Figure 4.2: CAREC Countries—Average Worldwide Governance Indicator Scores, 2010 and 2018

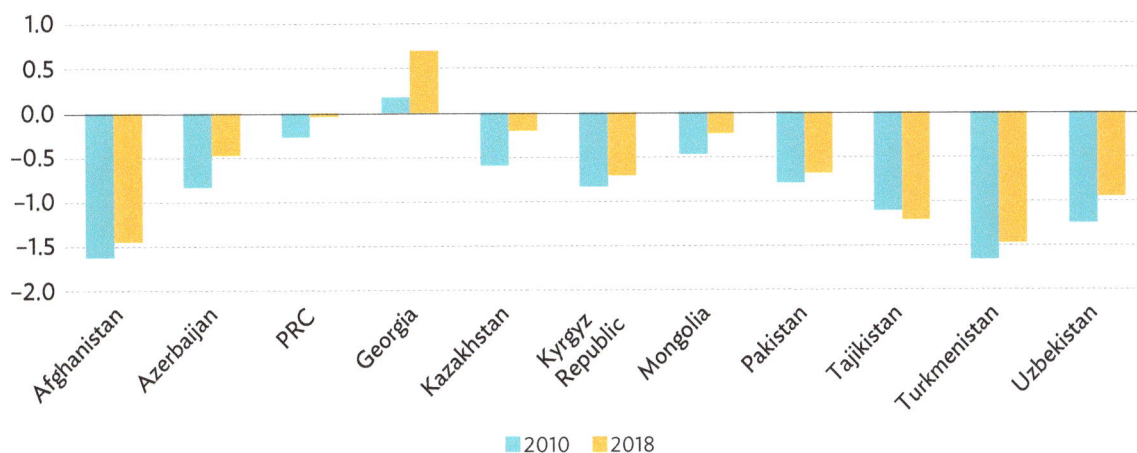

CAREC = Central Asia Regional Economic Cooperation, PRC= People's Republic of China.

Notes: The average scores are the arithmetic means of the Worldwide Government Indicator scores for government effectiveness, regulatory quality, rule of law and control of corruption. The scores range from −2.5 to 2.5, with a greater score corresponding to better governance. The median performer has a score of 0. The indicators are available for 200 countries and territories.

Sources: World Bank. Worldwide Government Indicators. https://info.worldbank.org/governance/wgi/ and authors' computations.

Figure 4.3: CAREC Countries—Selected Global Competitiveness Index 2019 Components Relating to Quality of Institutions

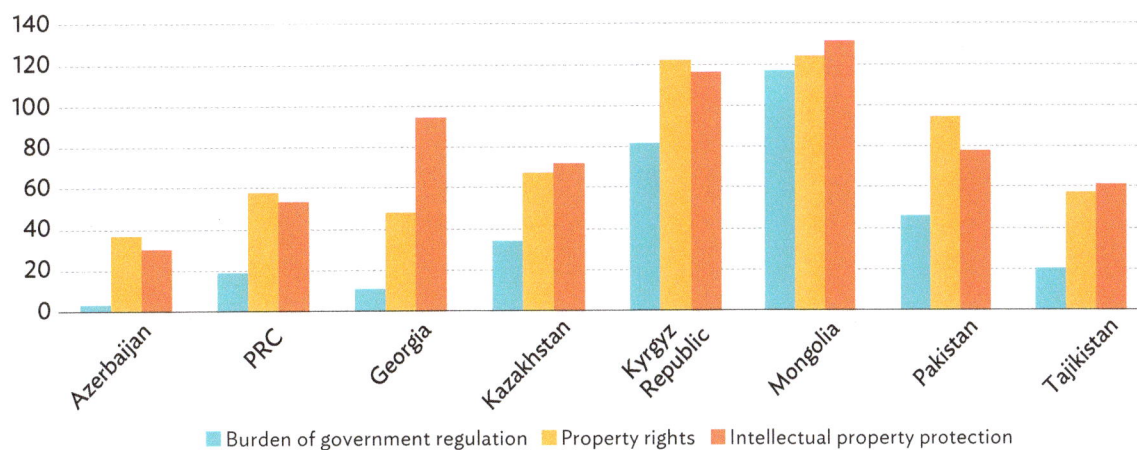

CAREC = Central Asia Regional Economic Cooperation, PRC= People's Republic of China.

Note: The Global Competitiveness Index 2019 covers 141 countries. It does not cover Afghanistan, Turkmenistan, and Uzbekistan.

Source: Schwab. 2019. The Global Competitiveness Report 2019. Geneva.

Regulatory quality, which has a major effect on development in the services sector, remains relatively low in most CAREC countries. Only two CAREC countries (Georgia and Kazakhstan) have a percentile ranking of greater than 60 in the 2019 Worldwide Governance Indicators for regulatory quality.[33] It is not uncommon for CAREC countries to enact business regulations that are not the most effective and efficient means to achieve the intended policy goals. Many of these regulations (e.g., regulations that restrict healthy foreign competition) impede the development of the services sector. Undertaking regulatory impact assessment would help CAREC countries improve regulatory quality (Box 4.1).

Box 4.1: Regulatory Impact Assessment

A regulatory impact assessment (RIA) is both a process and tool for informing policy makers on whether and how to regulate to achieve public policy goals. An RIA provides a systematic advance appraisal (ex-ante) of the positive and negative effects of a proposed new regulation. It also compares alternative means of achieving policy goals and identifies the approach that is likely to deliver the greatest net benefit to society.

An RIA can help promote policy coherence by pointing to the trade-offs inherent in regulatory proposals, improve the use of evidence in policy making, and help avoid regulatory weaknesses. To be effective, however, RIAs require substantial availability and commitment of resources and expertise. An RIA is sometimes mistaken as a substitute for policy making, when in fact it is intended to facilitate and strengthen the policy making process.

RIA processes should be closely linked with the general consultation processes in the development of new regulations through, for example, road maps that give early notice of possible regulatory initiatives and related consultations and impact assessment work. To ensure a high level of transparency and reduce the risks of regulatory capture, the results of the consultations, together with individual contributions, should as far as possible be made publicly available (including online, where appropriate). Experience shows that governments must lead strongly to overcome inbuilt inertia, risk aversion, and a regulate-first-ask-questions-later culture. To ensure that public policy objectives are attained, care must also be taken when deciding to use light-handed approaches such as self-regulation.

For an RIA to be successful, it must:

- start at the inception phase of the regulation-making process;
- clearly identify the problem being addressed and desired goals of the regulatory proposal;
- identify and evaluate all potential alternative solutions, including nonregulatory ones;
- attempt to assess all potential costs and benefits, both direct and indirect;
- be based on all available evidence and scientific expertise; and
- be developed transparently with stakeholders and communicate its results clearly.

Sources: Organisation for Economic Co-operation and Development (OECD). 2012. Recommendation of the Council on Regulatory Policy and Governance. Paris: OECD. https://www.oecd.org/governance/regulatory-policy/2012-recommendation.htm; and OECD. 2020. Best Practice Principles for Regulatory Policy: Regulatory Impact Assessment. Paris: OECD. https://www.oecd-ilibrary.org/docserver/663f08d9-en.pdf?expires=1636101021&id=id&accname=guest&checksum=DB403BDDD4BCC2429C5BCBAC783428AB.

---

[33] A country's percentile rank indicates the percentage of countries that score below (more poorly) that it does. For instance, a percentile rank of 60 means that the country scored above 60% of the countries on the indicator.

CAREC countries should pay special attention to strengthening governance in those services subsectors and indsutries where development is critical to economic diversification. For CAREC countries, governance needs to be improved in the transport sector (including air and rail transport) to foster growth of transport services and tourism. Better governance in terms of prudential regulation and supervision is also needed to enhance soundness and ensure robust development of the finance sector. Many CAREC countries need to stimulate the development of quality testing and certification services and improve their acceptability in other jurisdictions. All CAREC countries should enhance the incentive framework for research, development, and innovation. This is especially important in telecommunication and information, finance, and education sector.[34]

Enhancing Market Competition

Market competition leads to lower prices, higher quality and greater variety of goods and services, better firm management, more innovation, higher productivity, and faster economic growth when there are no market failures or policy-induced distortions. Even where market failure or a policy-induced distortion exist, enhancing competition generally leads to better outcomes than restricting competition.[35] Buccirossi et.al. (2013) estimated the impact of competition policy in 12 OECD countries during 1995–2005 on the growth of total factor productivity for 22 industries (including transport, storage, finance, hotels and restaurants, and professional services) and identified a significant positive relationship between the two variables. Boylaud and Nicoletti (2000) found that the prospect of competition and actual competition raise productivity in the telecommunications sector in OECD countries, improve the quality of services, and lower their prices. Arvis, Raballand, and Marteau (2010) developed a quantitative model of a transit supply chain to simulate the impact of changes in freight market organization in landlocked developing countries. They found that transitioning from cartel control of transit freight allocation to an efficient trucking market (which decreases truck turnaround time) reduces the truck and labor components of transport costs for landlocked economies by more than 30%. In the Philippines for example, the World Bank (2018c) estimated that enhancing competition in the energy, professional services, transport, and telecommunication sectors could lead to additional annual GDP growth of 0.2%.

Competition is currently weak in many sectors in the CAREC countries. Five of the eight CAREC countries covered by the Global Competitiveness Index 2019 fell below 60 (out of 141 countries) on the extent of market dominance, and seven ranked 80th or lower on competition in services (Figure 4.4). Competition in the banking sector is weaker in all CAREC countries than in the OECD countries on average (Table 4.1). State-owned entities dominate key services subsector (including air transport, banking, and education services) in many CAREC countries.

---

[34] See, for instance, ADB (2019a) for a discussion of governance reforms needed in the road transport sector of the CAREC countries; ADB (2017) for a discussion of legal and regulatory reforms needed in the railway transport sector of the CAREC countries; ADB (2019b) for a discussion of governance reforms needed in the education sector of the CAREC countries; and IMF (2018c and 2018d) and Morgan, Zhang, and Kydyrbayev (2018) for a discussion of governance reforms needed in the finance sector of the countries of Central Asia and the South Caucasus.

[35] See, for instance, World Bank (2017c) for a review of empirical literature on effects of market competition. Among more recent empirical studies, EBRD (2019), for example, finds that firms that face greater competitive pressures tend to have better management practices.

Figure 4.4: CAREC Countries—Selected Global Competitiveness Index 2019 Components Relating to Domestic Competition

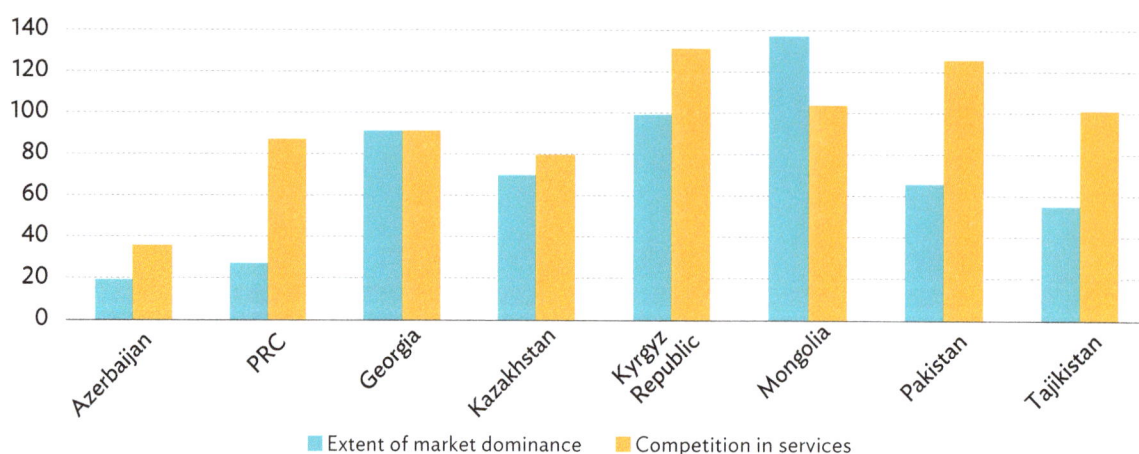

CAREC = Central Asia Regional Economic Cooperation, PRC= People's Republic of China.

Note: The Global Competitiveness Index 2019 covers 141 countries. It does not cover Afghanistan, Turkmenistan, and Uzbekistan.

Source: Schwab. 2019. The Global Competitiveness Report 2019. Geneva.

Table 4.1: CAREC Countries—Measures of Concentration and Competition in Banking Sector

Country	Measures of Concentration[a]		Measures of Competition[b]	
	3-Bank Asset Concentration[c]	5-Bank Asset Concentration[d]	Lerner Index[e]	Boone Indicator[f]
Afghanistan	55.6	73.7	0.34	−0.06
Azerbaijan	55.6	72.5	0.38	−0.07
China, People's Republic of	37.2	52.5	0.35	−0.03
Georgia	77.8	86.2	0.36	−0.02
Kazakhstan	38.1	52.8	0.29	0.19
Kyrgyz Republic	50.1	70.1	...	−0.10
Mongolia	86.2	95.9	...	−0.05
Pakistan	44.1	60.0	...	−0.15
Uzbekistan	59.5	71.7	...	0.03
Comparator country group				
OECD countries	65.5	81.0	0.29	−1.20

... = data not available, CAREC = Central Asia Regional Economic Cooperation, OECD = Organisation for Economic Co-operation and Development.

[a] Data is for 2017.

[b] Data is for 2014 (except for Afghanistan where data is as of 2013).

[c] Assets of the three largest commercial banks as a percentage of total commercial banking assets.

[d] Assets of the five largest commercial banks as a percentage of total commercial banking assets.

[e] The Lerner index compares output pricing and marginal costs (that is, markup) in the market for banking services. An increase in the index indicates a deterioration of the competitive conduct of banks. Larger index values indicate lower levels of competition.

[f] The Boone indicator is a measure of competition based on profit-efficiency in the market for banking services. It is calculated as the elasticity of profits to marginal costs. An increase in the Boone indicator implies a deterioration of the competitive conduct of banks. Larger index values indicate lower levels of competition.

Sources: World Bank. Global Financial Development Database. https://www.worldbank.org/en/publication/gfdr/data/global-financial-development-databasen (accessed September 2020); and authors' computations.

International experience indicates that liberalizing trade and leveling the playing field in the services sector is an effective way to enhance competition in service industries. Lowering barriers to FDI is especially impactful.[36] Using firm-level data from 27 emerging market economies, Gorodnichenko, Svejnar, and Terrell (2010) showed that there is a positive relationship between foreign competition and innovation. Miroudot, Sauvage, and Shepherd (2012) found that opening up services markets to foreign competition increases competitive pressure on producers and leads to reallocation of resources from less productive firms to more productive ones. As a result, overall productivity in service subsectors increases. Shepherd (2019) compared the effects of a notional 10% reduction in applied tariffs with those of a notional 10% reduction in the restrictiveness of services policies and found that the latter has significantly larger positive effects on trade and real output than the former. Sahoo and Dash (2017) concluded that FDI has a significantly positive impact on India's exports of modern services. Francois and Hoekman (2010) showed that FDI in the services sector has positive effects on productivity in the economy by inducing greater competition and providing access to higher quality, more varied, and cheaper services. A few empirical studies have found that liberalization of trade in services boosts output and exports of service-intensive industries by providing firms in these industries with access to a greater variety of services of better quality at lower prices (Barone and Cingano 2011; Hoekman and Shepherd 2017; World Bank 2017b; and World Bank 2017c).

Some CAREC countries maintain comparatively high barriers to FDI in many services subsectors. Based on the OECD FDI Restrictiveness Index 2020, the PRC's barriers to FDI in transport, telecommunication, financial, and business services are substantially higher than the corresponding OECD country averages (Table 4.2). This is also true for FDI in financial services in Azerbaijan, Kazakhstan, and Tajikistan, in business services in Azerbaijan, the Kyrgyz Republic, Tajikistan, and Uzbekistan, and in telecommunication in Kazakhstan.

GATS commitments among the CAREC countries

Eight of the 11 CAREC countries are members of the WTO and have schedules of specific commitments under the General Agreement on Trade in Services (GATS). Except for Pakistan, which is a contracting party of the WTO (original member) since 1 January 1995, the GATS schedules were established for the rest of the seven CAREC member countries during their WTO accession.[37] Unlike the WTO's Harmonized Commodity Description and Coding Systems used for goods, the GATS schedules of specific commitments do not follow a uniform system of nomenclature. This makes it difficult to compare the commitments of individual CAREC countries. Moreover, GATS commitments tend to be regulatory in nature and, unlike tariff commitments in the case of goods, are not easily expressed numerically. This, too, makes country comparisons less straightforward.

GATS schedules have four columns. The first is for the service product description, the second for market access commitments under GATS Article XVI, the third for national treatment commitments under GATS Article XVII, and the fourth for additional commitments that do not fit smoothly under

---

[36]   Lowering barriers to FDI in service industries is tantamount to reducing barriers to Mode 3 imports of services.

[37]   Afghanistan acceded to the WTO on 29 July 2016, the People's Republic of China on 11 December 2001, Georgia on 14 June 2000, Kazakhstan on 30 November 2015, the Kyrgyz Republic on 20 December 1998, Mongolia on 29 January 1997, and Tajikistan on 2 March 2013.

Table 4.2: CAREC Countries—Foreign Direct Investment Restrictiveness Index for Selected Sectors, 2020

Country	Overall Index	Transport	Communication	Finance	Business
Azerbaijan	0.077	0.079	0.01	0.207	0.16
China, People's Republic of	0.214	0.395	0.733	0.05	0.225
Georgia	0.018	0.133	0	0	0
Kazakhstan	0.113	0.09	0.14	0.118	0.04
Kyrgyz Republic	0.137	0.188	0.055	0.087	0.298
Mongolia	0.072	0.171	0.06	0.06	0.06
Tajikistan	0.12	0.18	0.03	0.127	0.273
Uzbekistan	0.068	0.041	0.02	0.095	0.265
Comparator country group					
OECD countries	0.063	0.204	0.079	0.032	0.06

CAREC = Central Asia Regional Economic Cooperation, OECD = Organisation for Economic Co-operation and Development.

Note: The FDI Restrictiveness Index measures the restrictiveness of a country's FDI rules by looking at four main types of restrictions: foreign equity restrictions, discriminatory screening or approval mechanisms, restrictions on key foreign personnel, and operational restrictions. Implementation issues are not addressed and factors such as the degree of transparency or discretion in granting approvals are not taken into account. The value of the index and its sector components range from 0 (open) to 1 (closed). The index does not cover CAREC member countries that are excluded from the table.

Source: OECD. 2021. FDI restrictiveness (indicator). doi: 10.1787/c176b7fa-en (accessed 11 August 2021).

Articles XVI and XVII. Market access and national treatment commitments are both expressed in terms of modes of delivery: Mode 1 for cross-border supply for domestic consumption, Mode 2 for consumption abroad, Mode 3 for commercial presence, and Mode 4 for individual service suppliers. The commitments in members' GATS schedules are divided into two categories and sections: horizontal commitments that apply more generally to all or most sectors, and sector-specific commitments that focus on individual products and subsectors. This distinction is made for convenience. A horizontal commitment covering a broad area eliminates the need to repeat this specific commitment for each product or subsector. From an analytical perspective, the horizontal section of the GATS schedules is especially useful, since it sketches the general outlines of the extent to which members are willing to open or shield their services and service suppliers in terms of international competition. Precise analysis of the more detailed sector-specific commitments helps complete the picture.

Horizontal commitments

The horizontal commitments undertaken by the eight CAREC members of the WTO are summarized in Appendix 4. One pattern indicates broad reservations against commitments regarding subsidies for services subsectors or industries. All the countries that mention subsidies in their horizontal schedules tend to avoid commitments governing the use of this policy instrument. Commitments that would provide foreign enterprises the same subsidy support as local ones are also avoided in the countries' sector-specific schedules. This is not surprising, since CAREC countries are generally seeking to diversify their economic structure in every way possible, including through subsidies, and to encourage domestic participation in these efforts.

Apart from the subsidy-related exemptions on national treatment permitted by the "unbound" entries in the horizontal schedules, the bulk of the remainder of the limitations in commitments relate mostly to Mode 3 and 4 service transactions. Foreign commercial presence is encouraged in the case of Mode 3 but frequently limited in certain ways. These can include restrictions on foreign equity shares in certain sectors and on foreign participation in privatization exercises, as well as prohibitions on commercial activities when presence only involves a representative office. Limitations are also common on the ownership and use of land.

In Mode 4, intra-corporate transferees of a certain standing (executives, managers, and specialists) are generally permitted under specified criteria to provide services in the host country. Limitations typically relate to the length of stay (renewable work permits) and the status and place of work of the transferee. Arrangements of this kind are contemplated in all CAREC member countries but exclude less-skilled service suppliers. Business visitors can obtain short-term visas but are forbidden from undertaking any commercial activity.

Sector-specific commitments

Appendix 5 summarizes the incidence of commitments made by CAREC WTO members in the 11 sectors used in the listing of sector-specific commitments. Afghanistan, Georgia, the Kyrgyz Republic, and Tajikistan have made commitments in all 11, Kazakhstan in 10, the PRC in nine, and Mongolia and Pakistan in six. The numbers might be taken as an indication of the breadth of each country's commitments but do not tell anything about their significance quantitatively.

Appendix 6 examines the commitments at the subsector level and records the more disaggregated schedule entries of each CAREC WTO member. The theoretical maximum number of sector-specific commitments in the Appendix's table is 161. Table 4.3 below shows the number of actual commitments made by each CAREC member when they joined or acceded to the WTO.

Table 4.3: Number of CAREC WTO Member-Specific Subsectoral Commitments

Country	Number of Subsector Commitments	Share of Possible Commitments (%)
Afghanistan	103	58
China, People's Republic of	93	52
Georgia	125	70
Kazakhstan	112	63
Kyrgyz Republic	140	78
Mongolia	37	21
Pakistan	42	24
Tajikistan	110	62

CAREC = Central Asia Regional Economic Cooperation, WTO = World Trade Organization.

Note: Commitments are as of entry into force of the WTO Agreement for Pakistan or accession dates of WTO member countries (e.g., as of 29 July 2016 for Afghanistan). The table does not reflect any change after 15 August 2021.

Source: World Trade Organization. Schedules of specific commitments and lists of Article II exemptions. https://www.wto.org/english/tratop_e/serv_e/serv_commitments_e.htm (accessed September 2020).

Compared with international averages of the specific GATS commitments undertaken by WTO members, the totals for Afghanistan, Georgia, Kazakhstan, the Kyrgyz Republic, the PRC, and Tajikistan, are high. These six CAREC WTO members have committed more than 50% of the sectors covered by the GATS schedules at a significantly disaggregated subsector level.

Appendix 4 also shows how the subsector commitments of the CAREC WTO members are distributed. Variations are inevitable, but certain patterns do emerge. Other than service transactions excluded more generally through broad horizontal schedule entries, or when service supply through these modes is technically impracticable, much of Modes 1 and 2 trade is largely unrestricted. One exception is Mode 1 restrictions designed to assert governmental regulatory responsibility in such matters as insurance.

Mode 3 is the next most open in most of the schedules. Mode 4 is by far the most closed. Mode 4 restrictions (on the temporary movement of natural persons) are clearly spelled out in the horizontal commitments summarized in Appendix 4. The paucity of commitments on Mode 4 transactions, with permitted movements typically limited to professional personnel and strictly defined, is a feature shared by GATS schedules across the WTO membership.

A pattern appearing in the subsector spread of commitments by all the CAREC countries is one of fewer restrictions in what might be termed infrastructure-related commitments related (among other things) to business, ICT, construction, and to some extent financial services (less in insurance, more in banking).[38] Other relatively open subsectors include computer-related, research and development, and education services (except when it comes to protecting state-funded education), as well as tourism. Although consistent patterns do not hold for all CAREC WTO members, other subsectors where one might find a higher degree of restriction are in the category of 'other' business services, environmental services, and certain transport services.

Concluding observations on the GATS schedules of CAREC members

Most CAREC countries have committed to a higher level of discipline in services trade than many others. This level in fact approaches that of the developed nations. Adlung and Roy (2005) compared commitment levels across different country categories. At the time, the average number of subsector commitments by WTO members was 52, an average that was brought down significantly by the lower numbers of commitments by many least developed and developing countries. This changed when transition economies—which, in WTO parlance, covered most of the CAREC countries with the exceptions of Pakistan and the PRC—were considered on their own. The average jumped to 105; the developed country average was 106. The transition economy average would be higher still with the inclusion of the commitment numbers of the two CAREC countries that acceded to the WTO after 2005, notably those of Kazakhstan (2015) and Tajikistan (2013).

---

[38]   This pattern was also remarked upon in a much earlier analysis (Adlung and Roy, 2005).

Whether the commitments made have had a policy impact that has supported or hindered a more open approach to the service subsectors that are key to diversify the region's economies remains an issue. Soprana (2016) argued that some relatively far-reaching commitments of countries such as Kazakhstan and Tajikistan were more about signaling than committing to real reform. However, successful signaling will carry economic consequences and could further influence policy decisions.

It has been argued—by Eschenbach and Hoekman (2006), for example—that a statistically significant correlation exists in transition economies between policy reforms and FDI in such service subsectors as finance, telecommunications, power, and transport. FDI inflows to most CAREC countries have exceeded average world levels during 2001–2019 (Figure 2.1). Deeper analysis would be required to establish any actual relationship between these inflows and CAREC countries' GATS commitments.

GATS commitments can be both a signaling device and a harbinger of policy reform. In addition, GATS schedules set a baseline, predicated upon an international obligation, below which a country's policy cannot go unless it is willing to disregard this obligation and risk the repercussions of a challenge by a WTO trading partner. It seems reasonable to argue that the degree of certainty implicit in setting a policy bottom line is worth something.

On the other hand, the only level of GATS commitment (or a tariff binding on the goods side for that matter) is free trade. A thorough policy analysis cannot rest on a GATS-determined bottom line unless it is set at zero intervention, least of all in terms of an actual policy stance. Only with a zero-intervention commitment can the relationship between status quo policy and a WTO access commitment be fully established. First, governments may apply policies that offer better treatment than the underlying GATS obligation. Plenty of evidence exists of cases where actual market access exceeds what has been committed to in legally binding WTO commitments. Second, at the end of the day, there is no substitute for assessing the use of the policies themselves. Causality conclusions are difficult to make. On the face of it, GATS commitments might in some cases do more to prevent the worst in policy outcomes rather than to drive the best.

This cautionary note about how to read and understand GATS schedules in terms of economic outcomes does not invalidate the utility of WTO mechanisms that fix bottom-line policy positions and raise awareness of what these are in an international context. Indeed, some work on the effects of WTO commitments on policy outcomes—looking at tariff bindings on goods (Bacchetta and Piermartini 2011; Jakubik and Piermartini 2019)—shows that commitments and the levels at which they are set influence policy behavior and reduce uncertainty. There is no reason to believe that the story would be different for services trade policy. However, a supplementary consideration for both goods and services trade in terms of the relationship between policy commitments and actual policy environments on the ground concerns the design and application of regulatory frameworks. This is an issue already discussed at some length above in relation to regulatory outcomes. Regulation is often more opaque than access commitments because of the scope it affords the administering officials for discretionary action, sometimes on a daily basis. This can make it harder to be sure that policy commitments are consistently reflected in practice. This potential gap and ways of filling it fall squarely under the kind of governance considerations alluded to above.

While liberalizing trade in services is likely to yield significant benefits for CAREC countries, it will also entail certain costs and risks. Notably, it is likely to cause closure or downsizing of inefficient domestic firms and a temporary increase in unemployment. Liberalizing trade in financial services will make the financial sectors of CAREC countries more vulnerable to financial crises in other countries. Liberalizing trade in telecommunication and information services poses certain security risks.

CAREC countries should proceed carefully in liberalizing their services sector. As they liberalize their services trade, they should strengthen labor market institutions and vocational training to help the people who lose their jobs as a result acquire new skills and/or find new employment. Before liberalizing trade in transport, telecommunication, information, and financial services, CAREC countries need to set up robust systems for effectively managing the attendant security risks. They also should strengthen prudential regulation and supervision of financial institutions before, or in parallel with, the liberalization of trade in financial services.

Following a preannounced schedule in liberalizing services trade (e.g., in line with the country's GATS commitments in the case of CAREC countries that are WTO members) would make economic policies more transparent and predictable and help domestic firms, regulatory bodies, and labor market institutions better prepare for greater competition, higher risks, and possible layoffs. Postponing liberalization of services trade, on the other hand—to, for example, give domestic firms more time to become internationally competitive—is likely to perpetuate inefficiencies in the services sector and hinder its growth.

Deepening Regional Cooperation and Integration

CAREC countries can speed up the development of their services sector through stronger regional cooperation and integration.[39] They can foster growth of telecommunication and information services through cooperation in developing their digital infrastructure, pilot-testing new technologies, and managing cross border data flows. They can boost the development of education, research, and experimental development services by establishing joint universities, research centers, as well as exchange programs for students, teachers, and researchers.[40] CAREC countries can also work together to promote tourism and its many related services by introducing common tourist visas and developing regional tourism products.[41] They can spur growth of transport and storage services by harmonizing transport regulations and standards, modernizing border crossing infrastructure, and developing logistics centers and cold storage facilities in a coordinated manner.

---

[39]   See, for instance, ADB (2017, 2018, 2019c, 2019d, and 2019e), Kohli, Linn and Zacker (2019), and World Bank (2019b) for discussions of the opportunities for developing various service industries in CAREC countries within the frameworks of the CAREC Program or the PRC's Belt and Road Initiative.

[40]   See ADB (2019b) for a review of benefits and examples of regional cooperation in education. See WTO (2019b) for a discussion of the opportunities for regional collaboration in services trade and regulation within the WTO framework.

[41]   See ADB (2019a) for a review of examples of successful regional collaboration in tourism development and for a discussion of opportunities for cooperation between Kazakhstan and the Kyrgyz Republic in developing tourism along the Almaty–Bishkek Economic Corridor.

The CAREC Program

The CAREC program provides a strong platform that can bring about policy alignment and creation of mutual trust to improve regulations and facilitate liberalization of the services sector in the region. The *CAREC Integrated Trade Agenda 2030* includes capacity-building activities and mechanisms to bring together trade officials, regulators, and other stakeholders to discuss cooperation and reforms (Box 4.2).

Box 4.2: Expanding Trade in Services under the CAREC Trade Agenda

The prospects for CAREC economies to grow, develop, and prosper in services sector development depend not only on the policy choices of national governments, but also successes in regional cooperation. It is in this context that the *CAREC Integrated Trade Agenda 2030* aims to support reforms to enhance policy and regulatory environments and link CAREC countries with regional and global value chains. Supported by investments, policy dialogues, and knowledge products and services, the agenda includes a number of measures to:

- promote consistent and open foreign investment policies and measures to develop domestic financial markets;
- adopt policy reforms and measures to match the demand and supply of skills to support cross-border mobility;
- support business development and provide other support services;
- support regional collaboration on training and education services, mutual recognition of skills arrangements, and development of a regional labor market information system and skills upgrading;
- develop tourism and travel-related services, including facilitated visa regimes for business people (e.g., business cards and special arrangements for traders, driver mobility, and temporary movement of workers);
- conduct policy work to develop telecommunication, financial, transport, logistics, education, and other business services including an analysis of CAREC countries' services restrictiveness in relation to their commitments under the General Agreement on Trade in Services and other trade agreements;
- share good practices in promoting regulatory convergence and coherence; and
- build capacity and share knowledge on free trade agreements, including through inter-subregional sharing of experience with these agreements and issues beyond trade in goods such as trade in services, investment, competition policy, intellectual property, economic and technical cooperation.

CAREC = Central Asia Regional Economic Cooperation.

Sources: ADB. 2019a. *CAREC Integrated Trade Agenda 2030 and Rolling Strategic Action Plan 2018–2020*. Manila. https://www.adb.org/documents/carec-trade-agenda-2030-action-plan-2018-2020; ADB. 2019e. CAREC Integrated Agenda Issues Paper. Manila. https://www.adb.org/publications/carec-trade-agenda-2030-issue-papers.

Other Regional Cooperation Arrangements

CAREC countries are participating in several regional initiatives, some of which include cooperation in the services sector. Currently, CAREC countries are members and/or participants in numerous other regional organizations and economic cooperation initiatives within which they collaborate with one another and countries beyond the region (Table 4.5). Regional cooperation within the frameworks of these organizations, initiatives, and agreements has, at varying degrees, aimed to facilitate and foster growth of the CAREC region's services sector (Table 4.6). The extent through which these have effectively supported regional cooperation and integration remains to be seen.

Table 4.5: CAREC Countries—Membership/Participation in Selected Regional Organizations and Regional Cooperation Initiatives

Country	BRI	CIS	EAEU	ECO	EU AA	SCO	SPECA	TRACECA
Afghanistan	Yes	No	No	Yes	No	No[a]	Yes	No
Azerbaijan	Yes	Yes	No	Yes	No[b]	No[c]	Yes	Yes
China, People's Republic of	Yes	No	No	No	No	Yes	No	No
Georgia	Yes	No	No	No	Yes	No	No	Yes
Kazakhstan	Yes	Yes	Yes	Yes	No	Yes	Yes	Yes
Kyrgyz Republic	Yes	Yes	Yes	Yes	No	Yes	Yes	Yes
Mongolia	Yes	No	No	No	No	No	No	No
Pakistan	Yes	No	No	Yes	No	Yes	No	No
Tajikistan	Yes	Yes	No	Yes	No	Yes	Yes	Yes
Turkmenistan	Yes	Yes	No	Yes	No	No	Yes	No
Uzbekistan	Yes	Yes	No	Yes	No	Yes	Yes	Yes

BRI = Belt and Road Initiative, CAREC = Central Asia Regional Economic Cooperation, CIS = Commonwealth of Independents States, EAUE = Eurasian Economic Union, ECO = Economic Cooperation Organization, EU AA = European Union Association Agreement, SCO = Shanghai Cooperation Organization, SPECA = United Nations Special Programme for the Economies of Central Asia, TRACECA = Transport Corridor Europe–Caucasus–Asia program.

Note: Afghanistan's membership as listed does not reflect any change, if any, after 15 August 2021.

[a] Observer.
[b] Being negotiated.
[c] Dialogue partner.

Sources: Belt and Road Initiative, https://www.beltroad-initiative.com/; Commonwealth of Independent States, http://www.cisstat.com/eng/site-map.htm; Eurasian Economic Union, http://www.eaeunion.org/?lang=en; Economic Cooperation Organization, http://www.eco.int/; European Commission, https://ec.europa.eu/trade/policy/countries-and-regions/negotiations-and-agreements/; Shanghai Cooperation Organization, http://eng.sectsco.org/; United Nations Special Programme for the Economics of Central Asia, https://unece.org/speca; Transport Corridor Europe-Caucasus-Asia, http://www.traceca-org.org/en/home/.

Table 4.6: Service Industry Coverage of Selected Regional Organizations and Regional Cooperation Initiatives

Industry	BRI	CAREC	CIS	EAEU	ECO	EU AA[a]	SCO	SPECA	TRACECA
Tourism and related services and infrastructure	√	√	√	√	√	√	√		
Transport and storage services and related infrastructure	√	√	√	√	√	√	√	√	√
Information and communication services and digital infrastructure	√	√	√	√				√	
Financial services	√	√	√	√			√		
Education, research and development	√	√	√	√		√		√	√
Quality testing and certification services	√	√	√	√		√			
Other agriculture-related services	√	√	√	√		√			

BRI = Belt and Road Initiative, CAREC = Central Asia Regional Economic Cooperation, CIS = Commonwealth of Independents States, EAUE = Eurasian Economic Union, ECO = Economic Cooperation Organization, EU AA = European Union Association Agreement, SCO = Shanghai Cooperation Organization, SPECA = United Nations Special Programme for the Economies of Central Asia, TRACECA = Transport Corridor Europe-Central Asia program.

Note: Afghanistan's membership as listed does not reflect any change, if any, after 15 August 2021.

[a] Refers to the European Union's Association Agreement with Georgia.

Sources: Belt and Road Initiative, https://www.beltroad-initiative.com/; Commonwealth of Independent States, http://www.cisstat.com/eng/site-map.htm; Eurasian Economic Union, http://www.eaeunion.org/?lang=en; Economic Cooperation Organization, http://www.eco.int/; European Commission, https://ec.europa.eu/trade/policy/countries-and-regions/negotiations-and-agreements/; Shanghai Cooperation Organization, http://eng.sectsco.org/; United Nations Special Programme for the Economics of Central Asia, https://unece.org/speca; Transport Corridor Europe-Caucasus-Asia, http://www.traceca-org.org/en/home/.

Regional Trade Agreements

Several CAREC countries are pursuing reciprocal liberalization of trade in services in their regional trade agreements. Among those notified to the WTO where services are covered in the agreements are those signed by Georgia, Kazakhstan, the Kyrgyz Republic, Mongolia, Pakistan, and the PRC (Table 4.7). Most of these agreements are of recent vintage and tend to add to GATS commitments. CAREC is also in the early stages of exploring the feasibility of a regional free trade agreement. Trade in services has been identified among the priority sectors that could yield an early harvest. Preparations are underway to promote common understanding and improve capacities among trade officials.

When services commitments are included in these regional agreements, they are likely to contribute to closer economic relationships among the parties concerned. Parties to regional trade agreements tend, on average, to go well beyond their services commitments under the GATS (WTO 2019) (Box 4.3). In November 2020, the Regional Comprehensive Economic Partnership (RCEP) Agreement—which accounts for 29% of world GDP, 30% of global population and 25% of trade in goods and services—was signed by 15 countries including the PRC. Its comprehensive coverage

Table 4.7: Regional Trade Agreements Entered into by CAREC Countries with Services Commitments

Regional Trade Agreements Notified to the WTO	With at Least 2 CAREC Members	Entry into Force of Services Agreement
ASEAN – People's Republic of China		2007
People's Republic of China – New Zealand		2008
People's Republic of China – Singapore		2009
People's Republic of China – Pakistan	Yes	2009
Chile – People's Republic of China		2010
People's Republic of China – Peru		2010
People's Republic of China – Costa Rica		2011
Asia Pacific Trade Agreement	Yes	2013
European Union – Georgia		2014
People's Republic of China – Iceland		2014
People's Republic of China – Switzerland		2014
Australia – People's Republic of China		2015
Republic of Korea – People's Republic of China		2015
Eurasian Economic Union (Customs Union) – includes Kazakhstan and Kyrgyz Republic	Yes	2015
Japan – Mongolia		2016
European Free Trade Agreement – Georgia		2017
People's Republic of China – Georgia	Yes	2018
Hong Kong, China – Georgia		2019
Georgia – United Kingdom		2021
People's Republic of China – Mauritius		2021

CAREC = Central Asia Regional Economic Cooperation, WTO = World Trade Organization.
Note: Excludes those where implementation period has ended and where an early announcement has been made to the WTO.
Source: WTO. Regional Trade Agreements Database. http://rtais.wto.org/UI/PublicAllRTAList.aspx (accessed July 2021).

Box 4.3: GATS Commitments in Regional Trade Agreements

The World Trade Organization's database on regional trade agreements (RTAs) lists 303 such agreements, 153 of which cover services as well as goods. Many RTAs with services provisions have come into being since 2000. Based on the countries that have signed these RTAs, Roy, Marchetti, and Lim (2006) find that they potentially cover more than 80% of world services trade. The patterns and content of services obligations vary considerably between agreements. Analyses reveal that these RTAs both add to and subtract from General Agreement on Trade in Services (GATS) commitments (Miroudot, Sauvage and Sudreau 2010; Adlung and Miroudot 2012; Zhou and Whalley 2014). GATS-plus commitments are deeper and fuller than those found in GATS in terms of market access and/or sector coverage. GATS-minus commitments are the opposite, and GATS-neutral commitments replicate what is in the GATS.

Zhou and Whalley (2014) concluded that while GATS-plus and GATS-neutral RTA commitments have a significantly positive effect on trade flows between preferential partners, the negative effect on trade of GATS-minus commitments was not significant. The authors attributed this result mainly to the existence of two other characteristics of the RTAs concerned. The first is reliance on liberal rules of origin to determine eligibility for preferential treatment. The second is a "non-party most-favored-nation provision," which guarantees equally favorable treatment to non-parties to the agreement concerned.

Based on work by Miroudot, Sauvage and Sudreau (2010), in a sample of 56 RTAs and 155 service subsectors, Zhou and Whalley (2014) estimated that around 60% of the services subsectors covered contained GATS-plus commitments. These commitments were found predominantly in Mode 4 (movement of service providers), Mode 1 (cross-border transactions), and Mode 2 (consumption abroad); and to a lesser extent in Mode 3 (commercial presence). It is perhaps not surprising that Mode 4 is the best served means of delivery in RTAs; GATS commitments here are relatively sparse, and nearer neighbors are granted better access for their natural services suppliers. Mode 1 is relatively open in GATS but has attracted deeper RTA commitments. In the case of Mode 2, few restrictions apply under GATS—which is effectively an export activity for the committing country (e.g., tourism)—so there is little additional advantage left to give RTA partners. As for Mode 3, limited additional commitments under RTAs would seem to reflect general caution about opening markets to foreign investors. In terms of sector coverage, GATS-plus commitments were more prominent in health and social services, transport, recreational services, and other services. They were less common in communication and financial services.

Adlung and Miroudot (2012) analyzed GATS-minus provisions in 66 free trade agreements covering 80,000 commitments. They found GATS-minus commitments in most of the agreements examined, mainly in Modes 3 and 4, less so in Modes 1 and 2. Financial services, communication services, and business services were the subsectors most affected. The least affected were construction and engineering, education, tourism, distribution, environmental services, and recreational services. These patterns reflect the degrees of sensitivity prevalent in particular modes and subsectors.

Finally, the architecture of many RTAs differs from that of GATS schedules in several ways, and the differences can influence the degree of openness provided. Mention has already been made of rules of origin and the use of non-party most-favored-nation provisions. One of two other factors is the contrast between RTAs and the GATS in the use of positive and negative approaches to commitments. Each commitment is specified and expressed positively in the GATS schedules. By contrast, some RTAs use negative listing by specifying only exemptions from GATS obligations. While in a formal sense the two approaches should produce the same outcome, in practice negative listings are more transparent; what is not mentioned as an exception in a negative listing is subject by default to agreed disciplines. A second difference is the use of separate texts by several RTAs in detailing financial sector commitments. This tends to lay out a more extensive regime beyond the market access and national treatment provisions inscribed in their schedules of commitments. Due to these architectural differences, RTAs by and large offer more enhanced access than the GATS.

Sources: R. Adlung and S. Miroudot. 2012. Poison in the Wine? Tracing GATS-minus Commitments in Regional Trade Agreements. *WTO Staff Working Paper* ERSD2012-04. Geneva: WTO. https://www.wto.org/english/res_e/reser_e/ersd201204_e.pdf; Roy, M., J. Marchetti, and H. Lim. 2006. Services Liberalization in the New Generation of Preferential Trade Agreements (PTAs): How Much Further than the GATS? *Staff Working Paper* ERSD-2006-07. Geneva: World Trade Organization. https://www.wto.org/english/res_e/reser_e/ersd200607_e.pdf; Miroudot, S., J. Sauvage and M. Sudreau. 2010. Multilateralizing Regionalism: How Preferential Are Services Commitments in Regional Trade Agreements. *OECD Trade Policy Papers* No.106. https://developing-trade.com/wp-content/uploads/2014/11/DTC-Article-Chapter-2011-1.pdf; Zhou and Whalley. 2014. How Do the "GATS-Plus" and "GATS-Minus" Characteristics of Regional Service Agreements Affect Trade in Services? Cambridge, Massachusetts: National Bureau of Economic Research. *Working Paper* 20551 https://www.nber.org/papers/w20551.

extends beyond the signatories' previous trade agreements. RCEP promotes greater services trade by lifting the most restrictive and discriminatory barriers to activity. It contains modern and comprehensive provisions including rules on market access, national treatment, most favored-nation treatment, and local presence, and adopts a negative list approach, where member economies will be open to foreign service suppliers unless they appear on the list (Kang et al. 2020). The agreement has a chapter for the temporary movement of natural persons that will allow access to RCEP countries for business persons engaged in trade in goods, the supply of services, and the conduct of investment activities. The experience and coverage of other regional trade agreements' GATS-plus provisions and RCEP may provide useful lessons for CAREC countries to consider including similar chapters to expand and liberalize their trade in services.

Other Forms of Cooperation

With the rapid rise of e-commerce and digital trade amid the pandemic, regional agreements have emerged at the forefront of rulemaking to seize the opportunities they bring. Notably, the Australia-Singapore Digital Economic Partnership Agreement; Digital Economy Partnership Agreement between Chile, New Zealand, and Singapore; and the Comprehensive and Progressive Trans-Pacific Partnership, aim to reduce trade barriers in the digital economy, build comparative standards, and promote regulatory harmonization in domestic legal frameworks governing electronic transactions and cross-border business (ADB 2021e).

Digital services trade—while concentrated in few economies—has demonstrated resilience compared with non-digital services. CAREC countries can begin to study reforms in domestic services regulations as well as taxation and other cooperation arrangements (e.g., mutual recognition) to unlock the potential to expand digital services. For example, the PRC has established cross-border e-commerce pilot zones in 28 provinces and cities including Beijing, Hainan, and Shanghai—some of which have adopted the negative list approach to cross-border services trade—to promote the digital economy and opening-up of the services sector.[42] The PRC has also been organizing annual fairs for trade in services to share new business models and has proposed the establishment of the Global Alliance for Trade in Services.

Regional cooperation can help align policy and regulatory reforms and nurture closer links with global and regional value chains. Box 4.4 illustrates how greater regional cooperation, government policy, and the support of development partners can offer effective responses to challenges in supporting a particular industry grow, diversify an economy, and develop value chain within the region and beyond.

---

[42] State Council of the PRC. 2021. China Releases Negative List for Cross-border Services Trade in Hainan. http://english.www.gov.cn/statecouncil/ministries/202107/26/content_WS60fe1051c6d0df57f98dd933.html; State Council of the PRC. 2020. Pilot Project Approved to Innovate and Develop Services Trade. http://english.www.gov.cn/policies/latestreleases/202008/11/content_WS5f32852cc6d029c1c263792c.html.

Box 4.4: Regional Cooperation: Implications for the Kyrgyz Republic Garment Industry

The development of the Kyrgyz Republic's garment industry illustrates how a national specialization can be promoted to diversify an economy and fit smoothly into a broadly beneficial regional value chain (RVC). It also highlights challenges where greater regional cooperation, government policy, and development partners can support effective responses.

The country's apparel sector began under the former Soviet Union as a vertically integrated sheep breeding–fabric production–finished clothing industry. It has greatly changed and now contributes 15% of gross domestic product, employs about the same share of the nation's labor force, and is a sizeable export earner in an economy otherwise overly reliant on gold production and fluctuating remittance inflows. Small and medium-sized enterprises (SMEs), key drivers in all the CAREC economies, dominate the industry and operate mainly on low-value-added cut-make-trim sewing contracts for women's wear, as well as in some cases for garment parts (e.g., pockets and sleeves) and final stitching of ready-made clothing. Only some larger SMEs have graduated to the higher-value design, shipping, distribution, and retail opportunities the industry and international export markets can offer.

Much of the industry's trade with its biggest export markets—Kazakhstan and the Russian Federation—is done through ethnic Kyrgyz business owners in the two countries, but regional and international cooperation and trade agreements have also greatly helped. After the textile industry collapsed following independence in 1991, the opening by the Kyrgyz Republic and the People's Republic of China (PRC) of their common border brought the flow of fabrics and technical equipment from the PRC needed to build a new garment sector to replace it. Low or zero tariffs and harmonized regulatory regimes due to the 1998 accession to the World Trade Organization have spurred exports, and these have been protected in the industry's two principal foreign markets at the RVC's demand end since the Kyrgyz Republic joined the Eurasian Economic Union in 2015. The PRC has in the meantime remained the main source of material and sewing machine inputs.

An easing of taxes and taxation requirements on SMEs has helped small garment producers grow. So have the trade-friendly policies and plans for industry expansion under the National Export Strategy launched in 2013. The government has collaborated on stepped-up worker training and brand development with two national sector business associations. One advocates on the garment sector's behalf; the other has attracted foreign buyers to annual fashion trade shows since 2006 and expands sales abroad through offices in the two major export markets.

The vital next steps—for instance, adopting more modern technology to upgrade from the prevalent low-value-added cut-make-trim model, and accessing broader and higher-value export markets—will require more of the skills training, capacity building, and trade promotion that has already been well supported by the government and international development partners such as the Asian Development Bank. This support and these services—and wherever possible, greater collaborative action by CAREC members—are also essential to fulfill other needs that are common to the efforts across the region to diversify national economies by building specialized industries and RVCs. Greater SME access to finance is critical. So are stronger business associations, a better understanding between countries of how to develop and deepen complementary and mutually beneficial RVCs, and further simplification and harmonization of regulations and cross-border procedures to form and further develop CAREC value chains.

Source: CAREC Institute. 2019. Regional Value Chains in CAREC: The Case of Kyrgyzstan Garment Industry. Working Paper. Urumqi:CAREC Institute.

Raising the Efficiency and Quality of the Labor Market

The efficiency of the CAREC country labor markets is constrained by a few factors. International labor mobility is often low, and/or it is not easy in some countries to hire foreign workers (Table 4.8). As a result, firms have difficulty finding workers with the right skills. Labor tax rates, including employers' social security contributions, are high in most CAREC countries, as are redundancy costs. This raises labor costs significantly and discourages firms from employing workers formally. These constraints hinder development across CAREC economies but are particularly harmful to the growth of labor-intensive industries, including many in the services sector.[43]

Table 4.8: CAREC Countries—Ranking in Global Competitiveness Index 2019 Components Relating to Labor Market

Country	Internal Labor Mobility	Ease of Hiring Foreign labor	Labor Tax Rate	Redundancy Costs	Hiring and Firing Practices
Azerbaijan	58	3	107	57	4
China, People's Republic of	73	39	139	116	26
Georgia	123	9	1	17	25
Kazakhstan	61	41	36	17	41
Kyrgyz Republic	65	92	88	78	94
Mongolia	95	126	43	17	79
Pakistan	66	78	64	64	39
Tajikistan	119	102	119	47	37

CAREC = Central Asia Regional Economic Cooperation.
Notes: The Global Competitiveness Index 2019 covers 141 countries. It does not cover Afghanistan, Turkmenistan and Uzbekistan.
Source: Schwab. 2019. The Global Competitiveness Report 2019. Geneva.

Labor market efficiency must be raised to stimulate the development of the services sector in the CAREC region. CAREC countries need to increase internal labor mobility and/or lower their labor tax rates and redundancy costs. The focus of their labor market policies needs to shift from protecting jobs to protecting workers and creating a flexible labor market that works in combination with a reliable, predictable social security system.[44] The capacity of labor market institutions to identify emerging skills shortages and inform planning for tertiary education and vocational training—including from mutual recognition to a qualifications reference framework— also needs strengthening.

---

[43] The inefficiencies of the labor markets partly explain the high incidence of informal employment and outward labor migration in many CAREC countries.

[44] Such a combination, which has roots in Denmark and other European countries, is referred to as "flexicurity" (Campbell and Ronnas 2019; Humlum and Munch 2017).

Developing Physical and Digital Infrastructure

Services sector development—including the growth of the services industries important to economic diversification in the CAREC countries—requires good physical and digital infrastructure (Ghani 2010; Linn 2015; Sahoo and Dash 2016). A reliable and cost-effective electricity supply is essential to developing most service industries. Freight transportation and storage services require well-maintained roads, railways, and airports as well as adequate facilities and logistics centers. Tourism services demand good passenger transport infrastructure (including train and bus stations), hotels, convenience facilities, and entertainment centers. Telecommunication and information services must be served by up-to-date networks and secure internet servers.

Infrastructure deficiencies affect CAREC's competitiveness. All eight CAREC countries covered by the Global Competitiveness Index 2019 ranked low on at least some infrastructure-related components of the index. Only Georgia escaped a low ranking in tourist service infrastructure in the Travel and Tourism Competitiveness Index 2019 (Table 4.9). These international rankings underscore some weaknesses in the operation and maintenance of physical infrastructure in the CAREC countries.

Table 4.9: CAREC Countries—Ranking in Selected Global Competitiveness Index 2019 and Travel and Tourism Competitiveness Index 2019 Components Relating to Infrastructure

Country	Road Connectivity	Quality of Road Infrastructure	Railroad Density	Airport Connectivity	Electricity Supply Quality	Tourist Service Infrastructure
Azerbaijan	88	27	34	79	59	96
China, People's Republic of	10	45	61	2	18	86
Georgia	65	81	44	81	36	41
Kazakhstan	56	93	66	72	19	90
Kyrgyz Republic	110	113	86	104	115	128
Mongolia	112	112	96	97	73	105
Pakistan	52	67	54	41	99	112
Tajikistan	137	50	72	121	107	131

CAREC = Central Asia Regional Economic Cooperation.

Note: Data is out of 141 countries covered in the Global Competitiveness Index 2019 except for tourist services infrastructure which is out of 140 countries covered in the Travel and Tourism Competitiveness Index 2019.

Source: World Economic Forum. 2019a. *The Global Competitiveness Report 2019*. Geneva; World Economic Forum. 2019b. *The Travel and Tourism Competitiveness Report 2019: Travel and Tourism at a Tipping Point*. Geneva.

Improvements to physical and digital infrastructure are critical across the board if the CAREC countries are to facilitate greater development in their services sector. It is also critical to enhance connectivity and sustainability of transportation networks along the CAREC corridors. This is being addressed under the *CAREC Transport Strategy 2030*, which includes the strategic pillar of cross-border transport and logistics facilitation and identifies priority investments for better connectivity (ADB 2020).

In terms of digital infrastructure, while technical capacity for accessing the internet is high in most CAREC countries, barriers—such as affordability and low levels of digital literacy—create a gap between access and actual use. The basic data infrastructure is also underdeveloped in most CAREC countries. It is encouraging to note that all CAREC countries have digital strategies that aim to provide universal access to digital technologies. Recommendations for internet infrastructure in CAREC countries include expanding last-mile coverage, launching 5G networks as appropriate, enhancing digital literacy, developing business-oriented infrastructure, and establishing backbone networks, internet exchange points, data centers and cloud computing (Minges 2021).

Chapter 5

CONCLUSION, RECOMMENDATIONS, AND POSSIBLE PROJECTS

Conclusion

The services sector is a key driver of economic development and crucial for diversification in CAREC countries. The services sector expanded rapidly and made a significant contribution to economic growth in all CAREC countries over the last 2 decades. CAREC countries could further intensify development in the services sector by fostering growth of the services subsectors or industries critical to economic diversification and sustainable development. The COVID-19 pandemic heightened the need for diversification and resilience and at the same time, demonstrated the potential for certain service subsectors and/or industries to flourish amid the changing trade landscape.

Several services subsectors are particularly important to achieving diversification in the CAREC country economies. They are telecommunication and information services (including software development and data processing); financial services (including insurance and other nonbank services); education and research and development services (including agricultural extension services, vocational training, scientific research and development, and market research); tourism-related services (including passenger transport, travel agency, and accommodation services); freight transport and storage services (including logistics services and cold storage services for horticulture products); quality (including food quality) testing and certification services; and other agriculture-related services. Efforts should be focused on these crucial services subsectors, away from primary production, and toward manufacturing and high value-added economic activities.

CAREC countries need to create an enabling environment for robust growth in the services sector in the region. This includes a coherent and comprehensive approach that pursues a balanced development of the services sector in view of the interdependence that exists between many service industries. The sluggish growth of some services subsectors stifles growth of other service industries. Critical elements for an enabling environment are improving governance, enhancing market competition, deepening regional cooperation and integration, raising the efficiency and quality of the labor market, and developing physical and digital infrastructure.

Regional cooperation and integration between CAREC countries can facilitate and accelerate the development of the services sector and regional value chains. The *CAREC Integrated Trade Agenda 2030* and other cluster or sector strategies under the broad CAREC 2030 Strategy is a strong platform for promoting policy and regulatory coherence, reducing trade barriers through reciprocal liberalization of trade in services, and building and expanding cross-border digital services trade.

Policy Recommendations

Governments need to adopt a **coherent and comprehensive approach** to promote the development of the services sector in CAREC countries. To achieve this they should:

- **Institute independent midterm and final evaluations of government strategies, programs, and road maps, including those aimed at developing service industries.** This will help increase the effectiveness of government efforts through a whole-of-government approach in developing the services sector.

- **Improve the legal, regulatory, and institutional framework for the services sector.** The CAREC countries should undertake a diagnostic assessment of the legal, regulatory, and institutional framework for each service industry critical to economic diversification and development whenever such an assessment has not been recently carried out. Countries may take measures to reduce regulatory burdens (e.g., through the so-called regulatory guillotine) and facilitate innovation (e.g., through the establishment of regulatory sandboxes and innovation hubs).

- **Set up a systematic process for conducting regulatory impact assessments of proposed new laws and regulations, including those affecting the services sector.** This will help the CAREC countries establish and maintain a favorable legal and regulatory framework for the services sector that is likely to deliver the greatest net benefit.

- **Strengthen the protection of property rights.** Given the importance of the protection of intellectual property rights for the robust development of the services sector, CAREC countries should undertake a diagnostic assessment, and prepare and implement a road map for strengthening the protection of such rights.

- **Do more to involve the private sector.** CAREC members should take steps to enable the private sector to play a greater role in the development of producer services. The emphasis should be on creating a level playing field on which state-owned enterprises and private entities can compete.

- **Liberalize trade in services, while minimizing side-effects.** CAREC countries should liberalize trade in services, lowering trade costs and barriers to FDI, while taking measures to minimize the attendant costs and risks.

- **Review commitments under the GATS.** CAREC countries should review their GATS obligations to ensure that their commitments are not currently weaker than their actual policies. They should also consider whether making additional GATS commitments might be desirable as a lock-in mechanism for policy reforms.

- **Deepen and expand regional cooperation and integration in the areas related to services.** Knowledge sharing including cooperation to strengthen trade in services statistics, policy alignment, and coordinated infrastructure development can be very useful in developing the services sector. The pursuit of liberalization of trade in services is likely to generate significant net benefits for all countries involved, especially when it is a part of deep regional economic integration.

- **Make labor markets more efficient.** The efficiency of labor markets in the CAREC region should be raised by increasing internal labor mobility, reducing labor tax rates and redundancy costs, strengthening labor market institutions, and shifting the focus of labor policies from protecting jobs to protecting workers.

- **Build and upgrade critical infrastructure.** CAREC countries need to address the deficiencies of physical and digital infrastructure that impede the development of the services sector.

Table 5.1 is a list of projects that could foster the development of the services sector in CAREC countries and that the development partners could further support through lending projects and technical assistance. [45]

---

[45]   ADB placed on hold its assistance in Afghanistan effective 15 August 2021.

Table 5.1: Possible Projects for CAREC Countries

Services Industry or Thematic Area	Project Scope or Component	Project Type	Countries	Priority
Telecommunication and information services	Update, implement, and roll-out of actions on comprehensive national digital development strategy	National TA projects	Kazakhstan, the Kyrgyz Republic, Mongolia, Tajikistan, and possibly some other CAREC countries	Near- to medium-term
	Formulate a roadmap for the development of information services such as software development, data processing, and "mining" for blockchain technology	National TA projects	Kazakhstan, the Kyrgyz Republic, Tajikistan, Uzbekistan, and possibly some other CAREC countries	Near- to medium-term
	Formulate a comprehensive regional digital development strategy for CAREC countries	Regional TA project	All CAREC countries	Medium-term
	Develop CAREC digital highways and domestic fiber-optic networks with the aim of increasing the supply of bandwidth, improving the quality of internet connections, and reducing the cost of Internet access	Regional and/or national public investment projects	All CAREC countries	Medium- to long-term
Financial services	Establish a public credit registry or a private credit bureau, or expand the coverage of existing public registry or private credit bureau	Regional or national TA projects	All CAREC countries except Georgia and the PRC	Near-term
	Establish regulatory sandboxes for development of innovative financial products	Regional TA project	Georgia, the Kyrgyz Republic, Uzbekistan, and possibly some other CAREC countries	Near- to medium-term
	Establish digital banks or neobanks and online and mobile banking services	National TA and/or private sector projects	CAREC-10 countries	Medium- to long-term
	Develop insurance services, including credit insurance services for SMEs and farms	National public investment and/or private sector projects	All CAREC countries	Medium- to long-term
	Develop securities markets	National TA projects, policy-based operations and/or private sector projects	Kazakhstan, Pakistan, the PRC, and possibly some other CAREC countries	Medium- to long-term
	Establish venture capital funds	Regional or national private sector projects	All CAREC countries	Medium- to long-term
	Formulate and/or implement financial literacy strategies (among SMEs, farms, and households) to stimulate growth of financial services from the demand side	National TA projects and/or policy-based operations	All CAREC countries	Medium- to long-term

continued on next page

Table 5.1 *continued*

Services Industry or Thematic Area	Project Scope or Component	Project Type	Countries	Priority
Education, research, and experimental development services	Improve the quality of primary and secondary education (including through greater private sector involvement, use of modern technologies and teaching methods, introduction of results-oriented management and financing, and participation in international assessments)	National public investment projects, possibly leading to PPP	CAREC-10 countries	Near- to medium-term
	Modernize higher education and vocational training (in particular through greater involvement of the private sector, use of modern technologies and teaching methods, introduction of results-oriented management and financing, and participation in international university rankings) to improve the quality of higher education and vocational training, address the mismatch between the demand for and supply of skills, foster lifelong learning, and promote quality research at institutions of higher education	National public investment projects, possibly leading to PPPs	All CAREC countries	Near- to medium-term
	Introduce and/or expand vocational training in business internationalization for SMEs	National TA and/or public investment projects	All CAREC countries	Medium- to long-term
	Develop vocational training programs based on the German apprenticeship model	National TA and/or public investment projects	Uzbekistan, and some other CAREC countries	Medium- to long-term
	Establish/strengthen a lifelong education system	National TA and/or public investment projects	All CAREC countries	Medium- to long-term
	Introduce a transparent system for stimulating (e.g., through grants and tax credits) private sector investment in training, research, and development	National TA projects and/or policy-based operations	CAREC-10 countries	Medium- to long-term
	Establish research, development, and production clusters/networks (comprising universities, research institutions, and producers) in key sectors (e.g., agriculture and food, petrochemical, and pharmaceutical industries)	National public investment and/or private sector projects	CAREC-10 countries	Medium- to long-term

continued on next page

Table 5.1 *continued*

Services Industry or Thematic Area	Project Scope or Component	Project Type	Countries	Priority
	Establish innovation facilitators (such as innovation hubs, incubators, and accelerators) to support the development and adoption of new information and communication technologies	National public investment and/or private sector projects	All CAREC countries	Medium- to long-term
	Strengthen agricultural research and development (particularly through greater involvement of the private sector)	National public investment projects, possibly leading to PPPs	CAREC-10 countries	Medium- to long-term
Tourism-related services	Develop and market regional tourism products	Regional TA project	All CAREC countries	Near to medium-term
	Develop medical screening and testing services for people entering the country	National TA and/or public investment projects	CAREC-10 countries	Near- to medium-term
	Develop emergency assistance and health care services for tourists	National TA and/or public investment projects	CAREC-10 countries	Near- to medium-term
	Modernize border crossing infrastructure and procedures for people	Regional TA and public investment projects	The Kyrgyz Republic, Tajikistan, Turkmenistan, Uzbekistan, and possibly some other CAREC countries	Near- to medium-term
	Construct new airports and/or passenger terminals	National public investment projects, possibly leading to PPPs	Mongolia, Turkmenistan, Uzbekistan, and possibly some other CAREC countries	Medium- to long-term
	Construct and rehabilitate secondary and tertiary roads connecting tourist sites with primary roads	National public investment projects	Azerbaijan, Georgia, Kazakhstan, the Kyrgyz Republic, Mongolia, Pakistan, Tajikistan, Turkmenistan, and Uzbekistan	Medium- to long-term
	Develop roadside services	Private sector projects and/or public investment projects leading to PPPs	Azerbaijan, Georgia, Kazakhstan, the Kyrgyz Republic, Mongolia, Pakistan, Tajikistan, Turkmenistan, and Uzbekistan	Medium- to long-term
	Improve road transport connectivity among major tourism sites	Regional public investment projects	All CAREC countries	Medium- to long-term
	Develop tourist service infrastructure (including hotels, resorts, and entertainment facilities) and tourism clusters (including cross-border clusters)	Regional or national private sector projects	Azerbaijan, Georgia, Kazakhstan, the Kyrgyz Republic, Mongolia, Pakistan, Tajikistan, Turkmenistan, and Uzbekistan	Medium- to long-term

continued on next page

Table 5.1 continued

Services Industry or Thematic Area	Project Scope or Component	Project Type	Countries	Priority
	Develop tourism-related education and training, with programs based on common—across countries—curricular and qualification standards	Regional TA and possibly public investment projects	All CAREC countries	Medium- to long-term
Freight transport and storage services	Implement legal, regulatory, and institutional reforms in the transport sector (including railway and air transport) with the aim of improving the availability, affordability and quality of transport and storage services	National TA projects and/or policy-based operations	All CAREC countries	Near- to medium-term
	Modernize border crossing infrastructure and procedures for trucks and trains	Regional TA and public investment projects	The Kyrgyz Republic, Tajikistan, Turkmenistan, Uzbekistan, and, other interested CAREC countries	Near- to medium-term
	Introduce the electronic TIR system	Regional TA and/or public investment project	All CAREC countries	Medium- to long-term
	Introduce the CAREC Advanced Transit System and the Information Common Exchange	Regional TA and/or public investment projects	Azerbaijan, Georgia, and Kazakhstan as pilot countries Other interested CAREC countries	Medium- to long-term
	Introduce intelligent transport systems (including automated weigh-in-motion stations) in road traffic management to improve operation and maintenance of roads and enhance road safety	Regional or national public investment projects, possibly leading to PPPs	All CAREC countries	Medium- to long-term
	Modernize and extend railway infrastructure (in particular through introduction of modern information and communication technologies, such as radio frequency identification technology)	Regional or national public investment projects, possibly leading to PPPs	All CAREC countries	Medium- to long-term
	Implement electronic cargo processing systems in air transport	Regional or national public investment projects, possibly leading to PPPs	All CAREC countries	Medium- to long-term
	Establish a network of logistic centers, including multimodal logistic centers and agro-logistics centers with primary processing (e.g., sorting, calibration, and packaging) capacity, and cold storage facilities	Regional or national public investment projects, possibly leading to PPPs	All CAREC countries	Medium- to long-term

continued on next page

Table 5.1 *continued*

Services Industry or Thematic Area	Project Scope or Component	Project Type	Countries	Priority
Quality testing and certification services	Implement legal, regulatory, and institutional reforms to eliminate conflicts of interest and enhance competition in the market for quality testing and certification services	National TA projects and/or policy-based operations	Kazakhstan, Tajikistan, Turkmenistan, and Uzbekistan	Near- to medium-term
	Establish or strengthen training programs in food quality and safety, improve the availability of experts, and increase demand for food quality and safety services	Regional TA project	All CAREC countries	Near to medium-term
	Develop a regional network of internationally accredited quality (including food quality) testing laboratories	Regional or national public investment projects, possibly leading to PPPs	All CAREC countries	Medium- to long-term
Other agriculture-related services	Develop a regional network of internationally accredited veterinary and phytosanitary laboratories	Regional or national public investment projects	All CAREC countries	Medium- to long-term
Governance	Carry out a diagnostic assessment of protection of IPRs with subsequent formulation and implementation of a roadmap for strengthening IPR protection	National TA projects and/or policy-based operations	All CAREC countries	Near- to medium-term
	Establish a systematic process for conducting RIAs of proposed new laws and regulations, including those affecting the services sector	National TA projects and/or policy-based operations	All CAREC countries	Near- to medium-term
Labor market efficiency	Modernize labor market policies, regulations, and institutions to enhance the efficiency of the labor market and shift the focus of labor policies from protecting jobs to protecting workers	National TA projects and/or policy-based operations	All CAREC countries	Near- to medium-term

CAREC = Central Asia Regional Economic Cooperation, CAREC-10 = all CAREC countries except the People's Republic of China, IPR = intellectual property rights, PPP = public–private partnership, RIA = regulatory impact assessment, SMEs = small and medium-sized enterprises, TA = technical assistance, TIR = Transports Internationaux Routiers.

Source: Authors' proposals based on analysis of CAREC countries' development priorities and various CAREC studies and documents.

Appendix 1

CAREC COUNTRIES' EXPORTS AND IMPORTS OF SERVICES BY VALUE

Table A1.1: Afghanistan—Exports and Imports of Services, 2005–2019
($ million)

Afghanistan	2005		2008		2012		2015		2019		Growth 2005–2019 (%)	
	Export	Import	Export	Import	Export	Import	Export	Import	Export	Import	Export	Import
Total Services	88.9	551.0	1,290.6	747.9	1,853.3	1,767.5	839.4	1,171.3	696.8	1,261.4	14.7	5.9
Manufacturing services on physical inputs owned by others	0.0	0.0	0.0	0.0	0.0	0.0	0.0	0.0	0.0	0.0		
Maintenance and repair	0.0	0.0	1.3	1.3	0.0	5.1	0.0	3.6	0.0	21.9		28.1[a]
Transport	6.3	285.5	148.0	516.1	256.8	1,103.9	94.5	849.5	93.7	909.7	19.3	8.3
Travel	1.6	53.2	16.7	35.8	101.7	105.0	79.4	147.2	190.3	190.3	34.1	9.1
Construction	47.3	33.9	578.6	22.5	778.1	47.6	291.0	17.3	91.0	0.4	4.7	–31.7
Insurance and pension	0.0	11.9	0.0	8.4	58.6	16.9	6.2	10.4	0.1	16.6		2.4
Financial services	7.6	0.1	105.9	2.4	95.3	16.4	54.3	3.9	3.9	1.3	–4.8	18.3
Charges for the use of intellectual property	0.1	0.0	0.6	0.3	0.0	10.7	0.0	0.2	0.0	4.1		–21.6[b]
Telecommunication, computer, and information services	4.2	74.1	109.4	51.3	124.7	184.8	82.2	52.4	51.9	25.5	18.0	–7.6
Other business	19.3	55.3	299.9	45.9	390.0	222.7	142.9	35.9	163.9	40.9	15.3	–2.2
Personal, cultural, and recreational	0.3	0.0	3.9	0.1	1.7	9.6	28.9	7.3	5.0	0.0	20.1	0.0
Government goods and services	2.4	37.1	26.2	63.8	46.4	44.8	60	43.6	96.8	50.7	26.4	2.2

[a] 2008 to 2019.
[b] 2010 to 2019.

Source: World Trade Organization. WTO Data. https://data.wto.org/ (accessed March 2021).

Table A1.2: Azerbaijan—Exports and Imports of Services, 2005–2019
($ million)

Azerbaijan	2005 Export	2005 Import	2008 Export	2008 Import	2012 Export	2012 Import	2015 Export	2015 Import	2019 Export	2019 Import	Growth 2005–2019 (%) Export	Growth 2005–2019 (%) Import
Total Services	741.5	2,658.8	1,668.6	3,916.3	4,808.7	7,429.6	4,444.0	8,672.9	3,761.5	6,377.1	11.6	6.2
Manufacturing services on physical inputs owned by others	49.3	0.9	97.4	0.0	267.9	0.0	0.9	0.0	0.5	1.4	-32.8	3.2
Maintenance and repair	9.2	5.0	23.3	25.1	260.0	225.0	69.3	75.8	13.6	62.9	2.8	18.1
Transport	239.2	378.9	793.9	682.5	741.0	969.5	1,518.3	1,009.6	1,108.0	1,458.4	11.0	9.6
Travel	77.7	164.0	191.2	342.8	2,433.3	2,476.9	2,309.5	2,603.1	1,791.5	1,702.5	22.4	16.7
Construction	9.4	1,498.8	109.1	1,440.8	245.0	485.2	23.0	3,519.7	31.6	1,034.2	8.7	-2.7
Insurance and pension	7.8	40.6	4.9	52.8	10.4	163.4	17.5	142.3	26.6	159.3	8.8	9.8
Financial services	0.1	10.4	0.1	12.5	2.4	11.2	2.7	16.4	7.3	46.7	30.6	10.7
Charges for the use of intellectual property	0.0	0.0	0.0	4.8	0.0	28.2	0.0	0.0	0.0	0.0		
Telecommunication, computer, and information services	35.7	12.5	55.4	39.5	95.4	127.7	86.8	138.6	58.4	97.9	3.5	14.7
Other business	251.7	514.9	296.5	1,245.5	625.6	2,843.1	3,87.8	1,027.7	666.5	1,723.5	7.0	8.6
Personal, cultural, and recreational	3.0	5.0	3.9	6.6	0.0	0.0	7.2	20.1	22.5	16.0	14.4	8.3
Government goods and services	58.3	27.9	92.9	63.4	127.7	99.5	20.9	119.4	34.9	74.2	-3.7	7.0

Source: World Trade Organization. WTO Data. https://data.wto.org/ (accessed March 2021).

Table A1.3: Georgia—Exports and Imports of Services, 2005–2019
($ million)

Georgia	2005		2008		2012		2015		2019		Growth 2005–2019 (%)	
	Export	Import	Export	Import	Export	Import	Export	Import	Export	Import	Export	Import
Total Services	737.9	635.8	1,270.9	1,246.2	2,562.0	1,453.8	3,087.1	1,683.0	4,600.5	2,431.7	13.1	9.6
Manufacturing services on physical inputs owned by others	14.9	0.2	9.5	1.2	14.8	0.3	18.8	0.4	14.1	1.1	-0.4	12.2
Maintenance and repair	7.9	4.1	0.9	5.6	3.5	4.3	2.6	7.2	0.1	5.9	-31.2	2.6
Transport	333.0	288.5	615.3	642.4	852.9	804.7	952.1	956.9	1,006.7	1,276.4	7.9	10.6
Travel	241.4	168.8	446.6	203.5	1,410.9	256.4	1,868.5	329.6	3,268.7	657.1	18.6	9.7
Construction	0.0	16.0	2.2	17.8	7.6	6.1	9.2	10.2	5.1	7.1	4.3	-5.8
Insurance and pension	11.0	58.9	15.1	150.7	18.3	136.8	18.2	127.0	12.0	117.3	0.6	4.9
Financial services	20.3	2.2	9.7	17.4	19.8	21.1	11.0	11.7	23.5	23.4	1.0	16.9
Charges for the use of intellectual property	9.3	5.3	6.2	8.4	3.5	7.6	0.6	7.0	0.9	40.7	-16.7	14.6
Telecommunication, computer, and information services	18.6	17.9	25.5	23.3	49.7	32.1	45.0	39.9	113.8	85.1	12.9	11.1
Other business	10.8	26.1	27.1	74.2	68.4	93.1	58.5	109.9	49.9	131.8	10.9	11.6
Personal, cultural, and recreational	3.2	0.0	8.9	17.9	15.9	12.6	14.0	11.3	14.9	14.3	11.0	5.8[a]
Government goods and services	67.4	47.5	103.8	83.8	96.8	78.8	88.7	71.8	90.8	71.5	2.1	2.9

a from 2007.

Source: World Trade Organization. WTO Data. https://data.wto.org/ (accessed March 2021).

Table A1.4: Kazakhstan—Exports and Imports of Services, 2005–2019
($ million)

Kazakhstan	2005 Export	2005 Import	2008 Export	2008 Import	2012 Export	2012 Import	2015 Export	2015 Import	2019 Export	2019 Import	Growth 2005–2019 (%) Export	Growth 2005–2019 (%) Import
Total Services	2,087.3	7,521.3	4,292.4	11,218.9	5,430.9	14,344.5	6,177.4	10,897.7	7,773.6	11,428.5	9.4	3.0
Manufacturing services on physical inputs owned by others	0.0	14.0	0.0	0.0	0.0	0.0	14.3	56.5	70.1	185.4		18.5
Maintenance and repair	1.4	25.6	6.6	99.8	7.4	40.9	50.4	248.6	117.2	387.5	31.6	19.4
Transport	1,024.4	1,171.2	2,245.6	2,373.6	2,585.5	2,733.7	3,516.9	1,840.9	3,964.6	2,464.6	9.7	5.3
Travel	700.9	753	1,011.6	1,077.8	1,929.3	3272	1,632	2,867.3	2,463.3	2,763.1	9.0	9.3
Construction	2.0	1,941.4	18.2	3,187.7	19.0	2,755.4	36.0	571.9	51.0	194.7	23.1	−16.4
Insurance and pension	3.8	173.4	83.2	263.3	95.8	217.4	79.3	48.8	97.4	39.6	23.2	−10.5
Financial services	18.3	47.5	112.5	323.5	44.8	244.5	24.3	138.2	83.1	201.1	10.8	10.3
Charges for the use of intellectual property	0.0	30.9	0.0	86.7	0.0	152.4	0.9	149.1	2.8	141.3		10.9
Telecommunication, computer, and information services	71.1	121.6	102.4	205.3	124.4	240.2	142.8	341.7	129.9	401.4	4.3	8.5
Other business	178.6	3,105.8	407.1	3,371.7	400.8	4,513.2	411.3	4,368.4	512.3	4,471.4	7.5	2.6
Personal, cultural, and recreational	0.2	16.5	0.8	25.1	1.3	60.6	1.2	68.1	3.6	47.3	20.6	7.5
Government goods and services	86.6	120.4	304.5	204.6	222.6	114.3	268	198.3	278.4	131.0	8.3	0.6

Source: World Trade Organization. WTO Data. https://data.wto.org/ (accessed March 2021).

Table A1.5: Kyrgyz Republic—Exports and Imports of Services, 2005–2019
($ million)

Kyrgyz Republic	2005 Export	2005 Import	2008 Export	2008 Import	2012 Export	2012 Import	2015 Export	2015 Import	2019 Export	2019 Import	Growth 2005–2019 (%) Export	Growth 2005–2019 (%) Import
Total Services	259.4	290.3	806.5	909.8	987.4	1,323.1	853.6	1,055.7	1,162.7	974.7	10.7	8.7
Manufacturing services on physical inputs owned by others	0.0	0.0	0.0	0.0	0.0	0.0	0.0	11.8	0.0	0.0	0.0	
Maintenance and repair	0.0	0.0	0.0	0.0	0.0	0.0	0.4	2.8	0.0	0.0		
Transport	60.6	126.0	146.5	483.3	181.3	643.2	188.9	446.6	251.5	440.9	10.2	8.9
Travel	73.0	58.4	514.5	304.4	434.4	349.9	425.6	399.2	666.6	365.8	15.8	13.1
Construction	19.0	2.1	20.8	10.5	33.4	8.9	65.9	28.7	23.2	10.0	1.4	11.1
Insurance and pension	0.2	14.9	8.3	10.8	0.9	16.9	0.2	8.4	0.7	5.8	8.9	-6.7
Financial services	3.8	4.4	13.5	9.1	3.5	8.0	14.7	19.4	7.5	15.4	4.9	8.9
Charges for the use of intellectual property	1.7	6.0	0.0	0.0	2.7	7.8	1.4	6.0	1.0	4.4	-3.8	-2.2
Telecommunication, computer, and information services	7.6	7.7	17.7	27.2	13.1	19.2	42.4	25.2	11.6	21.9	3.0	7.5
Other business	61.0	45.5	4.1	20.9	182.4	204.5	81.3	43.8	104.0	42.6	3.8	-0.5
Personal, cultural, and recreational	6.7	21.0	69.4	38.1	120.1	55.9	25.2	52.3	94.2	53.1	18.9	6.6
Government goods and services	25.9	4.2	11.6	5.5	15.5	8.8	7.6	11.6	2.4	14.9	-17.0	9.0

Source: World Trade Organization. WTO Data. https://data.wto.org/ (accessed March 2021).

Table A1.6: Mongolia—Exports and Imports of Services, 2005–2019
($ million)

Mongolia	2005		2008		2012		2015		2019		Growth 2005–2019 (%)	
	Export	Import	Export	Import	Export	Import	Export	Import	Export	Import	Export	Import
Total Services	414.4	400.8	519.4	628.6	651.5	2077.5	688.8	1,404.3	1,368.3	2,972.2	8.5	14.3
Manufacturing services on physical inputs owned by others	0.0	0.0	19.9	0.0	3.0	0.0	6.4	0.0	3.3	7.0		
Maintenance and repair	0.0	0.0	0.0	18.3	0.0	3.8	0.0	2.7	0.0	0.0		
Transport	199.2	147.9	165.4	258.9	204.8	516.8	238.6	344.6	477.9	976.7	6.3	13.5
Travel	176.8	125.7	246.9	217.3	177.5	485.1	245.6	421.7	513.6	909.0	7.6	14.1
Construction	0.8	3.5	4.8	3.0	30.3	490.6	33.6	114.3	64.2	122.5	31.3	25.4
Insurance and pension	2.3	8.4	3.6	15.3	0.0	25.1	0.0	23.9	0	20.4		6.3
Financial services	5.0	7.9	0.6	1.4	19.3	52.4	7.0	58.9	4.1	114.2	-1.4	19.1
Charges for the use of intellectual property	0.0	0.0	12.5	1.3	1.5	12.0	2.4	15.6	2.4	26.4		29.6[a]
Telecommunication, computer, and information services	15.2	25.6	19.3	29.8	21.8	60.9	12.1	83.6	39.8	105.4	6.9	10.1
Other business	9.7	43.3	43.3	70.6	188.8	412.6	139.4	313.8	257.1	665.8	23.4	19.5
Personal, cultural, and recreational	0.1	30.6	0.5	0.7	0.2	1.1	0.8	4.3	1.3	0.9	18.3	-25.2
Government goods and services	5.3	8.0	2.5	12.2	4.5	17.0	3.0	20.9	4.6	23.7	-1.0	7.8

[a] Data is for 2008.

Source: World Trade Organization. WTO Data. https://data.wto.org/ (accessed March 2021).

Table A1.7: Pakistan—Exports and Imports of Services, 2005–2019
($ million)

Pakistan	2005		2008		2012		2015		2019		Growth 2005–2019 (%)	
	Export	Import	Export	Import	Export	Import	Export	Import	Export	Import	Export	Import
Total Services	3,664.0	7,592.0	4,249.0	9,797.0	6,582.0	8,517.0	5,897.0	8,807.0	5,418.4	9,304.4	2.8	1.5
Manufacturing services on physical inputs owned by others	0.0	0.0	0.0	0.0	0.0	0.0	0.0	0.0	0.0	0.0		
Maintenance and repair	1.0	90.0	3.0	84.0	7.0	92.0	2.0	113.0	9.0	62.0	15.7	–2.7
Transport	1,076.0	2,625.0	1,227.0	4,223.0	1,381.0	3,320.0	1,174.0	3,711.0	814.0	3,584.0	–2.0	2.2
Travel	182.0	1,280.0	316.0	1,518.0	339.0	1,414.0	317.0	1,658.0	483.0	1,602.0	7.0	1.6
Construction	18.0	132.0	42.0	55.0	33.0	47.0	44.0	18.0	94.0	27.0	11.8	–11.3
Insurance and pension	32.0	126.0	73.0	132.0	53.0	281.0	54.0	246.0	42.0	252.0	1.9	5.0
Financial services	47.0	124.0	55.0	214.0	43.0	120.0	108.0	230.0	108.0	209.0	5.9	3.7
Charges for the use of intellectual property	15.0	109.0	38.0	117.0	7.0	161.0	15.0	180.0	0.0	192.0	–5.9	4.0
Telecommunication, computer, and information services	343.0	107.0	277.0	225.0	582.0	374.0	789.0	406.0	1,203.0	426.0	9.0	9.9
Other business	313.0	2,689.0	483.0	2,797.0	754.0	1,822.0	939.0	1,646.0	1,453.0	2,480.0	11.0	–0.6
Personal, cultural, and recreational	2.0	8.0	3.0	1.0	6.0	3.0	17.0	7.0	11.0	1.0	12.2	–14.9
Government goods and services	1,635.0	302.0	1,732.0	431.0	3,377.0	883.0	2,438.0	592.0	1,201.0	469.0	–2.2	3.1

Source: World Trade Organization. WTO Data. https://data.wto.org/ (accessed March 2021).

Table A1.8: Tajikistan—Exports and Imports of Services, 2005–2019
($ million)

Tajikistan	2005 Export	2005 Import	2008 Export	2008 Import	2012 Export	2012 Import	2015 Export	2015 Import	2019 Export	2019 Import	Growth 2005–2019 (%) Export	Growth 2005–2019 (%) Import
Total Services	146.3	251.9	181.4	456.6	487.6	580.5	252.4	462.6	242.4	487.8	3.6	4.7
Manufacturing services on physical inputs owned by others	0.0	0.0	0.0	0.0	149.3	0.0	67.6	0.4	23.3	1.3	−23.1	
Maintenance and repair	0.0	0.0	0.0	0.0	0.0	5.8	0.0	5.2	0.0	4.6		
Transport	55.9	178.6	47.3	179.2	324.9	499.7	164.7	353.3	192.4	382.9	8.8	5.4
Travel	1.6	3.7	4.2	10.8	1.6	3.9	1.0	0	13.7	5.1	15.3	2.3
Construction	7.2	30.7	0.0	127.8	0.0	28.6	0	79.3	0.1	50.0	−30.5	3.5
Insurance and pension	0.0	14.3	0.0	23.5	0.0	1.4	0	1.0	0.0	0.6		−22.7
Financial services	8.3	4.1	17.3	25.4	1.5	10.9	3.1	2.1	0.8	7.4	−16.7	4.2
Charges for the use of intellectual property	1.2	0.3	1.0	0.3	0.0	0.0	0.0	0.0	0.0	0.0		
Telecommunication, computer, and information services	13.6	8.7	39.2	36.2	10.1	13.5	12.8	10.7	6.8	6.2	−5.0	−2.4
Other business	15.0	10.3	24.6	50.7	0.2	3.5	2.2	3.4	1.9	20.7	−14.8	5.0
Personal, cultural, and recreational	0.0	0.0	0.0	0.0	0.0	8.0	1.0	2.0	0.1	0.0		
Government goods and services	43.6	1.2	47.9	2.8	0.0	5.3	0.0	5.2	3.2	8.8	−18.7	14.2

Source: World Trade Organization. WTO Data. https://data.wto.org/ (accessed March 2021).

Table A1.9: Turkmenistan—Exports and Imports of Services, 2005-2019
($ million)

Turkmenistan	2005 Export	2005 Import	2008 Export	2008 Import	2012 Export	2012 Import	2015 Export	2015 Import	2019 Export	2019 Import	Growth 2005–2019 (%) Export	Growth 2005–2019 (%) Import
Total Services	1,413.1	2,131.1	2,121.9	2,745.2	3,945.3	4,907.3	3,431.8	4,616.6	3,392.1	9,013.7	6.3	10.3
Manufacturing services on physical inputs owned by others	0.0	0.0	0.0	0.0	0.0	0.0	0.0	0.0	0.0	0.0		
Maintenance and repair	0.0	0.0	0.0	0.0	0.0	0.0	0.0	0.0	0.0	0.0		
Transport	885.0	667.6	1,329.0	860.0	2,471.0	1,537.3	2,149.4	1,446.2	2,124.5	2,823.6	6.3	10.3
Travel	149.2	389.1	224.1	501.3	416.6	896.1	362.4	843.0	358.2	1,645.9	6.3	10.3
Construction	47.2	25.8	67.0	39.5	109.5	84.2	119.1	69.1	95.1	119.3	5.0	10.9
Insurance and pension	12.3	97.2	14.8	140.0	29.4	211.7	32.5	172.3	30.4	345.1	6.5	9.1
Financial services	21.8	101.2	51.8	131.6	83.1	203.1	80.4	220.0	81.5	434.2	9.4	10.4
Charges for the use of intellectual property	19.5	144.8	24.3	159.0	42.6	285.8	39.0	280.8	57.8	565.0	7.8	9.7
Telecommunication, computer, and information services	58.3	136.9	83.7	180.0	163.9	336.1	170.0	329.0	190.5	672.4	8.5	11.4
Other business	169.4	517.9	254.0	670.8	490.7	1,235.0	360.9	1,152.3	335.6	2,210.6	4.9	10.4
Personal, cultural, and recreational	8.8	29.5	11.1	36.0	22.8	69.8	17.6	58.5	18.9	108.7	5.5	9.3
Government goods and services	41.4	21.0	62.2	27.1	115.7	48.4	100.6	45.5	99.5	88.9	6.3	10.3

Source: World Trade Organization. WTO Data. https://data.wto.org/ (accessed March 2021).

Table A1.10: Uzbekistan—Exports and Imports of Services, 2005–2019
($ million)

Uzbekistan	2005		2008		2012		2015		2019		Growth 2005–2019 (%)	
	Export	Import	Export	Import	Export	Import	Export	Import	Export	Import	Export	Import
Total Services	659.9	425.5	1,195.5	427.0	2,343.1	942.6	2,357.4	3,093.3	3,095.1	5,360.9	11.0	18.1
Manufacturing services on physical inputs owned by others	0.0	0.0	0.0	0.0	0.0	0.0	65.0	1.4	11.6	0.5		
Maintenance and repair	0.0	0.0	0.0	0.0	0.0	0.0	11.8	8.6	11.4	17.5		
Transport	198.0	127.6	358.7	128.1	702.9	282.8	1,366.4	1,295.3	1,251.9	2,518.4	13.2	21.3
Travel	198.0	127.6	358.7	128.1	702.9	282.8	520.7	1,594.0	1,480.9	2,313.0	14.4	20.7
Construction	0.0	0.0	0.0	0.0	0.0	0.0	10.3	38.0	50.3	25.5		
Insurance and pension	4.6	71.9	8.6	72.9	18.2	166.3	8.4	66.4	7.4	162.6	3.4	5.8
Financial services	23.8	14.5	43.7	14.4	89.4	30.5	39.3	8.3	29.6	20.0	1.6	2.3
Charges for the use of intellectual property	2.0	0	3.4	0.0	5.6	0.0	1.0	15.2	0.1	87.1	−21.4	
Telecommunication, computer, and information services	165.5	48.0	298.7	47.5	576.7	100.1	206.6	27.1	165.4	71.8	0.0	2.9
Other business	68.1	35.8	123.8	36.0	247.0	80.2	100.3	28.4	65.8	107.7	−0.2	7.9
Personal, cultural, and recreational	0.0	0.0	0.0	0.0	0.3	0.0	0.6	0.1	1.0	9.7		
Government goods and services	0.0	0.0	0.0	0.0	0.0	0.0	27.1	10.5	19.7	27.0		

Source: World Trade Organization. WTO Data. https://data.wto.org/ (accessed March 2021).

CAREC COUNTRIES' EXPORTS AND IMPORTS OF SERVICES BY MODE OF SUPPLY

Table A2.1: Afghanistan—Exports and Imports of Services by Mode of Supply, 2017
($ million)

Afghanistan	Mode 1		Mode 2		Mode 3		Mode 4	
	Exports	Imports	Exports	Imports	Exports	Imports	Exports	Imports
Services in manufactures	–	–	–	–	–	–	–	–
Maintenance and repair	–	–	0.0	6.8	–	–	0.0	0.8
Transport	14.6	684.0	23.7	48.1	0.1	109.5	–	–
Tourism and business travel	–	–	0.8	66.4	–	4.2	–	–
Health	0.0	0.0	0.1	0.0	–	0.5	0.0	0.0
Education	0.0	0.0	0.0	29.5	0.0	17.6	0.0	0.0
Construction	–	–	–	–	0.0	148.6	0.0	0.9
Insurance and financial	9.3	135.7	–	–	5.6	143.3	–	–
Charges for the use of intellectual property	0.0	0.2	–	–	–	–	–	–
Telecom, computer, information, and audiovisual	57.9	31.3	0.0	0.0	16.5	874.2	0.1	0.3
Research and development	0.0	0.0	–	–	–	–	0.0	0.0
Professional and management consulting	78.8	19.5	–	–	–	–	26.3	6.5
Technical, trade-related, and other business	1.1	0.0	0.0	0.0	–	–	0.3	0.0
Heritage and recreational	0.0	0.0	–	–	0.2	0.2	0.0	0.0
Other personal	0.0	0.0	–	–	–	0.0	0.0	0.0
Trade-related (distribution)	30.4	270.9	–	–	2.9	76.4	–	–
TOTAL	192.1	1,141.6	24.6	150.8	25.3	1,374.5	26.7	8.5

Source: World Trade Organization. Trade in Services data by Mode of Supply (TISMOS) https://www.wto.org/english/res_e/statis_e/trade_datasets_e.htm (accessed September 2020).

Table A2.2: Azerbaijan—Exports and Imports of Services by Mode of Supply, 2017
($ million)

Azerbaijan	Mode 1		Mode 2		Mode 3		Mode 4	
	Exports	Imports	Exports	Imports	Exports	Imports	Exports	Imports
Services in manufactures	–	–	1.9	1.3	–	–	–	–
Maintenance and repair	–	–	87.4	83.3	–	–	9.7	9.3
Transport	750.0	837.5	221.4	210.9	16.2	245.4	–	–
Tourism and business travel	–	–	2,225.7	1,654.6	1.3	52.9	–	–
Health	0.8	2.1	0.8	2.9		1.1	0.3	0.7
Education	0.7	2.6	44.4	264.5	0.4	23.3	0.2	0.9
Construction	–	–	–	–	103.7	1,588.7	33.0	1,241.1
Insurance and financial	30.0	162.7	–	–	91.8	594.0	–	–
Charges for the use of intellectual property	0.0	0.0	–	–	–	–	–	–
Telecom, computer, information, and audiovisual	65.0	82.1	0.0	0.0	46.4	455.6	1.5	8.4
Research and development	1.5	7.3	–	–	–	–	0.5	2.4
Professional and management consulting	17.9	27.2	–	–	–	–	6.0	9.1
Technical, trade-related, and other business	301.0	1,124.8	4.1	26.6	–	–	74.0	256.5
Heritage and recreational		2.7	–	–	4.1	5.8	–	0.9
Other personal	7.7	3.3	–	–	0.0	3.2	2.6	1.1
Trade-related (distribution)	654.9	626.2	–	–	96.2	696.4	–	–
TOTAL	1,829.5	2,878.5	2,585.7	2,244.2	360.1	3,666.4	127.8	1,530.5

Source: World Trade Organization. Trade in Services data by Mode of Supply (TISMOS) https://www.wto.org/english/res_e/statis_e/trade_datasets_e.htm (accessed September 2020).

Table A2.3: Georgia—Exports and Imports of Services by Mode of Supply, 2017
($ million)

Georgia	Mode 1		Mode 2		Mode 3		Mode 4	
	Exports	Imports	Exports	Imports	Exports	Imports	Exports	Imports
Services in manufactures	–	–	13.0	0.6	–	–	–	–
Maintenance and repair	–	–	1.3	3.3	–	–	0.2	0.4
Transport	742.0	1045.4	218.0	36.6	7.6	102.0	–	–
Tourism and business travel			2,029.0	351.8	0.4	15.8	–	–
Health	0.7	0.6	1.5	11.2	–	1.1	0.2	0.2
Education	0.6	0.7	8.4	100.6	0.3	16.1	0.2	0.2
Construction	–	–	–	–	31.0	177.1	2.8	4.5
Insurance and financial	28.0	141.7	–	–	55.0	411.9	–	–
Charges for the use of intellectual property	0.3	24.7	–	–	–	–	–	–
Telecom, computer, information, and audiovisual	85.0	57.0	0.8	0.5	46.0	436.7	12.0	6.8
Research and development	0.4	0.6	–	–	–	–	0.1	0.2
Professional and management consulting	20.0	25.6	–	–	–	–	6.6	8.5
Technical, trade-related, and other business	35.0	53.4	0.5	2.3	–	–	8.5	11.9
Heritage and recreational	–	2.6	–	–	1.7	2.6	–	0.9
Other personal	6.8	0.5	–	–	0.0	4.2	2.3	0.2
Trade-related (distribution)	146.0	299.3	–	–	29.0	323.4	–	–
TOTAL	**1,064.8**	**1,652.4**	**2,272.5**	**506.9**	**171.0**	**1,490.9**	**32.9**	**33.8**

Source: World Trade Organization. Trade in Services data by Mode of Supply (TISMOS) https://www.wto.org/english/res_e/statis_e/trade_datasets_e.htm (accessed September 2020).

Table A2.4: Kazakhstan—Exports and Imports of Services by Mode of Supply, 2017
($ million)

Kazakhstan	Mode 1		Mode 2		Mode 3		Mode 4	
	Exports	Imports	Exports	Imports	Exports	Imports	Exports	Imports
Services in manufactures	–	–	8.7	160.6	–	–	–	–
Maintenance and repair	–	–	55.0	307.9	–	–	6.1	34.2
Transport	3,163.0	1,482.2	296.0	253.2	188.0	1,186.9	–	–
Tourism and business travel	–	–	2,129.0	2,409.2	6.3	89.3	–	–
Health	0.0	14.7	0.5	13.4	0.0	9.4	0.0	4.9
Education	0.0	18.6	6.3	137.3	0.3	22.6	0.0	6.2
Construction	–	–	–	–	–	782.7	–	159.5
Insurance and financial	104.0	270.2	–	–	783.0	2,915.2	–	–
Charges for the use of intellectual property	0.7	117.1	–	–	–	–	–	–
Telecom, computer, information, and audiovisual	113.0	284.5	0.0	4.0	261.0	1,597.3	3.8	46.4
Research and development	4.3	7.6	–	–	–	–	1.4	2.5
Professional and management consulting	82.0	631.0	–	–	–	–	27.0	210.3
Technical, trade-related, and other business	190.0	2,522.8	10.0	59.6	–	–	53.0	575.2
Heritage and recreational	0.0	19.4	–	–	14.0	30.5	0.0	6.5
Other personal	0.0	23.1	–	–	0.3	24.6	0.0	7.7
Trade-related (distribution)	1,861.0	1,801.8	–	–	514.0	3,929.7	–	–
TOTAL	**5,518.0**	**7,193.0**	**2,505.5**	**3,345.2**	**1,766.9**	**10,588.2**	**91.3**	**1,053.4**

Source: World Trade Organization. Trade in Services data by Mode of Supply (TISMOS) https://www.wto.org/english/res_e/statis_e/trade_datasets_e.htm (accessed September 2020).

Table A2.5: Kyrgyz Republic—Exports and Imports of Services by Mode of Supply, 2017
($ million)

Kyrgyz Republic	Mode 1		Mode 2		Mode 3		Mode 4	
	Exports	Imports	Exports	Imports	Exports	Imports	Exports	Imports
Services in manufactures	–	–	0.0	0.0	–	–	–	–
Maintenance and repair	–	–	0.0	0.0	–	–	0.0	0.0
Transport	147.0	278.6	59.0	155.6	0.1	17.8	–	–
Tourism and business travel	–	–	313.0	237.0	–	4.1	–	–
Health	13.0	4.0	–	–	–	0.3	4.4	1.3
Education	6.3	5.2	–	–	0.1	12.2	2.1	1.7
Construction	–	–	–	–	13.0	68.5	9.5	5.4
Insurance and financial	27.0	37.0	–	–	8.0	110.2	–	–
Charges for the use of intellectual property	0.8	5.3	–	–	–	–	–	–
Telecom, computer, information, and audiovisual	39.0	20.9	–	–	5.8	176.2	0.7	3.2
Research and development	0.0	–	–	–	–	–	0.0	0.00
Professional and management consulting	6.7	37.9	–	–	–	–	2.2	12.6
Technical, trade-related, and other business	23.0	3.9	0.2	0.2	–	–	5.5	0.9
Heritage and recreational	9.4	18.9	–	–	0.3	0.2	3.1	6.3
Other personal	13.0	3.6	–	–	–	0.6	4.4	1.2
Trade-related (distribution)	74.0	161.5	–	–	4.0	111.2	–	–
TOTAL	359.2	576.8	372.2	392.8	31.3	501.3	31.9	32.6

Source: World Trade Organization. Trade in Services data by Mode of Supply (TISMOS) https://www.wto.org/english/res_e/statis_e/trade_datasets_e.htm (accessed September 2020).

Table A2.6: Mongolia—Exports and Imports of Services by Mode of Supply, 2017
($ million)

Mongolia	Mode 1		Mode 2		Mode 3		Mode 4	
	Exports	Imports	Exports	Imports	Exports	Imports	Exports	Imports
Services in manufactures	–	–	5.4	16.4	–	–	–	–
Maintenance and repair	–	–	–	0.0	–	–	–	0.0
Transport	197.0	553.4	124.0	50.3	1.6	49.4	–	–
Tourism and business travel	–	–	280.0	406.4	0.1	7.1	–	–
Health	0.6	0.1	2.6	27.6	–	0.5	0.2	0.0
Education	0.3	0.2	6.1	98.8	0.2	8.3	0.1	0.1
Construction	–	–	–	–	–	189.9	–	120.3
Insurance and financial	26.0	69.8	–	–	57.0	380.3	–	–
Charges for the use of intellectual property	1.0	15.7	–	–	–	–	–	–
Telecom, computer, information, and audiovisual	24.0	68.0	–	–	11.0	168.2	2.1	5.2
Research and development	1.0	0.7	–	–	–	–	0.3	0.2
Professional and management consulting	28.0	136.7	–	–	–	–	9.4	45.6
Technical, trade-related, and other business	102.0	333.9	0.8	7.9	–	–	24.0	76.1
Heritage and recreational	0.4	0.2	–	–	0.5	1.1	0.1	0.1
Other personal	0.6	0.21	–	–	–	2.4	0.2	0.1
Trade-related (distribution)	252.0	250.0	–	–	22.0	240.1	–	–
TOTAL	**632.9**	**1,428.8**	**419.0**	**607.4**	**92.4**	**1,047.3**	**36.4**	**247.7**

Source: World Trade Organization. Trade in Services data by Mode of Supply (TISMOS) https://www.wto.org/english/res_e/statis_e/trade_datasets_e.htm (accessed September 2020).

Table A2.7: Pakistan—Exports and Imports of Services by Mode of Supply, 2017
($ million)

Pakistan	Mode 1		Mode 2		Mode 3		Mode 4	
	Exports	Imports	Exports	Imports	Exports	Imports	Exports	Imports
Services in manufactures	–	–	–	–	–	–	–	–
Maintenance and repair	–	–	6.3	48.6	–	–	0.7	5.4
Transport	599.0	3726.7	330.0	304.4	24.0	1,223.6	–	–
Tourism and business travel	–	–	197.0	1,560.4	1.4	128.2	–	–
Health	0.8	1.0	0.6	0.0	0.0	14.2	0.3	0.3
Education	3.2	1.4	9.4	76.2	0.2	65.2	1.1	0.5
Construction	–	–	–	–	68.0	398.8	34.0	12.5
Insurance and financial	200.0	547.0	–	–	210.0	1,547.9	–	–
Charges for the use of intellectual property	10.0	227.0	–	–	–	–	–	–
Telecom, computer, information, and audiovisual	842.0	348.3	0.0	0.00	271.0	2,260.0	163.0	75.8
Research and development	7.5	0.8	–	–	–	–	2.5	0.3
Professional and management consulting	135.0	78.8	–	–	–	–	45.0	26.3
Technical, trade-related, and other business	890.0	1,906.8	26.0	83.34	–	–	221.0	423.9
Heritage and recreational	3.3	4.9	–	–	12.0	12.0	1.1	1.7
Other personal	4.8	0.9	–	–	0.0	97.2	1.6	0.3
Trade-related (distribution)	1,064.0	2586.1	–	–	378.0	2746.0	–	–
TOTAL	3,759.6	9,429.7	569.3	2,072.9	964.6	8,493.1	470.3	547.0

Source: World Trade Organization. Trade in Services data by Mode of Supply (TISMOS) https://www.wto.org/english/res_e/statis_e/trade_datasets_e.htm (accessed September 2020).

Table A2.8: Tajikistan—Exports and Imports of Services by Mode of Supply, 2017
($ million)

Tajikistan	Mode 1		Mode 2		Mode 3		Mode 4	
	Exports	Imports	Exports	Imports	Exports	Imports	Exports	Imports
Services in manufactures	–	–	47.0	0.2	–	–	–	–
Maintenance and repair	–	–	–	1.7	–	–	–	0.2
Transport	177.0	252.6	8.3	34.0	0.1	34.0	–	–
Tourism and business travel	–	–	3.1	1.8	–	0.7	–	–
Health	0.1	0.0	1.2	0.5	–	0.1	0.0	0.0
Education	0.1	0.0	3.4	1.1	0.0	10.4	0.0	0.0
Construction	–	–	–	–	–	84.6	–	26.2
Insurance and financial	1.1	11.4	–	–	0.5	17.8	–	–
Charges for the use of intellectual property	0.0	0.1	–	–	–	–	–	–
Telecom, computer, information, and audiovisual	5.4	4.1	–	–	2.6	203.8	0.0	0.1
Research and development	–	–	–	–	–	–	–	–
Professional and management consulting	0.6	1.8	–	–	–	–	0.2	0.6
Technical, trade-related, and other business	0.0	3.8	0.0	0.2	–	–	0.0	0.8
Heritage and recreational	0.1	0.1	–	–	0.3	0.3	0.0	0.0
Other personal	0.1	0.0	–	–	–	1.8	0.0	0.0
Trade-related (distribution)	34.0	93.2	–	–	0.3	47.8	–	–
TOTAL	**218.5**	**367.1**	**63.0**	**39.5**	**3.8**	**401.3**	**0.2**	**27.9**

Source: World Trade Organization. Trade in Services data by Mode of Supply (TISMOS) https://www.wto.org/english/res_e/statis_e/trade_datasets_e.htm (accessed September 2020).

Table A2.9: Turkmenistan—Exports and Imports of Services by Mode of Supply, 2017
($ million)

Turkmenistan	Mode 1 Exports	Mode 1 Imports	Mode 2 Exports	Mode 2 Imports	Mode 3 Exports	Mode 3 Imports	Mode 4 Exports	Mode 4 Imports
Services in manufactures	–	–	–	–	–	–	–	–
Maintenance and repair	–	–	–	–	–	–	–	–
Transport	1,803.0	1,126.0	462.0	392.3	34.0	171.4	–	–
Tourism and business travel	–	–	375.0	608.2	2.0	29.4	–	–
Health	2.7	4.0	1.4	6.6	–	2.8	0.9	1.3
Education	2.5	5.1	5.1	25.0	0.3	23.5	0.8	1.7
Construction	–	–	–	–	107.0	250.1	43.0	18.4
Insurance and financial	123.0	416.7	–	–	312.0	1,347.4	–	–
Charges for the use of intellectual property	60.0	299.9	–	–	–	–	–	–
Telecom, computer, information, and audiovisual	175.0	322.1	0.9	3.0	177.0	782.2	39.0	67.8
Research and development	25.0	133.3	–	–	–	–	8.2	44.4
Professional and management consulting	76.0	320.5	–	–	–	–	25.0	106.8
Technical, trade-related, and other business	164.0	471.2	8.7	11.1	–	–	46.0	107.4
Heritage and recreational	2.8	5.3	–	–	5.4	7.8	0.9	1.8
Other personal	3.1	6.3	–	–	0.0	4.8	1.0	2.1
Trade-related (distribution)	977.0	574.3	–	–	138.0	770.5	–	–
TOTAL	**3,414.1**	**3,684.6**	**853.1**	**1,046.3**	**775.8**	**3,389.8**	**164.9**	**351.8**

Source: World Trade Organization. Trade in Services data by Mode of Supply (TISMOS) https://www.wto.org/english/res_e/statis_e/trade_datasets_e.htm (accessed September 2020).

Table A2.10: Uzbekistan—Exports and Imports of Services by Mode of Supply, 2017
($ million)

Uzbekistan	Mode 1		Mode 2		Mode 3		Mode 4	
	Exports	Imports	Exports	Imports	Exports	Imports	Exports	Imports
Services in manufactures	–	–	–	–	–	–	–	–
Maintenance and repair	–	–	–	–	–	–	–	–
Transport	737.0	217.6	315.0	75.8	3.6	146.9	–	–
Tourism and business travel	–	–	712.0	201.7	0.2	16.7	–	–
Health	3.4	0.7	13.0	2.2	–	1.3	1.1	0.2
Education	1.6	0.8	44.0	8.3	0.1	26.6	0.6	0.3
Construction	–	–	–	–	62.0	220.9	45.0	3.0
Insurance and financial	201.0	68.1	–	–	119.0	695.5	–	–
Charges for the use of intellectual property	61.0	49.0	–	–	–	–	–	–
Telecom, computer, information, and audiovisual	256.0	52.6	1.1	0.5	67.0	826.7	59.0	11.1
Research and development	56.0	21.8	–	–	–	–	19.0	7.3
Professional and management consulting	212.0	52.3	–	–	–	–	71.0	17.5
Technical, trade-related, and other business	272.0	77.0	2.2	1.8	–	–	64.0	17.6
Heritage and recreational	2.4	0.9	–	–	3.3	3.1	0.8	0.3
Other personal	3.5	1.0	–	–	–	8.5	1.2	0.3
Trade-related (distribution)	474.0	483.1	–	–	48.0	392.3	–	–
TOTAL	**2,279.9**	**1,024.9**	**1,087.3**	**290.3**	**303.2**	**2,339.4**	**261.7**	**57.6**

Source: World Trade Organization. Trade in Services data by Mode of Supply (TISMOS) https://www.wto.org/english/res_e/statis_e/trade_datasets_e.htm (accessed September 2020).

CONTRIBUTION OF SERVICE INDUSTRIES TO OUTPUT AND EXPORTS OF SELECTED SECTORS IN CAREC AND OECD COUNTRIES

The information presented in Appendix 2 indicates that the following non-service sectors or subsectors are among the priority services subsectors for at least some Central Asia Regional Economic Cooperation (CAREC) countries:

- agriculture (in particular horticulture and animal husbandry);
- food industry,
- textile and apparel industry,
- chemical/pharmaceutical industry,
- electronics industry, and
- production of transport equipment.

To assess the importance of various services industries for the above sectors/subsectors, the contribution of several business services industries to gross output (at basic prices) and exports (in value added terms) of these sectors/subsectors in Kazakhstan, the People's Republic of China (PRC), and comparator Organisation for Economic Co-operation and Development (OECD) countries were estimated. In doing so, OECD Statistics (https://stats.oecd.org/) was used, which includes input–output tables and data on exports in value-added terms for all OECD countries, Kazakhstan, and the PRC, and 26 countries and territories that are members of neither the OECD, nor the CAREC Program. For each non-services subsector or industry, three OECD countries with the largest share of the sector/subsector in total exports of goods and services were chosen as the comparator countries.

The results presented in Tables A3.1–A3.6 suggest that transport and storage services, telecommunication and information services, financial services, and various other business services (such as research, experimental development, and quality assurance services) are important for the development of the non-service sectors/subsectors that are among the priority sectors/subsectors for CAREC countries. These service industries generally contribute more to gross output and exports of the non-service sectors/subsectors in the comparator OECD countries than in Kazakhstan and the PRC. Moreover, they generally contribute more to exports than gross output. This underscores the importance of business services for exports and economic diversification.

Table A3.1: Contribution of Services Industries to Gross Output and Exports of Agriculture, Forestry, and Fishing in Selected Countries, 2015
(%)

| Industry | Gross Output at Basic Prices | | | | | Exports in Value-added Terms | | | | |
| | CAREC Countries | | OECD Countries[a] | | | CAREC Countries | | OECD Countries[a] | | |
	PRC	Kazakhstan	New Zealand	Latvia	Chile	PRC	Kazakhstan	New Zealand	Latvia	Chile
Transport and storage	1.2	1.1	1.8	3.0	2.3	1.9	1.4	2.6	4.1	3.0
Telecommunication and information	0.1	0.1	0.2	0.4	0.3	0.4	0.2	0.6	1.3	0.7
Finance and insurance	1.7	1.5	2.7	2.9	1.5	3.4	1.9	4.2	4.1	2.4
Other business sector services[b]	0.8	1.9	3.7	2.0	3.3	1.6	2.8	6.9	4.9	6.4

CAREC = Central Asia Regional Economic Cooperation, OECD = Organisation for Economic Co-operation and Development, PRC = People's Republic of China.

[a] The OECD countries with the largest share of agriculture, forestry and fishing in total exports of goods and services.

[b] The business sector services, excluding transport and storage services, accommodation and food services, communication and information services, finance and insurance services, and real estate activities.

Source: Organisation for Economic Co-operation and Development. OECD.Stat https://stats.oecd.org/ (accessed September 2020).

Table A3.2: Contribution of Services Industries to Gross Output and Exports of Food Industry in Selected Countries, 2015
(%)

| Industry | Gross Output at Basic Prices | | | | | Exports in Value-added Terms | | | | |
| | CAREC Countries | | OECD Countries[a] | | | CAREC Countries | | OECD Countries[a] | | |
	PRC	Kazakhstan	New Zealand	Iceland	Chile	PRC	Kazakhstan	New Zealand	Iceland	Chile
Transport and storage	2.1	1.6	1.6	2.8	3.0	2.9	1.9	2.8	3.5	4.0
Telecommunication and information	0.1	0.1	0.2	0.8	0.3	0.5	0.3	0.7	1.5	0.9
Finance and insurance	0.6	0.7	1.2	1.7	0.8	3.3	1.5	3.7	3.3	2.4
Other business sector services[b]	1.0	3.1	5.2	3.3	4.1	2.1	4.0	8.6	5.4	8.4

CAREC = Central Asia Regional Economic Cooperation, OECD = Organisation for Economic Co-operation and Development, PRC = People's Republic of China.

[a] The OECD countries with the largest share of agriculture, forestry and fishing in total exports of goods and services.

[b] The business sector services, excluding transport and storage services, accommodation and food services, communication and information services, finance and insurance services, and real estate activities.

Source: Organisation for Economic Co-operation and Development. OECD.Stat https://stats.oecd.org/ (accessed September 2020).

Table A3.3: Contribution of Services Industries to Gross Output and Exports of Textile and Apparel Industry in Selected Countries, 2015

(%)

| | Gross Output at Basic Prices | | | | | Exports in Value-added Terms | | | | |
| | CAREC Countries | | OECD Countries[a] | | | CAREC Countries | | OECD Countries[a] | | |
Industry	PRC	Kazakhstan	Turkey	Portugal	Italy	PRC	Kazakhstan	Turkey	Portugal	Italy
Transport and storage	4.4	2.3	3.7	2.1	3.3	5.7	2.7	5.0	2.8	3.9
Telecommunication and information	0.3	0.2	0.3	0.8	0.8	0.9	0.5	0.9	1.3	1.4
Finance and insurance	1.4	1.5	0.6	1.9	2.3	4.8	2.5	1.8	3.3	4.3
Other business sector services[b]	1.3	3.6	1.0	2.7	4.4	2.9	4.6	3.3	5.1	7.5

CAREC = Central Asia Regional Economic Cooperation, OECD = Organisation for Economic Co-operation and Development, PRC = People's Republic of China.

a   The OECD countries with the largest share of agriculture, forestry and fishing in total exports of goods and services.

b   The business sector services, excluding transport and storage services, accommodation and food services, communication and information services, finance and insurance services, and real estate activities.

Source: Organisation for Economic Co-operation and Development. OECD.Stat https://stats.oecd.org/ (accessed September 2020).

Table A3.4: Contribution of Services Industries to Gross Output and Exports of Chemical/Pharmaceutical Industry in Selected Countries, 2015

(%)

| | Gross Output at Basic Prices | | | | | Exports in Value-added Terms | | | | |
| | CAREC Countries | | OECD Countries[a] | | | CAREC Countries | | OECD Countries[a] | | |
Industry	PRC	Kazakhstan	Ireland	Switzerland	Belgium	PRC	Kazakhstan	Ireland	Switzerland	Belgium
Transport and storage	2.5	1.9	1.1	1.6	2.4	3.9	2.3	1.5	2.8	3.3
Telecommunication and information	0.4	0.1	0.6	0.3	0.6	1.0	0.4	0.9	1.0	1.3
Finance and insurance	2.1	0.9	7.4	0.2	1.7	5.6	1.7	7.9	2.0	3.7
Other business sector services[b]	2.8	3.6	18.9	8.0	6.5	4.1	4.6	8.3	10.4	9.7

CAREC = Central Asia Regional Economic Cooperation, OECD = Organisation for Economic Co-operation and Development, PRC = People's Republic of China.

a   The OECD countries with the largest share of agriculture, forestry and fishing in total exports of goods and services.

b   The business sector services, excluding transport and storage services, accommodation and food services, communication and information services, finance and insurance services, and real estate activities.

Source: Organisation for Economic Co-operation and Development. OECD.Stat https://stats.oecd.org/ (accessed September 2020).

Table A3.5: Contribution of Services Industries to Gross Output and Exports of Electronics Industry in Selected Countries, 2015
(%)

| Industry | Gross Output at Basic Prices | | | | | Exports in Value-added Terms | | | | |
| | CAREC Countries | | OECD Countries[a] | | | CAREC Countries | | OECD Countries[a] | | |
	PRC	Kazakhstan	South Korea	Mexico	Israel	PRC	Kazakhstan	South Korea	Mexico	Israel
Transport and storage	3.1	2.4	1.3	2.9	0.9	4.8	3.1	2.9	4.3	1.5
Telecommunication and information	0.5	0.2	0.6	0.2	0.2	1.4	0.4	1.2	0.9	0.5
Finance and insurance	1.5	0.9	0.8	0.3	0.3	5.7	1.3	3.1	2.7	1.4
Other business sector services[b]	3.1	4.5	2.7	4.1	1.2	5.4	5.0	5.8	7.3	3.6

CAREC = Central Asia Regional Economic Cooperation, OECD = Organisation for Economic Co-operation and Development, PRC = People's Republic of China.

a   The OECD countries with the largest share of agriculture, forestry and fishing in total exports of goods and services.

b   The business sector services, excluding transport and storage services, accommodation and food services, communication and information services, finance and insurance services, and real estate activities.

Source: Organisation for Economic Co-operation and Development. OECD.Stat https://stats.oecd.org/ (accessed September 2020).

Table A3.6: Contribution of Services Industries to Gross Output and Exports of Transport Equipment Industry in Selected Countries, 2015
(%)

| Industry | Gross Output at Basic Prices | | | | | Exports in Value-added Terms | | | | |
| | CAREC Countries | | OECD Countries[a] | | | CAREC Countries | | OECD Countries[a] | | |
	PRC	Kazakhstan	Slovak Republic	Mexico	Czech Republic	PRC	Kazakhstan	Slovak Republic	Mexico	Czech Republic
Transport and storage	2.3	2.2	2.0	4.5	1.1	4.1	2.9	4.0	5.5	3.0
Telecommunication and information	0.6	0.1	0.5	0.4	0.6	1.0	0.3	1.3	0.8	1.3
Finance and insurance	1.9	0.6	0.5	0.4	0.4	6.0	1.4	2.7	2.3	2.6
Other business sector services[b]	2.4	2.0	2.0	3.1	1.8	4.3	3.1	6.1	7.3	5.7

CAREC = Central Asia Regional Economic Cooperation, OECD = Organisation for Economic Co-operation and Development, PRC = People's Republic of China.

a   The OECD countries with the largest share of agriculture, forestry and fishing in total exports of goods and services.

b   The business sector services, excluding transport and storage services, accommodation and food services, communication and information services, finance and insurance services, and real estate activities.

Source: Organisation for Economic Co-operation and Development. OECD.Stat https://stats.oecd.org/ (accessed September 2020).

HORIZONTAL COMMITMENTS OF CAREC COUNTRIES UNDER GATS

Country	Horizontal Commitments
Afghanistan	***Subsidies (all modes):*** Subsidies and other forms of state support unbound. ***Commercial presence (Modes 3 and 4):*** Foreign land ownership prohibited, renewable 90-year leases for land use available. ***Natural persons (Mode 4):*** Presence of natural persons unbound except for intra-corporate transferees (executives, managers, specialists) who can acquire 1-year renewable visas; Persons in the process of establishing commercial presence may not undertake commercial activity – visas for 1 year, renewable; Service sellers (business meetings etc.) may not undertake any commercial activity – visas for 180 days per year; Service suppliers who do not establish commercial presence may acquire visas for 180 days per annum. ***Procurement (all modes):*** Compulsory procurement of 'equivalent' Afghan services under Oil and Gas Law until 2021; Priority procurement of 'equivalent' Afghan services under Mineral Law until 2021.
China, People's Republic of	***Subsidies:*** Unbound with respect to existing subsidies in audiovisual, aviation, and medical service sectors. ***Commercial presence:*** Minimum of 25% of foreign capital in equity joint ventures; Establishment of branches unbound unless otherwise indicated in schedules; Most representative offices prohibited from engaging in profit-making activity; Standstill on restrictiveness of conditions of ownership, operation and scope of activities of foreign firms existing at accession; Time restrictions on use of land. ***Natural persons:*** Unbound except for managers, executives, and specialists, who may acquire long-term permission to stay or a 3-year visa, whichever is shorter; Nonresident salespersons not to receive local remuneration nor engage in direct selling and subject to 90-day visa.

Country	Horizontal Commitments
Georgia	*Subsidies:* Unbound in Modes 1 and 2, and generally unbound except in certain regions of the country. *Commercial presence:* No right to participate in privatizations where government has more than a 25% share; At least one manager of enterprise with limited liability must be domiciled in Georgia and the same requirement for the establishment of a branch; Limitations on real estate purchase, except for nonagricultural land, buildings for commercial services activities; Agricultural land may be leased for no more than 49 years and nonagricultural land for no more than 99 years; Agricultural land may be bought by joint ventures. *Natural persons:* Generally unbound, except for services salespersons (who do not undertake commercial activities, and intra-corporate transferees (executives, managers, specialists), subject to seniority conditions, entitled to a 3-year visa, renewable only once for 2 years.
Kazakhstan	*Subsidies:* Unbound in all modes. *Commercial presence:* Procurement of services within investment contracts for subsurface activities on preferential basis subject to employment of Kazakh nationals for qualified employees in sense of intra-corporate transferee criteria; Limitations on land ownership— no private ownership of trunk lines, railroad networks, and public highways or public areas in cities, towns, and villages except for privately owned buildings and constructions; Limitations on land use—only the state has the right to permanent land use; No limitations on private ownership of commercial and residential buildings but unbound for agricultural and forestry land, although foreigners may be allowed usage for production purposes for a maximum of 10 years; Commercial presence allowed for juridical persons including branches and representative offices but representative offices and nongovernment organizations are not allowed to engage in commercial activity. *Natural persons:* Unbound except for intra-corporate transferees (executives, managers, specialists) not engaged in actual provision of services, with a maximum share of 50% of foreign managers with a minimum of three individuals, permitted to remain for 3 years (with possible 1-year extension) and subject to an economics needs test for up to 5 years after accession; Businesspersons permitted to stay up to 90 days to conduct negotiations for service sales or establishment of commercial presence or business meetings, but no participation in direct selling or supply and no remuneration from local sources.
Kyrgyz Republic	*Natural persons:* Unbound except for salespersons receiving no local remuneration and not engaged in direct sales, with visas for up to 90 days; Intra-corporate transferees (executives, managers, specialists) though branches, subsidiaries of affiliates who have supervisory roles but do not perform direct sales operations, with 3-year visas that may be extended for a maximum of 2 further years.

Country	Horizontal Commitments
Mongolia	**Natural persons:** National treatment unbound under Mode 4 except where indicated elsewhere in the schedule of specific commitments; Market access unbound under Mode 4 except for entry and temporary stay of persons with technical or managerial skills falling within the category of intra-corporate transferees, business visitors, or professionals under a business contract.
Pakistan	**Commercial presence:** General equity share limitation of 51% unless otherwise specified; Expenses of representative offices must be paid for abroad and offices undertake liaison work only; Real estate ownership limited to Pakistani nationals only unless an exception is made on a case-by-case basis. **Natural persons:** Unbound except for executives and specialists, up to a maximum of 50% for such personnel in a services enterprise.
Tajikistan	**Subsidies:** Unbound under Modes 3 and 4 except for dispensations for particular regions or categories of disadvantaged persons. **Commercial presence:** Unbound for land ownership and some restrictions on land use; Unbound for privatization of certain assets; Representative offices prohibited from commercial activity; Unbound with respect to constitution, acquisition or maintenance of noncommercial organizations unless otherwise specified in the Schedule of Commitments. **Natural persons:** Unbound except for an annual quota of foreign workforce; Business visitors exempted for the quota system, can obtain visas for up to 90 days, but are employed by the entity in question, receive no local remuneration, and do not engage in the actual provision of the service; The quota system for intra-corporate transferees (executives, managers, specialists and graduate trainees) to be eliminated 5 years after accession; The stay for intra-corporate transferees is limited to 3 years (extendible), involving supervisory managerial work and technical work, and in the case of graduate trainees involved in learning programmes, to 1 year.

Notes: Dates of commitments are based on countries' membership or accession to the WTO: Afghanistan on 29 July 2016, the People's Republic of China on 11 December 2001, Georgia on 14 June 2000, Kazakhstan on 30 November 2015, the Kyrgyz Republic on 20 December 1998, Mongolia on 29 January 1997, Pakistan on 1 January 1995, and Tajikistan on 2 March 2013. Any changes after 15 August 2021 are not reflected.

Source: World Trade Organization. GATS Schedules of Specific Commitments. https://www.wto.org/english/tratop_e/serv_e/serv_commitments_e.htm (accessed September 2020).

Appendix 5

SUMMARY OF CAREC COUNTRIES' GATS COMMITMENTS BY SECTOR

Sector	Afghanistan	China, People's Republic of	Georgia	Kazakhstan	Kyrgyz Republic	Mongolia	Pakistan	Tajikistan	Total
Business services	X	X	X	X	X	X	X	X	8
Communication services	X	X	X	X	X	X	X	X	8
Construction and related engineering services	X	X	X	X	X	X	X	X	8
Distribution services	X	X	X	X	X	X		X	7
Educational services	X	X	X	X	X			X	6
Environmental services	X	X	X	X	X			X	6
Financial services	X	X	X	X	X	X	X	X	8
Health-related and social services	X		X		X		X	X	5
Tourism and travel-related services	X	X	X	X	X	X	X	X	8
Recreational, cultural and sporting services	X		X	X	X			X	5
Transport services	X	X	X	X	X			X	6
Total	**11**	**9**	**11**	**10**	**11**	**6**	**6**	**11**	**75**

CAREC = Central Asia Regional Economic Cooperation, GATS = General Agreement on Trade in Services.

Notes: The symbol X indicates the existence of a GATS commitment. Dates of commitments are based on countries' membership or accession to the WTO: Afghanistan on 29 July 2016, the People's Republic of China on 11 December 2001, Georgia on 14 June 2000, Kazakhstan on 30 November 2015, the Kyrgyz Republic on 20 December 1998, Mongolia on 29 January 1997, Pakistan on 1 January 1995, and Tajikistan on 2 March 2013. Any changes after 15 August 2021 are not reflected.

Source: World Trade Organization. GATS Schedules of Specific Commitments. https://www.wto.org/english/tratop_e/serv_e/serv_commitments_e.htm (accessed September 2020).

SUMMARY OF CAREC COUNTRIES' GATS COMMITMENTS BY SUBSECTOR

Code	Sector	Afghanistan	China, People's Republic of	Georgia	Kazakhstan	Kyrgyz Republic	Mongolia	Pakistan	Tajikistan	Total
1	**BUSINESS SERVICES**									
1.A	Professional services									
1.A.a	Legal services	X	X	X	X	X			X	**6**
1.A.b	Accounting, auditing, and bookkeeping services	X	X	X	X	X	X		X	**7**
1.A.c	Taxation services	X	X	X	X	X			X	**6**
1.A.d	Architectural services	X	X	X	X	X			X	**6**
1.A.e	Engineering services	X	X	X	X	X	X	X	X	**8**
1.A.f	Integrated engineering services	X	X	X	X			X	X	**6**
1.A.g	Urban planning and landscape architectural services	X	X	X	X	X			X	**6**
1.A.h	Medical and dental services		X	X	X	X		X	X	**6**
1.A.i	Veterinary services				X	X	X			**3**
1.A.j	Services provided by midwives, nurses, physiotherapists, and paramedical personnel					X				**1**
1.A.k	Others					X				**1**
1.B	Computer and related services									
1.B.a	Consultancy services related to the installation of computer hardware	X	X	X	X	X		X	X	**7**
1.B.b	Software implementation services	X	X	X	X	X		X	X	**7**
1.B.c	Data processing services	X	X	X	X	X		X	X	**7**
1.B.d	Database services	X		X	X	X		X	X	**6**
1.B.e	Others	X	X	X	X	X			X	**6**
1.C	Research and development services									
1.C.a	Research and development services on natural sciences	X		X		X		X	X	**5**
1.C.b	Research and development services on social sciences and humanities	X		X	X	X			X	**5**
1.C.c	Interdisciplinary research and development services	X		X		X			X	**4**

Code	Sector	Afghanistan	China, People's Republic of	Georgia	Kazakhstan	Kyrgyz Republic	Mongolia	Pakistan	Tajikistan	Total
1.D	Real estate services									
1.D.a	Involving own or leased property		X	X		X				3
1.D.b	On a fee or contract basis		X	X		X				3
1.E	Rental/leasing services without operators									
1.E.a	Relating to ships	X	X	X	X	X			X	6
1.E.b	Relating to aircraft		X	X	X	X			X	5
1.E.c	Relating to other transport equipment	X	X	X	X	X			X	6
1.E.d	Relating to other machinery and equipment	X	X	X	X	X			X	6
1.E.e	Others	X	X	X	X	X			X	6
1.F	Other business services									
1.F.a	Advertising services	X	X	X	X	X			X	6
1.F.b	Market research and public opinion polling services	X		X	X				X	4
1.F.c	Management consulting service	X	X	X	X	X	X		X	7
1.F.d	Services related to management consulting	X		X	X	X			X	5
1.F.e	Technical testing and analysis services	X	X	X	X	X	X	X	X	8
1.F.f	Services incidental to agriculture, hunting, and forestry		X	X	X	X		X	X	6
1.F.g	Services incidental to fishing	X	X	X	X	X			X	6
1.F.h	Services incidental to mining	X		X	X	X	X	X	X	7
1.F.i	Services incidental to manufacturing	X		X	X	X				4
1.F.j	Services incidental to energy distribution	X		X	X	X				4
1.F.k	Placement and supply services of personnel			X						1
1.F.l	Investigation and security				X					1
1.F.m	Related scientific and technical consulting services	X	X	X	X	X	X		X	7
1.F.n	Maintenance and repair of equipment (not including maritime vessels, aircraft)	X	X		X	X			X	5
1.F.o	Building-cleaning services	X								1
1.F.p	Photographic services	X	X	X	X					4
1.F.q	Packaging services	X	X	X	X				X	5
1.F.r	Printing, publishing			X		X			X	3
1.F.s	Convention services	X	X	X	X	X			X	6
1.F.t	Others		X	X		X			X	4

Code	Sector	Afghanistan	China, People's Republic of	Georgia	Kazakhstan	Kyrgyz Republic	Mongolia	Pakistan	Tajikistan	Total
2	**COMMUNICATION SERVICES**									
2.A	Postal services					X	X			**2**
2.B	Courier services	X	X	X	X	X	X		X	**7**
2.C	Telecommunication services									
2.C.a	Voice telephone services	X	X	X	X	X		X	X	**7**
2.C.b	Packet-switched data transmission services	X	X	X	X	X		X	X	**7**
2.C.c	Circuit-switched data transmission services	X	X	X	X	X		X	X	**7**
2.C.d	Telex services	X		X	X	X		X	X	**6**
2.C.e	Telegraph services	X		X	X	X		X	X	**6**
2.C.f	Facsimile services	X	X	X	X	X		X	X	**7**
2.C.g	Private leased circuit services	X	X	X	X	X		X	X	**7**
2.C.h	Electronic mail	X	X	X	X	X	X		X	**7**
2.C.i	Voice mail	X	X	X	X	X	X		X	**7**
2.C.j	Online information and data base retrieval	X	X	X	X	X	X	X	X	**8**
2.C.k	Electronic data interchange	X	X	X	X	X	X		X	**7**
2.C.l	Enhanced/value-added facsimile services, incl. store and forward, store and retrieve	X	X	X	X	X	X		X	**7**
2.C.m	Code and protocol conversion	X	X	X	X	X	X		X	**7**
2.C.n	Online information and/or data processing (including transaction processing)	X	X	X	X	X	X	X	X	**8**
2.C.o	Others	X	X	X	X	X		X	X	**7**
2.D	Audiovisual services									
2.D.a	Motion picture and video tape production and distribution services	X	X	X	X	X			X	**6**
2.D.b	Motion picture projection service		X	X	X	X			X	**5**
2.D.c	Radio and television services			X	X	X			X	**4**
2.D.d	Radio and television transmission services					X				**1**
2.D.e	Sound recording		X	X		X				**3**
2.D.f	Others									

Code	Sector	Afghanistan	China, People's Republic of	Georgia	Kazakhstan	Kyrgyz Republic	Mongolia	Pakistan	Tajikistan	Total
3	**CONSTRUCTION AND RELATED ENGINEERING SERVICES**									
3.A	General construction work for buildings	X	X	X	X	X			X	**6**
3.B	General construction work for civil engineering	X	X	X	X	X		X	X	**7**
3.C	Installation and assembly work		X	X	X	X	X		X	**6**
3.D	Building completion and finishing work		X	X	X	X	X		X	**6**
3.E	Others	X	X	X	X	X			X	**6**
4	**DISTRIBUTION SERVICES**									
4.A	Commission agents' services	X	X	X	X	X			X	**6**
4.B	Wholesale trade services	X	X	X	X	X	X		X	**7**
4.C	Retailing services	X	X	X	X	X	X		X	**7**
4.D	Franchising	X	X	X	X	X			X	**6**
4.E	Others									
5	**EDUCATIONAL SERVICES**									
5.A	Primary education services	X	X	X		X			X	**5**
5.B	Secondary education services	X	X	X		X			X	**5**
5.C	Higher education services	X	X	X	X	X			X	**6**
5.D	Adult education	X	X	X	X	X			X	**6**
5.E	Other education services	X	X		X				X	**4**
6	**ENVIRONMENTAL SERVICES**									
6.A	Sewage services	X	X	X	X	X			X	**6**
6.B	Refuse disposal services	X	X	X	X	X			X	**6**
6.C	Sanitation and similar services	X	X	X	X	X			X	**6**
6.D	Others	X	X	X	X	X			X	**6**
7	**FINANCIAL SERVICES**									
7.A	All insurance and insurance-related services									
7.A.a	Direct insurance (including co-insurance)									
7.A.a.01	Life insurance	X	X	X	X	X	X	X	X	**8**
7.A.a.02	Non-life insurance	X	X	X	X	X	X	X	X	**8**
7.A.b	Reinsurance and retrocession	X	X	X	X	X	X	X	X	**8**
7.A.c	Insurance intermediation, such as brokerage and agency	X	X	X	X	X			X	**6**
7.A.d	Services auxiliary to insurance, such as consultancy, actuarial, risk assessment, and claim settlement services	X	X	X	X	X			X	**6**

Code	Sector	Afghanistan	China, People's Republic of	Georgia	Kazakhstan	Kyrgyz Republic	Mongolia	Pakistan	Tajikistan	Total
7.B	Banking and other financial services (excluding insurance)									
7.B.a	Acceptance of deposits and other repayable funds from the public	X	X	X	X	X	X	X	X	8
7.B.b	Lending of all types, including, among other things, consumer credit, mortgage credit, factoring, and financing of commercial transaction	X	X	X	X	X		X	X	7
7.B.c	Financial leasing	X	X	X	X	X		X	X	7
7.B.d	All payment and money transmission services	X	X	X	X	X	X	X	X	8
7.B.e	Guarantees and commitments	X	X	X	X	X	X	X	X	8
7.B.f	Trading for own account or for account of customers, whether on an exchange, in an over-the-counter									
7.B.f.01	Money market instruments	X		X	X	X	X	X	X	7
7.B.f.02	Foreign exchange	X	X	X	X	X	X	X	X	8
7.B.f.03	Derivative products	X		X	X	X			X	5
7.B.f.04	Exchange rate and interest rate instruments	X		X	X	X	X		X	6
7.B.f.05	Transferable securities	X	X	X	X	X	X	X	X	8
7.B.f.06	Other negotiable instruments and financial assets	X		X	X	X	X	X	X	7
7.B.g	Participation in issues of all kinds of securities, including underwriting and placement	X		X	X	X	X	X	X	7
7.B.h	Money broking	X		X	X	X			X	5
7.B.i	Asset management, such as cash or portfolio management, all forms of collective	X		X	X	X	X	X	X	7
7.B.j	Settlement and clearing services for financial assets, including securities, derivative products	X		X	X	X		X	X	6
7.B.k	Advisory and other auxiliary financial services on all the activities listed in	X	X	X	X	X	X	X	X	8
7.B.l	Provision and transfer of financial information, and financial data processing and related	X	X	X	X	X	X	X	X	8
7.C	Others									
8	**HEALTH RELATED AND SOCIAL SERVICES (other than those listed under 1.A.h-j.)**									
8.A	Hospital services	X		X		X		X	X	5
8.B	Other human health services			X		X				2
8.C	Social services			X		X				2
8.D	Others					X				1

Code	Sector	Afghanistan	China, People's Republic of	Georgia	Kazakhstan	Kyrgyz Republic	Mongolia	Pakistan	Tajikistan	Total
9	**TOURISM AND TRAVEL-RELATED SERVICES**									
9.A	Hotels and restaurants (including catering)	X	X	X	X	X	X	X	X	8
9.B	Travel agencies and tour operators services		X	X	X	X	X	X	X	7
9.C	Tourist guides services					X	X		X	3
9.D	Other					X				1
10.A	Entertainment services (including theatre, live bands, and circus services)			X	X	X			X	4
10.B	News agency services			X	X	X			X	4
10.C	Libraries, archives, museums, and other cultural services				X	X				2
10.D	Sporting and other recreational services	X			X	X				3
10.E	Other					X				1
11	**TRANSPORT SERVICES**									
11.A	Maritime: Transport services									
11.A.a	Maritime: Passenger transportation	X	X		X	X				4
11.A.b	Maritime: Freight transportation	X	X	X	X	X				5
11.A.c	Maritime: Rental of vessels with crew	X		X	X	X				4
11.A.d	Maritime: Maintenance and repair of vessels	X		X	X	X				4
11.A.e	Maritime: Pushing and towing services	X		X		X				3
11.A.f	Supporting services for maritime transport	X			X	X				3
11.B	Internal waterways transport									
11.B.a	Inland waterways: Passenger transportation									
11.B.b	Inland waterways: Freight transportation		X							1
11.B.c	Inland waterways: Rental of vessels with crew				X					1
11.B.d	Inland waterways: Maintenance and repair of vessels				X					1
11.B.e	Inland waterways: Pushing and towing services									
11.B.f	Supporting services for internal waterway transport									
11.C	Air transport services									
11.C.a	Air: Passenger transportation					X				1
11.C.b	Air: Freight transportation					X				1
11.C.c	Rental of aircraft with crew					X				1
11.C.d	Maintenance and repair of aircraft	X	X	X	X	X			X	6
11.C.e	Supporting services for air transport	X	X	X	X	X			X	6

Code	Sector	Afghanistan	China, People's Republic of	Georgia	Kazakhstan	Kyrgyz Republic	Mongolia	Pakistan	Tajikistan	Total
11.D	Space transport									
11.E	Rail transport services									
11.E.a	Rail: Passenger transportation			X		X				2
11.E.b	Rail: Freight transportation		X	X		X				3
11.E.c	Rail: Pushing and towing services			X		X				2
11.E.d	Maintenance and repair of rail transport equipment			X	X	X			X	4
11.E.e	Supporting services for rail transport services					X				1
11.F	Road transport services									
11.F.a	Road: Passenger transportation					X				1
11.F.b	Road: Freight transportation		X	X		X			X	4
11.F.c	Rental of commercial vehicles with operator					X				1
11.F.d	Maintenance and repair of road transport equipment		X	X	X	X			X	5
11.F.e	Supporting services for road transport services					X			X	2
11.G	Pipeline transport									
11.G.a	Transportation of fuels					X			X	2
11.G.b	Transportation of other goods					X				1
11.H	Services auxiliary to all modes of transport									
11.H.a	Cargo-handling services	X	X	X	X	X			X	6
11.H.b	Storage and warehouse services	X	X	X	X	X			X	6
11.H.c	Freight transport agency services	X	X	X	X	X			X	6
11.H.d	Other		X	X	X	X				4
11.I	Other transport services									
12	**OTHER SERVICES NOT INCLUDED ELSEWHERE**									
	TOTAL	**103**	**93**	**125**	**112**	**140**	**37**	**42**	**110**	**762**

WTO = World Trade Organization.

Note: The symbol X indicates the existence of a scheduled WTO commitment. Dates of commitments are based on countries' membership or accession to the WTO: Afghanistan on 29 July 2016, the People's Republic of China on 11 December 2001, Georgia on 14 June 2000, Kazakhstan on 30 November 2015, the Kyrgyz Republic on 20 December 1998, Mongolia on 29 January 1997, Pakistan on 1 January 1995, and Tajikistan on 2 March 2013. Any changes after 15 August 2021 are not reflected.

Source: World Trade Organization. GATS Schedules of Specific Commitments. https://www.wto.org/english/tratop_e/serv_e/serv_commitments_e.htm (accessed September 2020).

REFERENCES

Adlung, R., and S. Miroudot. 2012. Poison in the Wine? Tracing GATS-Minus Commitments in Regional Trade Agreements. *Staff Working Paper ERSD-2012-04*. Geneva: World Trade Organization. http://www.wto.org/english/res_e/reser_e/ersd201204_e.pdf.

Adlung, R., and M. Roy. 2005. Turning Hills into Mountains? Current Commitments Under the GATS and the Prospects for Change. *Staff Working Paper ERSD-2005-01*. Geneva: World Trade Organization. https://www.wto.org/english/res_e/reser_e/ersd200501_e.htm.

Ahmed G., Baisakalov A., Hamrick D., Iskaliyeva A., Molochanovkiy V., Nahapetyan S., and Seidek S. 2017. *The Wheat Value Chain in Kazakhstan*. National Analytical Center, Nazarbayev University, Astana, and Duke University Global Value Chains Center, Duke University, Durham, North Carolina. https://gvcc.duke.edu/wp-content/uploads/Wheat-Report-R4-PRINT.pdf.

Ali, A. T. 2016. Malaysia's Move Toward a High-Income Economy: Five Decades of Nation Building—A View from Within. In R. Cherif, F. Hasanov and M. Zhu, eds. *Breaking the Oil Spell: The Gulf Falcons' Path to Diversification*. Washington, DC: IMF. https://doi.org/10.5089/9781513537863.071.

Amin, M. and A. Mattoo. 2006. Do Institutions Matter More for Services? *Policy Research Working Paper No. 4032*. Washington, DC: World Bank. https://openknowledge.worldbank.org/bitstream/handle/10986/9014/wps4032.pdf?sequence=1&isAllowed=y.

Arnold, J. M., B. S. Javorcik, and A. Mattoo. 2011. Does Services Liberalization Benefit Manufacturing Firms? Evidence from the Czech Republic. *Journal of International Economics* 85(1):136–146. https://www.sciencedirect.com/science/article/abs/pii/S0022199611000523?via%3Dihub.

Arvis, J. F., G. Raballand, and J. Marteau. 2011. Total Logistics Cost on a Transit Corridor. In J. F. Arvis and R. Carruthers, eds. *Connecting Landlocked Developing Countries to Markets: Trade Corridors in the 21st Century*. Washington, DC: World Bank. https://openknowledge.worldbank.org/handle/10986/2286.

Asian Development Bank (ADB). 2006. *Central Asia: Increasing Gains from Trade Through Regional Cooperation in Trade Policy, Transport, and Customs Transit.* Manila. https://www.adb.org/sites/default/files/publication/29927/central-asia-trade-policy.pdf.

_____. 2009. *Asian Development Outlook 2009: Rebalancing Asia's Growth.* Manila. https://www.adb.org/sites/default/files/publication/27704/ado2009.pdf.

_____. 2010. *Asian Development Outlook 2010: Macroeconomic Management Beyond the Crisis.* Manila. https://www.adb.org/sites/default/files/publication/27701/ado2010.pdf.

_____. 2013. *Developing the Service Sector as an Engine of Growth for Asia.* Manila. https://www.adb.org/sites/default/files/publication/31114/developing-service-sector-engine-growth-asia.pdf.

_____. 2015. *Digital Economy Study in Central and West Asia (Unleashing the Potential of the Internet in Central Asia, South Asia, the Caucasus and Beyond).* Consultant's report. Manila. https://www.adb.org/sites/default/files/project-document/178531/unleashing-internet-potential-central-asia-south-asia-caucasus-and-beyond.pdf.

_____. 2017. *Unlocking the Potential of Railways: A Railway Strategy for CAREC, 2017–2030.* Manila. https://www.adb.org/documents/railway-strategy-carec-2017-2030.

_____. 2018a. *Embracing the E-Commerce Revolution in Asia and the Pacific.* Manila. https://www.adb.org/sites/default/files/publication/430401/embracing-e-commerce-revolution.pdf.

_____. 2018b. *Completion Report: Uzbekistan: Small Business and Enterprise Development Project.* Manila. https://www.adb.org/sites/default/files/project-documents/42007/42007-014-pcr-en.pdf.

_____. 2018c. Republic of Uzbekistan: Horticulture Value Chain Infrastructure Project. Project Number: 51041-002. https://www.adb.org/projects/51041-002/main.

_____. 2019a. *CAREC Integrated Trade Agenda 2030 and Rolling Strategic Action Plan 2018–2020.* Manila. https://www.adb.org/sites/default/files/institutional-document/490576/carec-trade-agenda-2030-action-plan-2018-2020.pdf.

_____. 2019b. *Promoting Regional Tourism Cooperation Under CAREC 2030: A Scoping Study.* Manila. https://www.adb.org/sites/default/files/publication/490681/carec-2030-regional-tourism-cooperation-study.pdf.

_____. 2019c. *Education and Skills Development Under the CAREC Program: A Scoping Study.* Manila. https://www.adb.org/sites/default/files/publication/526901/education-skills-carec-program.pdf.

_____. 2019d. *Modernizing Sanitary and Phytosanitary Measures in CAREC: An Assessment and the Way Forward.* Manila. https://www.adb.org/sites/default/files/publication/506151/modernizing-sanitary-phytosanitary-carec.pdf.

_____. 2019e. *CAREC Integrated Agenda Issues Papers.* Manila. https://www.adb.org/publications/carec-trade-agenda-2030-issue-papers.

_____. 2020. *CAREC Tourism Strategy 2030.* Manila. https://www.adb.org/sites/default/files/institutional-document/668406/carec-tourism-strategy-2030.pdf.

_____. 2021a. *Asian Development Outlook (ADO) 2021 Supplement: Renewed Outbreaks and Divergent Recoveries.* https://www.adb.org/publications/ado-supplement-july-2021.

_____. 2021b. ADB Data Show the Extent of COVID-19 Trade Disruption in Developing Asia. https://www.adb.org/news/features/adb-data-show-extent-covid-19-trade-disruption-developing-asia.

_____. 2021c. *Asian Development Outlook (ADO) 2021 Update: Transforming Agriculture in Asia.* Manila. https://www.adb.org/publications/asian-development-outlook-2021-update.

_____. 2021d. Mongolia: Climate-Resilient and Sustainable Livestock Development Project. https://www.adb.org/projects/53038-001/main.

_____. 2021e. *E-Commerce in CAREC Countries: Laws and Policies.* Manila. https://www.adb.org/publications/e-commerce-carec-laws-policies.

Asian Development Bank Institute (ADBI). 2014. *Connecting Central Asia with Economic Centers.* Tokyo: ADBI. https://www.adb.org/sites/default/files/publication/159307/adbi-connecting-central-asia-economic-centers-final-report.pdf.

_____. 2019. *Leveraging Services for Development: Prospects and Policies.* Tokyo: ADBI. https://www.adb.org/publications/leveraging-services-development-prospects-policies.

Bacchetta, M. and R. Piermartini. 2011. The Value of Bindings. *Staff Working Paper ERSD-2005-01.* Geneva: World Trade Organization. https://www.wto.org/english/res_e/reser_e/ersd201113_e.htm.

Baldwin, R. E. 2019. *The Globotics Upheaval: Globalization, Robotics, and the Future of Work.* Oxford: Oxford University Press.

Barone, G. and F. Cingano. 2011. Service Regulation and Growth: Evidence from OECD Countries. *Economic Journal* 121(555):931–957. https://onlinelibrary.wiley.com/doi/abs/10.1111/j.1468-0297.2011.02433.x.

Baumol, W. J. and W. G. Bowen. 1965. On the Performing Arts: The Anatomy of Their Economic Problems. *American Economic Review* 55(1/2):495–502. http://www.jstor.org/stable/1816292.

Boylaud, O. and G. Nicoletti. 2001. Regulation, Market Structure and Performance in Telecommunications. *OECD Economics Department Working Papers.* No. 237. Paris: OECD Publishing. https://www.oecd.org/economy/outlook/2736298.pdf.

Buccirossi, P., L. Ciari, T. Duso, G. Spagnolo, and C. Vitale. 2013. Competition Policy and Productivity Growth: An Empirical Assessment. *The Review of Economics and Statistics* 95(4):1324–1336. https://direct. mit.edu/rest/article-abstract/95/4/1324/58286/Competition-Policy-and-Productivity-Growth-An?redirectedFrom=fulltext.

Calderwood L. and Soshkin M. 2019. *The Travel & Tourism Competitiveness Report 2019: Travel and Tourism at a Tipping Point.* Geneva: World Economic Forum. https://www3.weforum.org/docs/ WEF_TTCR_2019.pdf.

Campbell, D., and P. Ronnas. 2019. Good Jobs and the Labor Market. In G. Capannelli and R. Kanbur, eds. *Good Jobs for Inclusive Growth in Central Asia and the South Caucasus.* Manila: ADB. https://www.adb.org/sites/default/files/publication/489856/jobs-inclusive-growth-central-asia-caucasus.pdf.

Capannelli, G. and R. Kanbur, eds. 2019. *Good Jobs for Inclusive Growth in Central Asia and the South Caucasus.* Manila: ADB. https://www.adb.org/sites/default/files/publication/489856/jobs-inclusive-growth-central-asia-caucasus.pdf.

CAREC Institute. 2019. Regional Value Chains in CAREC: The Case of Kyrgyzstan Garment Industry. *Working Paper.* Urumqi: CAREC Institute. https://www.carecinstitute.org/wp-content/ uploads/2019/11/CI-KM-KGZ-Garment-Industry-GVC-14-Nov-2019.pdf.

Center for International Development of Harvard University. Atlas of Economic Complexity. https://atlas.cid.harvard.edu/rankings.

Cherif, R. and F. Hasanov. 2016. Soaring of the Gulf Falcons: Diversification in the GCC Oil Exporters in Seven Propositions. In R. Cherif, F. Hasanov and M. Zhu, eds. *Breaking the Oil Spell: The Gulf Falcons' Path to Diversification.* Washington, DC: IMF. https://doi.org/10.5089/9781513537863.071.

Cherif, R., G. Hasanov and M. Zhu, eds. 2016. *Breaking the Oil Spell: The Gulf Falcon's Path to Diversification.* Washington, DC: IMF. https://doi.org/10.5089/9781513537863.071.

Cheung, D., Low, P. and Sit D. *Case Study: Hong Kong-based Bakery Chain, FGI Services in Global Value Chains Project.* Hong Kong, China: Fung Global Institute (unpublished).

Clarke, G. R. G. 2008. Has the Internet Increased Exports for Firms from Low and Middle-Income Countries? *Information Economics and Policy* 20(1):16–37. https://www.sciencedirect.com/ science/article/abs/pii/S0167624507000418.

Cornell University, INSEAD and World Intellectual Property Organization. 2019. *Global Innovation Index 2019: Creating Healthy Lives—The Future of Medical Innovation.* Ithaca, Fontainebleau and Geneva. https://www.wipo.int/edocs/pubdocs/en/wipo_pub_gii_2019.pdf.

Demirgüç-Kunt, A., L. Klapper, D. Singer, S. Ansar, and J. Hess. 2018. *Global Findex Database 2017: Measuring Financial Inclusion and the Fintech Revolution*. Washington, DC: World Bank. https://openknowledge.worldbank.org/handle/10986/29510.

Dennis, A. and B. Shepherd. 2007. Trade Costs, Barriers to Entry, and Export Diversification in Developing Countries. *World Bank Policy Research Working Paper 4368*. https://openknowledge. worldbank.org/bitstream/handle/10986/7385/WPS4368.pdf?sequence=1&isAllowed=y.

Elms D. and Haines W. *Case Study: An Apparel Firm in Indonesia, FGI Services in Global Value Chains Project*. Hong Kong, China: Fung Global Institute (unpublished).

Eschenbach, F. and B. Hoekman. 2006. Services Policy Reform and Economic Growth in Transition Economies. *Review of World Economics* 142:746–764. https://link.springer.com/article/10.1007/ s10290-006-0091-7.

European Bank for Reconstruction and Development (EBRD). 2019. *Transition Report 2019–2020: Better Governance, Better Economies*. London: EBRD. https://www.ebrd.com/transition-report.

Faber, B. and C. Gaubert. 2019. Tourism and Economic Development: Evidence from Mexico's Coastline. *American Economic Review* 109(6):2245–2293. https://pubs.aeaweb.org/doi/ pdfplus/10.1257/aer.20161434.

Fisman, R. and J. Svensson. 2007. Are Corruption and Taxation Really Harmful to Growth? Firm Level Evidence. *Journal of Development Economics* 83(1):63–75 https://www.sciencedirect.com/ science/article/abs/pii/S0304387806001106?via%3Dihub.

Francois, J. and F. Eschenbach. 2002. Financial Sector Competition, Services Trade, and Growth. *Tinbergen Institute Working Paper No. 2002-089/2*. Netherlands: Tinbergen Institute. https://ssrn.com/abstract=335440.

Francois, J. and B. Hoekman. 2010. Services Trade and Policy. *Journal of Economic Literature* 48(3):642–692. https://pubs.aeaweb.org/doi/pdfplus/10.1257/jel.48.3.642.

Ganiev B. 2019. Growth Performance and Prospects of the Countries of Central Asia and the South Caucasus. In G. Capannelli and R. Kanbur, eds. *Good Jobs for Inclusive Growth in Central Asia and the South Caucasus*. Manila: ADB. https://www.adb.org/sites/default/files/publication/489856/ jobs-inclusive-growth-central-asia-caucasus.pdf.

Gatti, P. 2013. Tourism, Welfare and Income Distribution: The Case of Croatia. *Tourism: An Interdisciplinary Journal* 61(1):53–71. https://hrcak.srce.hr/101422.

Ghani, E. 2010. Is Service-Led Growth a Miracle for South Asia? In E. Ghani, ed. *The Service Revolution in South Asia*. Oxford: Oxford University Press.

GIZ and Euromonitor. 2017. *Analysis of Priority Markets for Diversification of Export of Products from Central Asia.* https://www.giz.de/de/downloads/GIZ%20-%20Euromonitor-%20Central%20 Asia%20Trade%20Facilitation_Fresh%20Fruit%20report%20-%20Eng_s.pdf.

Gorodnichenko, Y., J. Svejnar, and K. Terrell. 2010. Globalization and Innovation in Emerging Markets. *American Economic Journal* 2(2):194–226. https://www.jstor.org/stable/25760301.

Goyal, A. 2015. Growth Drivers: ICT and Inclusive Innovations. In P. Agrawal, ed. *Reviving Growth in India.* Cambridge: Cambridge University Press. https://www.cambridge.org/ core/books/abs/reviving-growth-in-india/growth-drivers-ict-and-inclusive-innovations/ C9745FAD2665EEDC6D8DE7FFDDE32FCE#.

Hajdinjak, S. 2014. Impact of Tourism on Economic Growth in Croatia. *Enlightening Tourism. A Pathmaking Journal* 4(1):30–51. http://www.uhu.es/publicaciones/ojs/index.php/et/article/ view/2427.

Hoekman, B. and B. Shepherd. 2017. Services Productivity, Trade Policy and Manufacturing Exports. *World Economy* 40(3):499–516. https://onlinelibrary.wiley.com/doi/10.1111/twec.12333.

Hoekman, B. and D. W. te Velde, eds. 2017. *Trade in Services and Economic Transformation: A New Development Policy Priority.* London: Overseas Development Institute. https://set.odi.org/wp-content/uploads/2017/02/SET-essays.pdf.

Hollweg, C. and M. H. Wong. 2009. Measuring Regulatory Restrictions in Logistics Services. *ERIA Discussion Paper Series 2009-14.* https://www.eria.org/ERIA-DP-2009-14.pdf.

Humlum, A. and J. R. Munch. 2019. Globalization, Flexicurity and Adult Vocational Training in Denmark. In M. Bacchetta, E. Milet and J. A. Monteiro, eds. *Making Globalization More Inclusive: Lessons from Experience with Adjustment Policies.* Geneva: World Trade Organization. https://www.wto-ilibrary.org/economic-research-and-trade-policy-analysis/making-globalization-more-inclusive_81bbf1f1-en.

International Labor Organization. ILOStat. https://www.ilo.org/shinyapps/bulkexplorer35/?lang=en&se gment=indicator&id=EMP_2EMP_SEX_ECO_NB_A.

International Monetary Fund (IMF). 2018a. *World Economic Outlook April 2018: Cyclical Upswing, Structural Change.* Washington, DC: IMF. https://www.imf.org/en/Publications/WEO/ Issues/2018/03/20/world-economic-outlook-april-2018.

_____. 2018b. Manufacturing Jobs: Implications for Productivity and Inequality. In *IMF World Economic Outlook 2018.* Washington, DC: IMF. http://governance40.com/wp-content/uploads/2018/12/ WEO-2018.pdf.

_____. 2018c. Opening Up in the Caucasus and Central Asia: Policy Frameworks to Support Regional and Global Integration. *Middle East and Central Asia Department Working Paper No. 18/07.* Washington, DC: IMF. https://www.elibrary.imf.org/view/journals/087/2018/007/087.2018.issue-007-en.xml.

_____. 2018d. Building Resilient Banking Sectors in the Caucasus and Central Asia. *Middle East and Central Asia Department Working Paper No. 18/08.* Washington, DC: IMF. https://www.elibrary.imf.org/view/journals/087/2018/010/article-A001-en.xml.

_____. 2020. *Georgia: Staff Report for the Sixth Review Under the Extended Arrangement.* IMF Country Report. No. 20/149. Washington, DC: IMF. https://www.imf.org/en/Publications/CR/Issues/2020/05/05/Georgia-Sixth-Review-Under-the-Extended-Arrangement-and-Requests-for-a-Waiver-of-49394.

_____. Direction of Trade Statistics. https://data.imf.org/regular.aspx?key=61013712.

International Organization for Standardization. ISO Survey 2019. https://isotc.iso.org/livelink/livelink?func=ll&objId=18808772&objAction=browse&viewType=1.

Jakubik, A. and R. Piermartini. 2019. How WTO Commitments Tame Uncertainty. *Staff Working Paper* ERSD-2019-06. Geneva: World Trade Organization. https://www.wto.org/english/res_e/reser_e/ersd201906_e.htm.

Jorgensen, D. W. and M. P. Timmer. 2011. Structural Change in Advanced Nations: A New Set of Stylised Facts. *Scandinavian Journal of Economics* 113(1):1–29. https://scholar.harvard.edu/files/jorgenson/files/sje_jorgenson_timmer_publication.pdf.

Kang, J., P. Crivelli, M. C. Tayag, and D. Ramizo. 2020. *Regional Comprehensive Economic Partnership: Overview and Economic Impact.* ADB Briefs No. 164. Manila. https://www.adb.org/sites/default/files/publication/664096/adb-brief-164-regional-comprehensive-economic-partnership.pdf.

Kellermann M. 2019. *Ensuring Quality to Gain Access to Global Markets: A Reform Toolkit.* Washington, DC: The World Bank Group https://thedocs.worldbank.org/en/doc/249621553265195570-0090022019/original/FullQIToolkitReport.pdf.

Khatiwada, S. and J. P. Flaminiano. 2019. What are the Prospects for Decent Work in Services? In ADBI. M. Helble and B. Shepherd, eds. *Leveraging Services for Development: Prospects and Policies.* Tokyo: ADBI. https://www.adb.org/sites/default/files/publication/506216/adbi-leveraging-services-development-prospects-policies.pdf#page=280.

Kohli, H. S., J. F. Linn, and L. M. Zucker, eds. 2020. *China's Belt and Road Initiative: Potential Transformation of Central Asia and the South Caucasus.* New Delhi: SAGE Publishing India. https://us.sagepub.com/en-us/nam/china%E2%80%99s-belt-and-road-initiative/ book272734#description.

Koren, M. and S. Tenreyro. 2007. Volatility and Development. *The Quarterly Journal of Economics* 122(1):243–287. https://doi.org/10.1162/qjec.122.1.243.

Lazaro, D., G. Samad, L. de Dios, and A. R. Tafgar. 2021. *Expanding Agri-Trade in Central Asia Through the Use of Electronic Certificates.* ADB Briefs No. 184. Manila. https://www.adb.org/publications/agri-trade-central-asia-electronic-certificates.

Levchenko, A. A. 2007. Institutional Quality and International Trade. *Review of Economic Studies* 74(3):791–819. https://www.jstor.org/stable/4626161.

Linn, J. F. 2015. Creating a Competitive and Innovative Manufacturing and Service Economy. In R. M. Nag, J. F. Linn and H. S. Kohli, eds. *Central Asia 2050: Unleashing the Region's Potential.* Nur-Sultan: National Analytical Center of Nazarbayev University. http://www.centennial-group. com/publication/central-asia-2050-unleashing-the-regions-potential/.

Low, P. and G. Pasadilla. 2016. *Services in Global Value Chains: Manufacturing-Related Services.* Singapore: World Scientific.

Madhur, S. 2016. Pursuing Open Regionalism for Shared Prosperity. In R. Nag, J. F. Linn, and H. S. Kohli, eds. *Central Asia 2050: Unleashing the Region's Potential.* Nur-Sultan: National Analytical Center of Nazarbayev University. https://doi.org/10.1177%2F0974910116634476.

Manyika, J. and C. Roxburgh. 2011. *The Great Transformer: The Impact of the Internet on Economic Growth and Prosperity.* New York: McKinsey Global Institute. October. https://www.mckinsey.com/ industries/technology-media-and-telecommunications/our-insights/the-great-transformer.

Mattoo, A., R. Rathindran, and A. Subramanian. 2006. Measuring Services Trade Liberalization and Its Impact on Economic Growth: An Illustration. *Journal of Economic Integration* 21(1):64–98. https://www.e-jei.org/upload/4Q358PDD5KW32JFU.pdf.

Mazhar, M. S., B. E. Bajwa, G. McEvilly, G. Palaniappan, and M. R. Kazmi. 2019. Improving Vegetable Value Chains in Pakistan for Sustainable Livelihood of Farming Communities. *Journal of Environmental and Agricultural Sciences* 18:1–9. https://core.ac.uk/reader/211026830.

Mercer-Blackman, V. and C. Ablaza. 2018. The Servicification of Manufacturing in Asia: Redefining the Sources of Labor Productivity. *ADBI Working Paper* No. 902. Tokyo: ADBI. https://www.adb.org/ sites/default/files/publication/471531/adbi-wp902.pdf.

Minges, M. 2021. Developing E-Commerce in CAREC Countries: Current State and Challenges in Infrastructure Development. *CAREC Institute Policy Brief.* Urumqi: CAREC Institute. https://www.carecinstitute.org/wp-content/uploads/2021/05/CI-e-commerce-infra-policy-brief-May-2021-1.pdf.

Ministry of Economy and Sustainable Development of Georgia and Georgian National Tourism Administration. 2015. *Georgian Tourism in Figures: Structure and Industry Data.* Tbilisi. https://gnta.ge/wp-content/uploads/2014/08/ENG-new.pdf.

Miroudot, S. 2019. Services and Manufacturing in Global Value Chains: Is the Distinction Obsolete? *ADBI Working Paper* No. 927. Tokyo: ADBI. https://www.adb.org/sites/default/files/publication/488556/adbi-wp927.pdf.

Miroudot, S., J. Sauvage, and B. Shepherd. 2012. Trade Costs and Productivity in Services Sectors. *Economics Letters* 114(1):36–38. https://developing-trade.com/wp-content/uploads/2014/11/DTC-Article-Chapter-2011-1.pdf.

Miroudot, S., J. Sauvage and M. Sudreau. 2010. Multilateralising Regionalism: How Preferential Are Services Commitments in Regional Trade Agreements? *OECD Trade Policy Papers* No.106. Paris: OECD Publishing. https://www.oecd-ilibrary.org/docserver/5km362n24t8n-en.pdf?expires=1634905749&id=id&accname=guest&checksum=92C9CA48143A8F563E5090C47F614D2F.

Morgan, P. J., Y. Zhang and D. Kydyrbayev. 2018. Overview of Financial Inclusion, Regulation, Financial Literacy, and Education in Central Asia and South Caucasus. *ADBI Working Paper* No. 878. https://www.adb.org/sites/default/files/publication/460221/adbi-wp878.pdf.

National Statistics Office of Georgia. 2021. https://www.geostat.ge/en.

National Statistics Committee of the Kyrgyz Republic. 2015. http://stat.kg/en/.

Nayyar, G. and M. Cruz. 2018. Developing Countries and Services in the New Industrial Paradigm. *World Bank Policy Research Working Paper* 8659. Washington DC: World Bank. https://openknowledge.worldbank.org/handle/10986/30981.

Nayyar, G., M. Cruz, and L. Zhu. 2018. Does Premature Deindustrialization Matter? The Role of Manufacturing Versus Services in Development. *World Bank Policy Research Working Paper* 8596. Washington DC: World Bank. https://doi.org/10.1596/1813-9450-8596.

Nunn, N. 2007. Relationship-Specificity, Incomplete Contracts, and the Pattern of Trade. *The Quarterly Journal of Economics,* 122(2):569–600. https://academic.oup.com/qje/article-abstract/122/2/569/1942086?redirectedFrom=fulltext.

Ookla. Speedtest Global Index. https://www.speedtest.net/global-index.

Organisation for Economic Co-operation and Development (OECD). 2011. *Developing Skills in Central Asia Through Better Vocational Education and Training Systems. Private Sector Development Policy Handbook.* Paris: OECD. https://www.oecd.org/global-relations/VocationalEducation.pdf.

OECD. 2012. Recommendation of the Council on Regulatory Policy and Governance. Paris: OECD. https://www.oecd.org/governance/regulatory-policy/2012-recommendation.htm.

OECD. 2013. The OECD-WTO Trade in Value Added (TiVA) Database. https://www.oecd.org/sdd/its/tiva-nowcast.htm.

OECD. 2018. *Enhancing Competitiveness in Central Asia.* In Competitiveness and Private Sector Development. Paris: OECD Publishing. https://www.oecd-ilibrary.org/docserver/9789264288133-en.pdf?expires=1634897058&id=id&accname=guest&checksum=757C9424B676B62C123752193531A294.

OECD. 2019. *PISA 2018 Results (Volume I): What Students Know and Can Do.* Paris: PISA, OECD Publishing. https://doi.org/10.1787/5f07c754-en.

OECD. 2020. Best Practice Principles for Regulatory Impact Analysis. In *Regulatory Impact Assessment.* Paris: OECD Publishing. https://www.oecd-ilibrary.org/docserver/663f08d9-en.pdf?expires=1636101021&id=id&accname=guest&checksum=DB403BDDD4BCC2429C5BCBAC783428AB.

Pavlić, I., M. Š. Tolić, and T. Svilokos. 2015. Tourism, Real Effective Exchange Rate and Economic Growth: Empirical Evidence for Croatia. *International Journal of Tourism Research* 17(3):282–291. https://onlinelibrary.wiley.com/doi/10.1002/jtr.1986.

Pillai, J. S., A. Sindila and A. Nagornova. 2018. Research and Development Transformation in Central Asia: University-Led Research Consortiums. *Eurasian Journal of Business and Economics* 11(22):1–27. https://www.ejbe.org/EJBE2018Vol11No22p001PILLAI-SINDILA-NAGORNOVA.pdf.

Price, N. A., J. P. Francisco, and C. E. Caboverde. 2016. IT-BPO in the Philippines: A Driver of Shared Prosperity? *Working Paper* 16-002. Manila: Asian Institute of Management. http://dx.doi.org/10.2139/ssrn.2880408.

Purdy, M. and P. Daugherty. 2016. *Why Artificial Intelligence is the Future of Growth.* Dublin: Accenture. https://dl.icdst.org/pdfs/files2/2aea5d87070f0116f8aaa9f545530e47.pdf.

Rillo, A. D. and S. Nugroho. 2016. Promoting Agricultural Value Chain Integration in Central Asia and the Caucasus. *ADBI Policy Brief No. 2016-4.* November. https://www.adb.org/publications/promoting-agricultural-value-chain-integration-central-asia-and-caucasus.

Rodrik, D. 2016. Premature Deindustrialization. *Journal of Economic Growth* 21:1–33. https://doi.org/10.1007/s10887-015-9122-3.

Roy, M., J. Marchetti, and H. Lim. 2006. Services Liberalization in the New Generation of Preferential Trade Agreements (PTAs): How Much Further than the GATS? *Staff Working Paper ERSD-2006-07*. Geneva: World Trade Organization. https://www.wto.org/english/res_e/reser_e/ersd200607_e.pdf.

Sahay, R., M. Čihák, P. N'Diaye, A. Barajas, S. Mitra, A. Kyobe, Y. N. Mooi, and S. R. Yousefi. 2015. Financial Inclusion: Can It Meet Multiple Macroeconomic Goals? *IMF Staff Discussion Note SDN/15/17*. September. https://www.imf.org/external/pubs/ft/sdn/2015/sdn1517.pdf.

Sahoo, P. and R. K. Dash. 2017. What Drives India's Surge in Service Exports? *The World Economy* 40(2):439–461. https://onlinelibrary.wiley.com/doi/epdf/10.1111/twec.12411.

Schwab, K. 2019. *The Global Competitiveness Report 2019*. Geneva: Word Economic Forum. https://www3.weforum.org/docs/WEF_TheGlobalCompetitivenessReport2019.pdf.

Shepherd, B. 2019. Services Policies and Manufacturing Exports. In ADBI. *Leveraging Services for Development: Prospects and Policies*. Tokyo: ADBI. https://www.adb.org/sites/default/files/publication/506216/adbi-leveraging-services-development-prospects-policies.pdf#page=171.

Silve, F. and A. Plekhanov. 2018. Institutions, Innovation and Growth. *Economics of Transition* 26(3):335–362. https://papers.ssrn.com/sol3/papers.cfm?abstract_id=3190743.

Soprana, M. 2016. Services Liberalization in Transition Economies: The Case of North and Central Asia. *UNESCAP ARTNeT Working Paper* No. 162. https://www.unescap.org/resources/services-liberalization-transition-economies-case-north-and-central-asia-awp-no-162.

State Council of the PRC. 2020. Pilot Project Approved to Innovate and Develop Services Trade. News release. 11 August.http://english.www.gov.cn/policies/latestreleases/202008/11/content_WS5f32852cc6d029c1c263792c.html.

_____. 2021. China Releases Negative List for Cross-border Services Trade in Hainan. News release. 26 July. http://english.www.gov.cn/statecouncil/ministries/202107/26/content_WS60fe1051c6d0df57f98dd933.html.

Tan, S. W. 2017. Digital Trade in Europe and Central Asia. *ADBI Working Paper Series No. 751*. Tokyo: ADBI. https://www.adb.org/sites/default/files/publication/324996/adbi-wp751.pdf.

Timmer, M. P. 2012. *The World Input-Output Database (WIOD): Contents, Sources and Methods*. http://dx.doi.org/10.13140/RG.2.1.2863.8802.

Transparency International. 2020. Corruption Perception Index. https://www.transparency.org/en/cpi/2020/index/nzl.

United Nations. 1990. International Standard Industrial Classification of All Economic Activities. Statistical Papers, Series M, Number 4, Revision 3. New York. https://unstats.un.org/unsd/classifications/Econ/ISIC#ISIC3.

United Nations Conference on Trade and Development (UNCTAD). UNCTADStat. https://unctadstat.unctad.org/wds.

_____. 2017. *The Role of the Services Economy and Trade in Structural Transformation and Inclusive Development.* Geneva: UNCTAD. https://unctad.org/system/files/official-document/c1mem4d14_en.pdf.

_____. 2020. The UNCTAD B2C E-Commerce Index 2020: Spotlight on Latin America and the Caribbean. *UNCTAD Technical Notes on ICT for Development* No. 17. Geneva: UNCTAD. https://unctad.org/system/files/official-document/tn_unctad_ict4d17_en.pdf.

Woo, M. 2016. Industrial Diversification in Korea: History in Search of Lessons. In Cherif, R., F. Hasanov and M. Zhu, eds. *Breaking the Oil Spell: The Gulf Falcons' Path to Diversification.* Washington, DC: IMF. https://doi.org/10.5089/9781513537863.071.

World Bank. World Development Indicators. https://databank.worldbank.org/source/world-development-indicators.

_____. Worldwide Government Indicators. https://info.worldbank.org/governance/wgi/.

_____. 2011a. *Learning for All: Investing in People's Knowledge and Skills to Promote Development.* Washington, DC: World Bank. https://openknowledge.worldbank.org/bitstream/handle/10986/27790/649590WP0REPLA00WB0EdStrategy0final.pdf?sequence=1&isAllowed=y.

_____. 2011b. *Harnessing Quality for Global Competitiveness in Eastern Europe and Central Asia.* Washington, DC: World Bank. https://openknowledge.worldbank.org/bitstream/handle/10986/2305/618960PUB0Harn000public00BOX358355B.pdf?sequence=1&isAllowed=y.

_____. 2015. *Global Financial Development Report 2015/2016: Long-Term Finance.* Washington, DC: World Bank. https://openknowledge.worldbank.org/handle/10986/22543.

_____. 2016. *World Development Report 2016: Digital Dividends.* Washington, DC: World Bank. https://www.worldbank.org/en/publication/wdr2016.

_____. 2017a. *Europe and Central Asia Economic Update: Trade in Transition.* Washington DC: World Bank. https://openknowledge.worldbank.org/bitstream/handle/10986/26497/9781464811135.pdf?sequence=5&isAllowed=y.

_____. 2017b. Economic Diversification: Guidance Note. Washington, DC: World Bank. https://ieg.worldbankgroup.org/sites/default/files/Data/reports/EconomicDiversification.pdf.

_____. 2017c. *A Step Ahead: Competition Policy for Shared Prosperity and Inclusive Growth.* Washington, DC: World Bank. https://openknowledge.worldbank.org/handle/10986/27527.

_____. 2018a. *Connecting to Compete 2018: Trade Logistics in the Global Economy.* Washington, DC: World Bank. https://openknowledge.worldbank.org/bitstream/handle/10986/29971/LPI2018.pdf?sequence=1&isAllowed=y.

_____. 2018b. *World Development Report 2019: The Changing Nature of Work.* Washington, DC: World Bank. https://www.worldbank.org/en/publication/wdr2019.

_____. 2018c. *Fostering Competition in the Philippines: The Challenge of Restrictive Regulations.* Washington, DC: World Bank. https://www.worldbank.org/en/country/philippines/publication/fostering-competition-in-the-philippines-the-challenge-of-restrictive-regulation.

_____. 2019a. Mongolia Central Economic Corridor Assessment: A Value Chain Analysis of the Cashmere-Wool, Meat, and Leather Industries. Report No. AUS0000216. Washington DC: World Bank. https://openknowledge.worldbank.org/bitstream/handle/10986/31767/Mongolia-Central-Economic-Corridor-Assessment-A-Value-Chain-Analysis-of-Wool-Cashmere-Meat-and-Leather-Industries.pdf?sequence=1&isAllowed=y.

_____. 2019b. *Belt and Road Economics: Opportunities and Risks of Transport Corridors.* Washington, DC: World Bank. https://www.worldbank.org/en/topic/regional-integration/publication/belt-and-road-economics-opportunities-and-risks-of-transport-corridors.

_____. 2020. *Beyond Arrivals: Emerging Opportunities for Georgian Firms in Tourism Value Chains.* Report No. AUS0000777. Washington DC: World Bank. https://documents1.worldbank.org/curated/en/264181575569238865/pdf/Georgia-Beyond-Arrivals-Emerging-Opportunities-for-Georgian-Firms-in-Tourism-Value-Chains.pdf.

World Trade Organization (WTO). Regional Trade Agreements Database. http://rtais.wto.org/UI/PublicAllRTAList.aspx.

_____. Trade in Services Data by Mode of Supply (TISMOS). https://www.wto.org/english/res_e/statis_e/trade_datasets_e.htm.

_____. WTO Data. https://data.wto.org/.

_____. 2010. Balanced International Trade in Services Extended Balance of Payments Services. https://www.wto.org/english/res_e/statis_e/trade_datasets_e.htm.

_____. 2015. *Trade Policy Review: Report by the Secretariat. Mauritius*. Geneva: WTO. WT/TPR/S/304/Rev.1.

_____. 2019a. *Trade Policy Review: Report by the Secretariat. East African Community (EAC)*. Geneva: WTO. https://www.wto.org/english/tratop_e/tpr_e/s384_e.pdf.

_____. 2019b. *World Trade Report 2019: The Future of Services Trade*. Geneva: WTO. https://www.wto.org/english/res_e/booksp_e/00_wtr19_e.pdf.

_____. 2020. *Trade in Services and Economic Diversification*. Discussion Paper for the G20 Trade and Investment Working Group. 14 February. https://www.wto.org/english/tratop_e/serv_e/trade_services_economic_diversification_e.pdf.

_____. 2021. *World Trade Statistical Review 2021*. Geneva: WTO. https://www.wto.org/english/res_e/statis_e/wts2021_e/wts21_toc_e.htm.

World Travel and Tourism Council. 2021. *Croatia: 2021 Annual Research: Key Highlights*. London: WTTC. https://wttc.org/Research/Economic-Impact/moduleId/704/itemId/96/controller/DownloadRequest/action/QuickDownload.

Young, A. 2014. Structural Transformation, the Mismeasurement of Productivity Growth, and the Cost Disease of Services. *American Economic Review* 104(11): 3635–3667. https://pubs.aeaweb.org/doi/pdfplus/10.1257/aer.104.11.3635.

Yusof, Z. A. 2013. *Economic Diversification: The Case of Malaysia*. New York: Revenue Watch Institute. https://resourcegovernance.org/sites/default/files/RWI_Econ_Diversification_Malaysia.pdf.

Zafar, A. 2011. Mauritius: An Economic Success Story. Chapter 5 in P. Chuhan-Pole and M. Angwafo, eds. *Yes Africa Can: Success Stories from a Dynamic Continent*. Washington DC: in World Bank. https://documents1.worldbank.org/curated/en/304221468001788072/930107812_2014082530900808/additional/634310PUB0Yes0061512B09780821387450.pdf.

Zhou, N. and J. Whalley. 2014. How Do the "GATS-Plus" and "GATS-Minus" Characteristics of Regional Service Agreements Affect Trade in Services? *Working Paper 20551*. Cambridge, Massachusetts: National Bureau of Economic Research. https://www.nber.org/papers/w20551.

www.ingramcontent.com/pod-product-compliance
Lightning Source LLC
Chambersburg PA
CBHW061235270326

41929CB00031B/3493

* 9 7 8 9 2 9 2 6 9 2 4 1 4 *